KEY PHILOSOPHERS IN CONVERSATION

The *Cogito* interviews

Edited by
Andrew Pyle

London and New York

First published 1999
by Routledge
11 New Fetter Lane, London EC4P 4EE

Simultaneously published in the USA and Canada
by Routledge
29 West 35th Street, New York, NY 10001

British Library Cataloguing in Publication Data
A catalogue record for this book is available from the British
Library

Library of Congress Cataloging in Publication Data
A catalogue record for this book has been requested

ISBN 0–415–18036–8 (hbk)
ISBN 0–415–18037–6 (pbk)

CONTENTS

Introduction   vii
ANDREW PYLE

1 Michael Dummett   1

2 Mary Warnock   8

3 Willard Van Orman Quine   17

4 Roger Scruton   26

5 Peter Strawson   36

6 Hilary Putnam   44

7 Stephan Körner   55

8 Richard Dawkins   65

9 Alasdair MacIntyre   75

10 Dan Dennett   85

11 Hugh Mellor   101

12 Richard Sorabji   114

13 David Gauthier   129

14 Bernard Williams   142

CONTENTS

15 Adam Morton   164

16 Derek Parfit   179

17 Nancy Cartwright   196

18 John Cottingham   215

19 Jean Hampton   231

20 Martha Nussbaum   239

INTRODUCTION

The journal *Cogito*, brainchild of Edo Pivcevic, was launched with a pilot issue in 1986, and had its first full issue in January 1987. For the first two years it was not only edited but also published by the Department of Philosophy of the University of Bristol; then in its third year it was taken on by Carfax of Abingdon. Although its precise form and contents have altered over the years, its mission has remained unchanged: to bring good quality philosophy to a non-specialist readership. Articles had to be short (less than 4,000 words) and clear (avoiding technical jargon), accessible to readers without a formal training in philosophy. There was also an editorial policy of including a more diverse range of materials than the normal scholarly journal: dialogues, short stories, polemics, paradoxes and puzzles have all found space on our pages. Successive editors also strove to preserve a light touch, to enliven the journal with pictures and the occasional dash of humour. We may not always have succeeded, but we have tried to ensure that the journal was never boring.

From the very first issue, a key feature of every number of *Cogito* has been the interview, invariably given pride of place at the front. Indeed, editors such as myself tend to identify a given number with its interviewee, so that Volume 3 No. 2 became 'Hilary Putnam' and Volume 8 No. 1 'Bernard Williams'. Over the years, the interview has consistently been one of our most popular features, read by philosophers and non-philosophers alike. Non-philosophers might find it hard to read and understand the books and articles on which the reputation of a given thinker depends, but anyone can skim through an informal ten-page interview and obtain some sense both of the gist of his or her work and of the personality that lies behind the writings. It is this last feature, surely, which explains the perennial appeal of the interview: however impersonal the arguments of a philosopher may appear, most readers find themselves drawn to look for the subjective factor, the bit of human (often, all-too-human) biography that 'explains' the philosophy. Even fellow-professionals found the interviews well worth reading: the interviewee might provide some insight into the philosophical motivation behind a piece of work, gives an overview emphasising some things at the expense of others, or indicate a change of mind, emphasis, or even direction.

The nature of *Cogito*'s readership allowed interviewers freedom to roam more widely than would be possible in a professional journal. Our interviewees thus find themselves invited to step outside the ivory tower of academia and address wider questions. They might be asked to explain why non-philosophers should care about the technical details of their work, or why the public purse should support their research. Or they might be asked how they became interested in modal logic, artificial intelligence, or Aristotelian ethics, and how their philosophy has affected more down-to-earth aspects of their life and thought. The interviews are by no means uniform in this regard, but none of them is exclusively professional and technical. As Hume said long ago, 'Be a philosopher; but, amidst all your philosophy, be still a man.' Or, we must add, a woman – it is good to see that the growing number of women in modern Anglo-American philosophy is well represented among our interviewees.

This volume contains twenty of the thirty interviews that appeared during the first ten years of the journal's existence, from 1987 until 1996. The nature of the interviews was not fixed during this period: as a rough generalisation, the earlier ones tend to be shorter, and to contain rather more biography and rather less philosophy. Interviewers were given considerable liberty to shape each interview as they thought fit, without much attempt at standardisation. So the interviews that make up this volume differ in terms of their length, their style, and their degree of philosophical difficulty. In every case, however, interviewer and interviewee alike were aware of the intended readership of the journal, and under instructions to try to keep the material accessible to the general reader. Some philosophers, the reader of this volume will soon discover, are better communicators of difficult thoughts than others.

We have been fortunate, over the years, to have obtained interviews with many of the great figures in modern Anglo-American philosophy. Some big names did escape us (e.g. Kripke, Rawls, Lewis) but our final list of twenty names will still look impressive to any modern philosopher. It also covers the field both geographically and intellectually. If there is a slight British bias, that is perhaps inevitable in a British-based journal, but does not preclude interviews with the Americans Quine, Putnam, Dennett, Cartwright, Nussbaum and Hampton, not to mention Canadians Morton and Gauthier. Intellectually, we cover virtually all aspects of the subject from logic and philosophy of science through metaphysics, epistemology and philosophy of mind to ethics and political philosophy, not forgetting parts of the history of philosophy. Anyone reading this volume will get a fair impression of the range of activities that go on in philosophy departments in the English-speaking world, and of the men and women engaging in those activities. Speaking from experience, I can say that our interviewees were without exception helpful and considerate, willing to give up their time both for the interview itself and for the subsequent editorial process. Our thanks to all these eminent people, who found time to fit in a *Cogito* interview, often into an already busy schedule.

In one or two of the earlier interviews, the name of the interviewer appeared alongside that of the interviewee. In the later issues of the journal, the anonymous 'Cogito' was found preferable. This anonymous form has been standardised in this volume. The point is of course to concentrate the minds of readers on the responses of the interviewee, and to make the role of the interviewer(s) as self-effacing as possible. The interview is not a true dialogue, but a sort of assisted monologue, in which the job of the interviewer is not to advance his or her views, but merely to draw out and clarify the opinions of the interviewee, to act as a sort of transparent medium between the interviewee and the readers. But the anonymous interviewers are not forgotten. In addition to thanking the interviewees we must also thank the interviewers, who gave equally of their time and labour, but whose names are not recorded here for posterity.

Updates on each interviewee have been added to the original introductions.

Andrew Pyle (Editor, 1992–96),
Department of Philosophy,
University of Bristol

1

MICHAEL DUMMETT

Philosophical doubts and religious certainties

Michael Dummett, Wykeham Professor of Logic at Oxford University, is one of the leading British philosophers of language, mathematics and logic. Apart from two major studies of the German thinker Gottlob Frege (1848–1925), *Frege: the Philosophy of Language* (1973) and *The Interpretation of Frege's Philosophy* (1980), he has published a range of books and articles, including numerous papers on the central problems of philosophical logic. Some of these are collected in his *Truth and Other Enigmas* (1978). He is also well known for his campaigning work outside philosophy, especially for his association with groups opposed to racial discrimination.

Professor Dummett (interview 1987) is one of the elder statesmen of Oxford philosophy. Since our interview, he has published a number of important philosophical works, notably *Frege: Philosophy of Mathematics* (1991), *The Origins of Analytical Philosophy* (1994) and *Frege and Other Philosophers* (1996). He has also published books on such non-philosophical topics as the correct use of English and the merits of different voting systems.

Cogito: Professor Dummett, it might seem strange to begin by asking you about the work of another philosopher, but since you have devoted so much time and attention to the work of Frege, perhaps you could tell us whether you have seen your role primarily as explaining Frege's views or as using them as a vehicle for the communication of your own philosophical doctrines?

Dummett: Well, it turned out to be both really. My original intention was to explore Frege's views because they seemed highly relevant to the current discussions within analytical philosophy. He was, of course, the grandfather of analytical philosophy, and it is striking how many of his concerns are still live ones. He speaks to modern philosophers in a way that's quite unusual, so that exposition seemed, in the first instance, precisely what was needed. But some of the issues he raised were not fully dealt with by him, and I suppose that in considering them further I put forward views of my own. That was not my original purpose. When I started writing about Frege he was still rather neglected. People knew him as a source for Wittgenstein, and in connection with Russell, but he wasn't then – as I think he is now – essential reading for anybody studying analytical philosophy. It was part of my purpose to make him so.

Cogito: Could you enumerate for our readers some of Frege's most important concerns?

Dummett: The fundamental idea for Frege was that the contents of what are now called 'propositional attitudes' – that is, things that are believed or known – which he called 'thoughts', are not *mental* contents. They are not ingredients of the stream of consciousness. Such ingredients are things that are purely subjective: mental images, sensations, feelings, and so forth. By 'thoughts', Frege means not particular acts of thinking but the contents of those acts; and these contents are objective, that is, common to all. One person can think, or consider, or deny just that very same thought which somebody else asserts. Frege made a sharp division between the subjective, which cannot be fully communicated, and the objective, which being independent of any particular mind must, Frege believed, exist independently of being grasped or thought about.

Cogito: This would seem to mark a sharp contrast between Frege and the school of Hegelian Idealism.

Dummett: Yes of course, enormously sharp. But the doctrine as I have just explained it remains a purely negative one. It just tells you that a thought should not be characterized in terms of mental operations. The question which then arises is 'In what terms *should* a thought be characterized?' There is an ambiguity in Frege's work on this point. He believed that thoughts and their constituent senses had an objective reality. They are not material objects in the physical world, but neither are they ingredients of consciousness. Towards the end of his life he referred to them as constituting the 'Third Realm'. Of course, one can object to all that as a piece of philosophical mythology. If one then searches around for something else which is external to consciousness, but which involves no mythologizing, what one finds is the social institution of language. It's thus very natural to make a move from Frege's position to the fundamental idea of analytic philosophy: that the path to the analysis of thought lies through the analysis of *language*.

2

This occurred to Frege himself in part. When he engages in detail, rather than in great generalities, the so-called 'linguistic turn' is exactly the move he makes.

Cogito: What would be an example of this move?

Dummett: You can see it in his *Foundations of Arithmetic* as early as 1884. There he raises the question of how numbers are given to us. They are not objects of sense or intuition, so how are we aware of them? He first makes the move, which he expresses linguistically, of saying that it is only in the context of a sentence that a word has a meaning – you can only think of an object in the course of thinking something about it. Then he argues that we are aware of numbers because we understand certain sentences in which number-words occur. What we have to do is give an explanation of the senses of these sentences. The account of thought he arrives at, then, is actually given as a theory of meaning for language.

Cogito: You have suggested that the relationship between thought and language is the most basic philosophical problem. The discipline which has been a traditional starting point for philosophy is metaphysics, but in your book *Intuitionism*, you argued strongly that – at least in the case of thinking about mathematics – one cannot start by considering the traditional metaphysical issue, the nature of mathematical objects, but that such questions too should be approached through the philosophy of language.

Dummett: There are many points within philosophy where it is useful to distinguish between a metaphysical issue – a question about how things are – and an epistemological issue – a question about how we know or understand something. But I don't think the term metaphysics is itself a useful piece of classification. One traditional metaphysical question concerns the status or character of certain kinds of objects; mathematical objects are one such category people worry about, and theoretical entities of science are another. Other questions which have interested me particularly are about the correctness or incorrectness of a *realistic* view of a certain subject matter. These are closely allied, obviously. It seems to me that there is a question of priority here. Should you first settle those metaphysical questions, and in the light of your results produce a theory of meaning for the part of language that talks about such things, or should you do it the other way around? I strongly believe that the metaphysical questions have no clear substance or content within themselves. If you are asked to settle the question whether we discover mathematical objects or invent them, whether they are creations of our mind or exist independently of us, metaphors are being brought into play which ask you to compare mathematics with one or other of two things it's obviously

3

pretty unlike. You don't know how to set about it. The proper procedure is to try to think about how we understand mathematical statements and how we come to form mathematical concepts; then, in the light of the account you've given, one or other metaphor will seem more appropriate. That's the way the metaphysical question will be settled, if ever, because we have no purchase on it the other way around. We don't know what we're trying to investigate even.

Cogito: So your general approach to questions about realism and the nature of reality is to say that they must be tackled by thinking about thought or language?

Dummett: Yes, by analysing what it is for us to have thoughts about such things; in particular, what notion of truth we have available for such thoughts or statements. When you can see that clearly, the other questions will very nearly answer themselves.

Cogito: As you told us earlier, Frege's work is associated with realism, that is the commitment to certain objective realities. Yet your own work in the philosophy of mathematics has been associated with what is called intuitionism. Could you explain what it is to be a realist, as opposed to an intuitionist, about mathematical objects?

Dummett: The simplest possible case is the theory of natural numbers, where we can describe in a very simple way the forms of expression we need: numerals, operations on them such as addition and multiplication, and expressions like 'and', 'if ... then ...', 'or', 'not', 'there is a number x ...', and 'for every number x ...'. With these simple resources you can construct a variety of statements, some of which are extremely difficult to prove, and some of which have persistently defied attempts to prove or disprove them. From a realist standpoint, these statements concern the elements of an infinite mathematical structure containing the natural numbers, and these elements determinately either possess or do not possess the properties attributed to them. So any statement we can construct using these resources, such as 'Every number is the sum of four squares', will be determinately true or false, whether it can be proved or not. On an anti-realist, or intuitionist view, we understand the notion of mathematical truth only in connection with what it is for something to be demonstrated as true. When we learn mathematics, what we actually learn is how to do calculations and how to prove or disprove statements. The only conception of truth we can acquire from this training is that under which, given a proof, we can say this statement is true, and, given a refutation, we can say it is false. And so the supposition that a statement is true can only amount to the supposition that there exists a proof of it.

We're not entitled to suppose that we are talking about a reality existing independently of ourselves, or that we have formed a conception of what it is for such a reality to render our statements true or false, regardless of whether we know or even can know if they are true or false.

Cogito: Has your concern with intuitionism been to see how far it can be worked through systematically as an alternative to the tradition Frege represents?

Dummett: Exactly. Intuitionism, so far as I know, is the only case of a fully worked-out anti-realist theory which has accepted the necessity of abandoning classical logic, and has developed a logic with which to replace it. If people wish to defend realism, they should do so against the strongest possible attack.

Cogito: You are indicating, then, that there are questions to be answered about the realist's understanding of mathematics. Now although it might seem odd to question our realist attitude to the external world, presumably similar difficulties none the less arise, and must be adequately addressed?

Dummett: That's how it seems to me. This was once a live issue for the phenomenalists, who said, 'There are only our sensations, and we construct the external world out of them.' Realism had a very easy victory, partly because it launched a perfectly correct attack on the notion of sense-data, but partly also because the phenomenalists never noticed that if they rejected the realistic interpretation of statements about the external world, they no longer had the right to assume that every such statement was true or false, made so by its agreement or disagreement with a reality existing independently of us. They continued to apply classical logic, which led to the reduction of their thesis to something completely empty: that here were just two forms of language for describing the reality. This need not have happened if, like intuitionists, the phenomenalists had noted that they needed to adopt some weaker logic in order to make their position coherent.

Realism may still be the correct view, but it's got to be defended against a more sophisticated attack if it's to be declared the champion.

Cogito: To lead you into quite a different area, may we ask whether as a Catholic philosopher you have ever found any cross-fertilization between your religious and philosophical views?

Dummett: I should like such cross-fertilization to occur, but I can't really pretend that it has, and part of the reason for that is I've never succeeded in getting as far in philosophy as I should have liked. I certainly had the ambition to carry my investigations from general considerations into a whole lot of areas within philosophy. I can't say I have abandoned that ambition, but it's all taken me much longer than I thought, partly because I keep revising my opinions about the foundations, and partly because of general teaching obligations. I had the ambition to write a book called *Realism* investigating a lot of different areas including much of what's traditionally called metaphysics. Natural theology, that part of philosophy which has to do with questions about the existence of God, is something to which I never have properly contributed, partly because my own ideas about it are in a pretty confused state, I admit, and partly because I think it's almost the most remote area from the foundations. You have to get so much else right first before you can even begin to tackle that.

Because I think there is this hierarchical order within philosophy, it would be wrong to allow any preconception of how things ought to come out to influence what one does lower down. You have to follow the argument and see where it leads. I'm not saying that pursuit of these ideas about anti-realism would lead to atheistic conclusions, but if they were to do so, although it would be very uncomfortable to me, I don't think it would matter very much. My religious belief would tell me I must have made a mistake somewhere.

Cogito: Would you extend that answer to cover your association with certain public issues and debates, with the Campaign Against Racial Discrimination for example? Do you set aside your philosophy when you become involved in such a project, because it touches on a remote part of the subject you have yet to reach?

Dummett: In that sense, I have been very bad at making those connections. It's not that I'm at all dubious about my own stance; I feel deeply certain that it's right. The connection there is more with my religious views. Obviously these are things one can talk about as a philosopher, but since I've worked in the more abstract parts of the subject, I've never got anywhere near that point.

Cogito: In conclusion, you've said in some of your writings that modern philosophy has become more scientific, in the sense that people are now working co-operatively on much the same projects. Would you still express confidence in conclusive achievements being made in the sort of fundamental areas we discussed earlier?

Dummett: I don't know that I am as confident as I was when I wrote that. To tell you the truth, I find some of the manifestations of the phenomenon you describe rather disagreeable. It manifests itself in a kind of loss of genuine philosophical curiosity. People take a whole set of views for granted, including a rather irritating scientism and materialism. Technical problems in semantics are of genuine relevance to philosophy, but they should always develop against a background of real philosophical puzzlement or wonder.

Cogito: One sometimes gets the sense that we become involved in a puzzle-solving game, and lose sight of what the original problem was.

Dummett: Exactly. Philosophy will never be a science, obviously, and I never meant to say that it was. But I thought at one time that a certain range of problems had been sufficiently isolated that there could be something resembling co-operative work on them. Now I feel a bit sceptical about that.

2

MARY WARNOCK

Existentialism, education and ethics

Baroness Warnock of Weeke, better known as **Dame Mary Warnock**, has written on a wide range of issues, from Existentialism in her early years, through the philosophy of education, to her most recent, and most public, work on the ethics of embryo research.

Dame Mary Warnock (interview 1987) is still best known for the *Warnock Report on Human Fertilization and Embryology*, which remains the basis for public discussion of the moral issues raised by the application of medical advances to human reproduction. Since our interview, she has published *Imagination and Time* (1994) and edited a volume on *Women Philosophers* (1996).

Cogito: May we begin by asking what interests originally led you to study philosophy?

Warnock: I read Classics at school, and had a brother ten years older than me who read Greats at Oxford and was the cleverest member of the family. I thought whatever he can do, I can do; so I read Greats at Oxford, and came to philosophy through Classics. I decided to stick to philosophy, in the end, largely because of the influence of J.L. Austin, then the most powerful figure in Oxford, and actually my examiner in Greats.

Cogito: Some years ago you wrote two books on Existentialism, and one on the philosophy of Sartre, which are still very popular among students looking for an introduction to that school of thought. What initially attracted you to it?

Warnock: Nothing. I was asked by the Oxford University Press to write a book about ethics since 1900, and was told that I ought to have a chapter on continental philosophy in it, so for one long vacation I killed myself reading up on it. I found it not uninteresting, but very unattractive. I did think that I had, in a way, understood what Sartre was up to, and that I might as well try to explain that. After all, there were some very close connections between continental philosophy and what was going on, for instance, at Oxford at that time.

Cogito: It might surprise people to find you making that connection. Perhaps you could say a bit more about it?

Warnock: When Oxford's Gilbert Ryle was a young man he went to Germany to study the philosophy of Edmund Husserl, and he did a review of Heidegger in *Mind*, also when he was quite young. He was interested in German philosophy, but hated it and wanted to expose it. But phenomenology, as expounded by Husserl, which was the philosophy which said you must look at experience direct – forget all presuppositions, assumptions and prejudices you've had and put them, as he said, into brackets – this appealed to Ryle very much indeed. It was also extremely influential on Sartre, so that the common German source of Husserl divided up; in England it became characteristically Anglo-Saxon Ryle, and in France highly French Sartre.

Cogito: The French branch, which developed as Existentialism, once enjoyed popularity among those people who felt it addressed itself to their emotions and passions as well as their rationality, and that in comparison the analytic philosophy practised in British and American circles was rather bloodless. Were you sympathetic to this view?

Warnock: Having been brought up in the somewhat austere atmosphere at Oxford, one of the most amazing things about first reading Sartre was that he was prepared to talk philosophically about passion and love, sex and obesity, cooking and all sorts of domestic subjects. There is an amazing passage in *Being and Nothingness* about the nature of the obscene, which would have been regarded in English philosophy as pornography. English philosophy has now moved in the direction of the everyday and the practical, but it would be misleading to say that even in the 1940s and 1950s it was an altogether detached and austere subject. John Austin was a great one for taking ordinary models of conversation and looking at their presumptions and presuppositions. I remember one of his Saturday mornings when he took a Design Institute catalogue, and we spent hours looking through the specification for teapots. What makes a good teapot? What are the aesthetic presuppositions of that? What does that judgement entail? There wasn't a great gap between the continentals who were interested in real life, and the Oxford people who were interested in the way language fitted onto real life, which I still think is the main business of philosophy.

9

Cogito: Is language still the place to start if you want to ask a philosophical question?

Warnock: Absolutely. The concern with language is essential, but I think in the 1950s people were so excited at having discovered this that some went over the top and just talked about language for its own sake, because it is very interesting. What we have carried on from that time is the notion that you can't do philosophy at all unless you concern yourself with the relation between the language you are using and the things you are talking about. To his credit, I think Sartre had a glimpse of this now and then; that you had to understand the way people use language before you could understand the way they thought, or the importance of what they thought. But he was such an appalling language-user himself, his writing is so ghastly, that these glimpses were lost.

Cogito: Despite the importance of language, you have said more recently that the philosophy of education should not be concerned with the definition of the concept of education, but rather with the effect of its practice. Could you explain this distinction?

Warnock: I taught in a school before I ever taught in university, and was a member of the Oxfordshire Education Committee, and involved in musical education within the county, so I was very much interested in education at the delivery end. I thought, perhaps snobbishly, that philosophers of education – having picked up the jargon of Oxford in the 1950s – were asking fake conceptual questions like 'What do you *mean* by "education"?'; whereas what one needed to know was where the power lay, where the money was to be spent, whether to have comprehensive schools, and so on. I held, rather aggressively, that the philosophy of education was, if anything, a branch of political philosophy.

Cogito: You did, however, suggest that there were three essential elements in education: the development of the imagination, preparation for a career, and the inculcation of a proper sense of morality.

Warnock: What you quote goes back a bit. When the Committee on the education of handicapped children came to write its report, which was published in 1978, we realized that we needed to make central to our findings a notion of 'educational needs' which would bridge the gap between the needs of children who are very bright and the needs of those who are particularly dim. This led us to try to outline some perfectly general goals for education, so that if children are not approaching those goals, however slowly, then the needs of these children are not being met. The necessity for defining such goals is even more acute in the 1980s because people are constantly complaining that schools are not delivering the goods even though nobody is quite prepared to say what goods ought to be delivered. I don't think I'd go back on the general-sounding goals that you quote. The goal of developing the imagination is something that I did pick up from Sartre. The faculty which enables us to envisage a world or future different from the world we are living in is essential to human freedom, and it is one of the main functions of education to open people's eyes, so that they do not assume that the way they live now is the way that everybody must live forever.

Cogito: It has been argued in some quarters that while education must be to do with allowing someone freely to develop their own potential, training for a specific task is quite another matter. Would you agree?

Warnock: No, I wouldn't, because learning how to do a specific thing is itself an expansion of your powers. Even if it is just producing a note on the flute that you have not been able to produce before, this can give you a new outlook on what you can do, on what lies within your power, and you may even begin to think of all the things you can do with the instrument as a kind of expansion of yourself. At the same time, I think it is very dangerous to say that you have got to teach people how to use a word-processor or computer at school because it will be useful. Technology changes incredibly quickly, so what they learn in school today probably won't be very much use to them the day after tomorrow. I don't believe in very specific tasks, so that pupils can slot into a job when they leave school, or indeed university; but if they can do something at the end of the lesson they couldn't do before, this gives them some confidence to go on, which can be tremendously beneficial.

Cogito: Do you think that a philosophy A-Level course can help develop individual potential?

Warnock: I am very much against having philosophy A-Level courses. The study of philosophy ought to be based on the history of the subject, it shouldn't be taken very fast, and it's awfully difficult. What I do believe in greatly is putting a powerful philosophical element into every course, whether it be science or literature or history; but you don't have to call it philosophy. To be critical of the language in which a text is written, and to raise constant questions about whether it means what it says – this is an essential part of any course. It is philosophy but it doesn't have to be called that.

Cogito: One of your central claims has been that the content of the curriculum is a more important issue than equality of opportunity to study the curriculum.

Warnock: I still believe that. Let me say that I am a great believer in comprehensive schools, but when people try to decide what children ought to be taught on the grounds of what is equal or just, then we have moved away from educational considerations and into political considerations that are irrelevant here.

Cogito: But do you believe that education is a political issue?

Warnock: Certainly it is because it is so expensive. But I don't think that all the decisions within education should be taken on political grounds.

Cogito: You said earlier that one question in the philosophy of education is where power is located – whether with the Secretary of State, the governors, the teachers or the parents. This is in a lot of people's minds at the moment.

Warnock: If old-fashioned political philosophy, like Locke's, is concerned with the relation between the governors and the governed, then I do think it is a philosophical question, in a loose sense, whether we should encourage 'parent-power' or whether, in a democratic society, we trust the Secretary of State with decision-making powers. And a whole area which political philosophy has not touched on is that of the status of local authorities. An awful lot of rather sentimental stuff is talked about local democracy, but I think individuals feel that, if anything, they have got more of a say in what central government is deciding. I mean, they can lobby their local MP probably a great deal better than they can lobby their local education authority.

Cogito: What about moral education? Does it hold an important place on the curriculum?

Warnock: Yes, I think so, in the sense that everybody hopes their child will emerge from school more morally alert, intelligent and sensitive. I don't believe in lessons specifically in morals or lessons in moral philosophy, but all the way through school there are endless opportunities for demonstrating virtues like justice, fairness, hope and faith. The school has a great responsibility for demonstrating them, but then I think the home has as well.

Cogito: One of the things the public now knows you best for is the report of the Committee of Enquiry into Human Fertilization and Embryology. It deals among many topics with surrogacy, the mothering of a child by a woman who usually provides the egg, and who is artificially inseminated with the man's sperm. On the face of it, providing a child for a couple unable to have one in any other way would seem to be beneficial. Yet the report strongly recommended the criminalization of surrogacy agencies. Why was this?

Warnock: At the time we wrote the report, there was a queue of agents from America wishing to set up in England and hire girls to offer their services as surrogates. It was the element of exploitation in such commercial agencies that we felt very strongly about. People in great distress about their infertility might be conned into paying a great deal of money, while the present state of the law, both here and in the US, is that a surrogacy agreement has no binding force and this has recently been confirmed in the courts. The girl who had the baby could, in principle, keep both the child and the money. We felt there was something extremely unethical about people making an enormous amount of money from the miseries of the infertile for a legally dubious outcome.

Cogito: What about the moral rights and wrongs of surrogacy itself?

Warnock: On the whole, we were not happy about it. Carrying a child and giving birth to it is not something to be taken on lightly, and there have been so many cases where the mother has gone on record as saying she should never have done it. We were certain, however, that surrogacy would go on anyway, between friends or sisters, but that, whatever the difficulties, such cases would not be very frequent; and as they would be unlikely to come to court, there was no question of setting up a law to say that the baby belongs to X or Y. Questions have recently arisen about the adoption of such babies by the commissioning parents but these are not insurmountable.

Cogito: It almost sounds like there are reasons for banning it completely.

Warnock: You can't ban it between friends, because it would be an incredibly obtrusive law that went poking around, saying 'Are you sure this baby is yours? It bears a curious likeness to your sister.' It would be like making adultery a criminal offence; it would mean having spies in the bedroom.

Cogito: The report also dealt with embryo research. The question here is what restriction should be placed on research on embryos created as a by-product of the technique of in-vitro fertilization?

Warnock: The further question is whether embryos should be especially produced by in-vitro fertilization for research; so it is not just a question about by-products, but about living human embryos deliberately brought into existence in the laboratory.

Cogito: How did you arrive at the conclusion that embryos should not be left alive for research beyond fourteen days?

Warnock: I was very anxious that there should be a date beyond which such research should be a criminal offence, countable from the day fertilization took place, so that the law could be perfectly specific and definite. Up to day fourteen or fifteen, the cluster of cells in question has not yet settled into a firm pattern that will produce either one or two babies or none at all. After this, there begins to develop a central collection of cells, the 'primitive streak', out of which one baby, or possibly an identical twin as well, will form. The other cells will form a protective coating to the embryo as placenta. Only from this date can you really begin to identify the ultimate human being that will emerge. Before that, it is quite likely that no human being will emerge, or it may be two, or even triplets. So we picked on the fourteen-day limit as the date before which it would be reasonable to think of the collection of cells as a pre-embryo, which may or may not lead to the development of an embryo, which would become a foetus, which would become a human being.

Cogito: Couldn't one say that the potential for a human being exists in the pre-embryo?

Warnock: I'm not terribly impressed by that, because after all the egg is potentially a human being in certain circumstances, as are each of the millions of sperm which are lost without any fuss. Potentiality is a rather difficult notion to use here.

Cogito: It has been suggested that research should be allowed until a later stage in the embryo's existence, because not until then does it develop neural structures and become able to feel pain.

Warnock: Here one comes up against a real philosophical question – whether the calculation of benefits and harms is really the whole of morality and whether embryos immediately after fertilization must count in the calculus. A Utilitarian would say that you are morally entitled to do something if the balance of the consequences comes out in favour of benefits. Thus Bob Edwards, who was responsible for the first test-tube baby, argues that the balance of utility is in favour of research because the embryo cannot feel any pain up to about three months, while the research may be of enormous benefit to the advance of knowledge. And he says this even though the embryo will be destroyed.

I strongly believe that Utilitarianism is not the whole of morality, but that you must also take into account a whole range of moral sentiments – feelings of outrage, shame, horror and fear. If we cut all of those out of the calculation, then we are no longer able to distinguish between what is morally right and what is expedient. In writing the report I was concerned to distinguish between the moral sentiments that were well-founded and those that were ill-founded, or perhaps founded on a religious dogma with which there was no arguing.

Cogito: If Utilitarianism is insufficient, does the idea of taking the moral sentiments of the general public into account constitute a new form of moral theory?

Warnock: In a way yes, but in another way it is far from new – I learned it from the philosopher David Hume. He said that morality is more properly felt than thought, and I strongly believe that unless people feel passionately about right and wrong then they haven't a morality at all; calculation is not enough. Stuart Hampshire is a modern philosopher who has said that within societies sentiments erect barriers beyond which one mustn't go. What hasn't yet been addressed is what the law is supposed to do in a society where people erect their barriers in different places. If this is not a new moral theory, then it is a great new moral problem that people have got to answer.

Cogito: Is this a particular problem for modern Britain, with its many different moralities and different cultures?

Warnock: I think it is a particular problem in the 1980s in Britain, with a decline of religion on the whole, but pockets of religion still all over the place and a whole lot of different ethical and ethnic cultures on all sides. I greatly fear the rise of fundamentalist religion. If parliament decides to reject the things we recommend to them, then it is absolutely right that they should do so, but I hope very much that they are not carried along on a mindless tide of fundamentalism, but that they actually think about the issues, and try to distinguish between things that differ. For example, that they distinguish their feelings about protecting children from their feelings about protecting a four cell-embryo.

Cogito: Finally, we should like to ask you about the philosopher's role in public life. Why should it be that a philosopher is chosen to chair committees of the kind we have been discussing?

Warnock: I suspect that somebody or other in government hopes that philosophers know the difference between right and wrong, and can produce cut and dried arguments to show what is the right course to take. Obviously, it is not like that at all; but all the same I think philosophers have two merits as chairmen. They are accustomed professionally to analysing what people say, picking out the arguments and seeing where there is contradiction and that kind of thing. Secondly, they benefit by not having a special subject of their own, in the sense that they are always dealing with other people's specialisms, standing back from them, understanding roughly what they are saying, and seeing what the unexamined assumptions are.

Cogito: Would you like to see more philosophers in this sort of role?

Warnock: Yes. I would like to see far more undergraduates reading philosophy at university, preferably combined with some other subject, and I would like to see them increasingly used, not only to chair committees, but to chair companies, and in other quite practical roles. I think they would be good at it; and that's a plug you can send to the schools!

3

WILLARD VAN ORMAN QUINE
Quine speaks his mind

There can be few philosophy undergraduates who have not experienced the impact of **Willard Van Orman Quine**'s views, particularly his criticisms of *a priori* knowledge, logical truth, meaning, analyticity, his theses of the indeterminacy of translation and ontological relativity and his insistence upon the close relationship between philosophy and science. His books, much thumbed, will be on their bookshelves: in particular, *Elementary Logic* (1941), *Methods of Logic* (1950), *From a Logical Point of View* (1953), *Word and Object* (1960), *Set Theory and its Logic* (1969), *Ontological Relativity and Other Essays* (1969) have been quoted in thousands of students' essays and have been subject to scrutiny in the leading philosophical journals. He has, further, the rare honour of being the subject of a volume in the *Library of Living Philosophers* (1976).

Professor Quine (interview 1988) holds the Edgar Pierce chair of philosophy at Harvard University, and remains the grand old man of American philosophy. To list his awards, prizes, and honorary degrees would take a small volume. Since our interview, he has published *The Pursuit of Truth* (1990) and *From Stimulus to Science* (1995). His philosophical correspondence with Rudolf Carnap has also appeared, under the editorship of Ricard Creath, as *Dear Carnap, Dear Van: The Quine–Carnap Correspondence and Related Work* (1991).

Cogito: Professor Quine, as an undergraduate you studied mathematics at Oberlin College, Ohio. Could you tell us how you developed an interest in philosophy?

Quine: Philosophical curiosity had touched me somewhat by about the age of ten, when I began to sense the implausibility of heaven and immortality. A few years later, having taken to reading the collected writings of

17

Edgar Allan Poe, my philosophical interest in the nature of things was fired by his eloquent and extravagant essay 'Eureka'. But I had conceived equally strong interests outside philosophy, notably in the origins of words. In school I did well also in mathematics. The result was indecision, in college, over choice of a major field. A knowledgeable older student had heard of Russell's 'mathematical philosophy', and this seemed to offer a way of combining two of my competing interests. So I arranged to major in mathematics and do my honours reading in 'mathematical philosophy', which turned out to be mathematical logic. It was not taught at Oberlin, but the mathematics professor consulted a colleague elsewhere and prepared me a reading list, which I pursued with mounting enthusiasm. It culminated in Whitehead and Russell's *Principia Mathematica*, for which my admiration was unbounded. After graduating I moved on to Harvard for graduate study in philosophy, for Whitehead was by then – 1930 – a professor of philosophy there. My change of field, from mathematics to philosophy, did not reflect a change in interest. The focus of my interest had come to be the intersection of the two.

Cogito: What was the subject of your post-graduate research at Harvard?

Quine: On becoming a candidate for a doctorate in philosophy I had to take on traditional philosophical studies, but in my own research I took the same line that I would have wanted to take if I had been going for a doctorate in mathematics. I was bent on improving the logic and set theory of *Principia Mathematica*, by enhancement of rigour, economy, and philosophical clarity. It is no disparagement of *Principia* that it cried out for such improvements; such is the way with pioneer works.

Cogito: Which particular sections of the *Principia* did you think were most in need of repair or improvement?

Quine: My improvements were limited to the Introduction and Part I, 'Mathematical Logic' – hence the first half of Volume I. These were the sections where the semantics of the system were set forth and the technical apparatus was developed for the derivation in Parts II–VI of classical mathematics. A fault on the semantic side was a persistent neglect of the distinction between use and mention, sign and object. As a result the conceptual background was nebulous and needlessly complex. A fault on the logical side was redundancy of symbols. Many notations were introduced by definition that could be paraphrased in prior notations with little or no loss of brevity. Such redundancy mounts exponentially, because each new notation generates a new sheaf of theorems relating it to previous expressions. I showed how some economy of notation could do away with scores of turgid pages and relieve the memory of a needless lot of ideograms.

Cogito: At one time you were strongly influenced by the German logician Rudolf Carnap, whom you first met, I believe, in Prague in 1933. Why did you go to Prague, and how long were you there?

Quine: A travelling fellowship from Harvard had taken me to Vienna in October 1932, on the heels of my PhD. I met young Gödel, who had lately clinched immortality with his great theorem, but there were no lectures on mathematical logic or kindred themes in philosophy. It was Carnap, major spokesman of the Vienna Circle, who pressed modern logic most vigorously into the service of philosophy, and he had moved from Vienna to Prague the year before. I wrote to him, and when he visited Vienna late in 1932 I talked with him. It was arranged that my wife and I would move to Prague on March 1, 1933. We stayed 37 intensive days. My months in Vienna, meanwhile, had strengthened my German to the point where those 37 days could be fully exploited, for with Carnap I spoke only German. The theme was philosophical, but the technique, a wonderfully effective one, was largely mathematical logic. Afterwards I went on to Warsaw and immersed myself in mathematical logic pure and simple. There again, for lack of Polish, German was my language.

Cogito: 1933 was of course the year of Hitler's accession to power. He became Chancellor on 30 January 1933, and Goebbels was appointed minister for propaganda in March of the same year. What was the atmosphere like in Prague at the time? How did the philosophical community react to these events?

Quine: In Prague our only intellectual contacts were Carnap, the philosopher–physicist Philipp Frank, their wives, and perhaps Karel Reach. Certainly all of us, unreservedly, found the Nazis scandalous, outrageous, and alarming – much as we do now in retrospect, even though not foreseeing then the horrors of the holocaust. We had already observed the anti-Jewish propaganda and the expulsion of Einstein. In Vienna, where Nazi graffiti and swastika confetti had already been widespread in 1932, my friends likewise saw matters as I did and do. Similarly in Warsaw, with two rather vacillating exceptions.

Cogito: Who were the vacillating exceptions?

Quine: *De mortuis nihil nisi bonum.*

Cogito: A number of German philosophers, especially those associated with the so-called 'Vienna Circle', emigrated to the States in the thirties. Tell us about those who came to Harvard.

Quine: Philipp Frank, Viennese in origin, and Carnap, Viennese by adoption, both were of the Vienna Circle. Frank came to Harvard and stayed. Carnap visited at Harvard but settled at Chicago. Gerald Holton, a younger philosopher–physicist and a Viennese with a changed name, came to Harvard and stayed, and a great teacher he has been; but he had been a little too young for the Vienna Circle. Herbert Feigl, a young member of the Vienna Circle, had come to Harvard on a fellowship before Nazi times, and had been instrumental to my choosing Vienna in 1932.

Cogito: Russell was there too at one time. In 1940 he gave a series of lectures at Harvard which were later published under the title *An Inquiry into Meaning and Truth*. Did you attend his lectures?

Quine: Yes, 1940 was a great year: Russell, Carnap and Tarski were all at Harvard. I did indeed attend Russell's lectures, and later I reviewed the resulting book, *Inquiry into Meaning and Truth*, for the *Journal of Symbolic Logic*.

Cogito: Russell was very scathing about the tendency to see philosophy purely as language analysis. What was the reaction to his lectures at the time? What was the discussion like in the seminar?

Quine: I shared Russell's reservations regarding Oxford's philosophy of ordinary language – 'the metaphysics of savages'. My review of his *Inquiry* was nevertheless very critical. Of his seminar, as distinct from his lectures, I recall nothing. I may even have neglected it. For all my admiration of Russell's earlier work, by 1940 I was finding my stimulation in Carnap, Tarski, Hempel, and a few of my local contemporaries.

Cogito: Russell of course was highly critical of the 'Wittgensteinean' view that the only proper topic for philosophy is language, and that the way to find out about the structure of the world is to analyse the language in which we talk about the world. What is your own view on this?

Quine: Epistemology, for me, is science self-applied. It is the scientific study of the scientific process. It explores the logical connections between stimulation of the scientist's sensory receptors and the scientist's output of scientific theory. Ontology, for me, is the inquiry into what it means to assume objects of one or another sort, and what such an assumption contributes to the logical connection between the scientist's sensory stimulation and his scientific output. Epistemology and ontology so conceived will indeed focus on language, as logical analysis must; but not necessarily on our pristine vernacular, any more than mathematical analysis does. 'In the scientific enterprise,' David Justice writes, 'man transcends his language

20

just as he transcends his untutored sense impressions'. Frege likened the use of technical notation to the discovery of how, by means of the wind, to sail against the wind.

Cogito: Let us turn again to your relations with Carnap. Eventually you parted ways with him philosophically. Why?

Quine: In Prague I was reading Carnap's *Logische Syntax der Sprache* fresh from Ina Carnap's typewriter. With the help of mathematical logic he brought new clarity to the philosophy of science. I became an ardent disciple. Central to the book was his Thesis of Syntax: Philosophy is the syntax of the language of science. After a couple of years we both saw, in our separate ways, that that theory was untenable. It was a vital matter of syntax versus semantics. Carnap's proposed remedy, moreover, was one that I could not accept either. It committed him to modal logic, a logic of necessity and possibility, which both of us had formerly deplored for its lack of intelligible foundation. Meanwhile, I had become critical of others of Carnap's tenets. One was his fundamental distinction between analytic sentences, that is sentences true purely by virtue of the meanings of their words, and synthetic sentences, which convey information about the world. Another was his sharp distinction between the meaningful and the meaningless, with relegation of metaphysics to the latter category. In the case both of the distinction between analytic and synthetic and the distinction between meaningful and meaningless, I became aware of a lack of criteria. Thus our divergence on philosophical points. But we remained firm friends, he ever the generous adversary and I ever the grateful pupil.

Cogito: You explained your views on the synthetic/analytic distinction in your paper on 'Two Dogmas of Empiricism'. It is perhaps not an exaggeration to say that this has been one of the most widely read and most influential papers in recent philosophy. Could you briefly summarize its contents for us?

Quine: Not an exaggeration, in view of some forty anthologizings and translations of 'Two dogmas' and hundreds of responses in the form of articles and books. The first of the two dogmas was the distinction between analytic and synthetic sentences. My attack on this was what raised most of the turmoil. The second dogma was to the effect that every synthetic sentence has its own empirical content, its own separable criteria in sense experience. Put negatively, the second dogma is a failure to appreciate the truth of *holism*, which says that synthetic sentences for the most part have empirical content only jointly as interlocking systems of sentences. In 'Two dogmas' I cited the second dogma only as helping to explain the widespread acceptance of the first dogma. Today I see the second dogma as the true villain of the piece.

Cogito: What are the advantages of the 'holistic' approach to knowledge, and in what way does your own 'holistic' approach differ from that of Hegel?

Quine: Holism is inevitable once we reflect on the experimental method. A scientific hypothesis rarely implies, single-handed, what observable results to expect from the observable conditions set up in an experiment. In order to clinch such an implication the scientist has to draw on his background of scientific theory, common sense, and mathematics. What implies the observables is thus a big bundle of stated and unstated assumptions and beliefs. It is not, however, the whole of science as Hegel would have had it, it is a question only of critical mass: a big enough fragment of science to imply what to expect from some observation or experiment. The size will vary from case to case. This moderate holism is scarcely debatable, irrespective of its advantages; but there are advantages too, in that it solves two riddles regarding mathematical truth. How, Carnap asked, can mathematics be meaningful despite lacking empirical context? His answer was that mathematics is analytic. Holism's answer is that mathematics, insofar as applied in science, imbibes the shared empirical content of the critical masses to which it contributes. Second riddle: why is mathematical truth necessary rather than contingent? Carnap's answer, again, was analyticity. Holism's answer is that when a critical mass of sentences jointly implies a false prediction, we are free to choose what component sentence to revoke so as to defuse the implication. In so choosing we choose to safeguard any purely mathematical truths among those sentences, since disturbing them would disturb science excessively in all its branches. We are guided by a maxim of minimum mutilation, and it is this sparing of mathematics that accounts for its apparent necessity. So we see how holism solves two riddles that had been primary motives for Carnap's insistence on the notion of analyticity, the first of the two dogmas. I said earlier that I now see the second dogma as the true villain of the piece, and this is why. Once we appreciate holism, even moderate holism, the notion of analyticity ceases to be vital to epistemology.

Cogito: All your books have been widely read and appreciated, especially in the English-speaking world. Which of your own books do you yourself regard as most successful from your own point of view? Which do you regard as most important?

Quine: The duality of my training – mathematics and philosophy – has carried over into my publications. My second book, *Mathematical Logic*, came out in 1940 and exerted some influence in that domain, to judge from the gratifying number of professional logicians who have told me that it drew them into the profession. But my eighth book, *Set Theory and Its Logic*, and at a more elementary level the fourth edition of my *Methods of Logic*, are my contributions to that rapidly developing subject that most please me now. On the more purely philosophical side, perhaps my most influential book has been *Word and Object*. But my later writings improve on it in sporadic ways.

Cogito: How do you see the role of philosophy in the general system of education?

Quine: Students who choose philosophy as a major field should also pursue a strong minor in a hard science, so as to get a true feeling of what it is to understand something or to prove something. Conversely, students majoring in other subjects need the perspective and critical detachment that can be fostered by philosophy at its best. How to contrive this in a curriculum is a baffling problem, calling for a rare combination of philosophical wisdom and pedagogical finesse.

Cogito: Is there anything that philosophy, as you view it, can usefully say about God? Are you yourself a religious man?

Quine: What my own philosophy can say about God is that there is no such thing, at any rate in any ordinary sense of the word; and there is no answering for extraordinary senses. I am not a religious man.

Cogito: Looking back on your life as a logician and a philosopher, would you say that you have achieved most of what you set out to achieve, or do you have any as yet unfulfilled intellectual ambitions?

Quine: It may be characteristic of a scientific or philosophical career that one can define a clearly intelligible goal for oneself only after being well on the way. I was pressing the vague quest for the basic elements of mathematics and the ultimate nature of reality without knowing what to look for or how to recognize it when I found it. At one stage, ontology seemed to me to be central to philosophy: what there is, and what being means. In later years I came to see that ontology, the positing of objects of one sort or another, is secondary to the relating of scientific theory to the stimulation of our sensory receptors. Yet even this was no reversal, no traumatic disillusionment. I kept pressing for further understanding, letting interim goals rise and tumble as they might. Currently I have gone on trying to clarify and integrate my views on communication, empirical content, and truth, and I have lately been rewarded by the dissolution of several nagging perplexities. But I still have no unfulfilled intellectual ambition clearly in mind, and I do have my full share of philosophical curiosity about matters that I am in no position to cope with. There are the baffling challenges that quantum physics levels at the concept of cause. I think here of the findings in connection with Bell's Inequality, and I think also of how some microphysical facts about the past are represented as depending, paradoxically, on present observation. The cosmology of the expanding universe is another matter in crying need of more light. Closer to home, there are the mysteries of the mechanism of memory; also of consciousness – I am even at a loss for a satisfactory statement of what consciousness is, though nothing is more familiar.

Cogito: You said that lately your efforts have been rewarded by the dissolution of several nagging perplexities. What did you have in mind?

Quine: For light on the nature of meaning, I have speculated over the years on how a linguist might break into a hitherto unknown language and achieve translations. I had represented his entering wedge as translation of certain native sentences into English sentences that respond to the same sensory stimulations. But this seemed to require equating the native's stimulations with those of the linguist; and how to equate them was one of my nagging perplexities. Lately I concluded that we need not. The linguist merely finds that he can get on with his translations by associating the 'Jungle sentence' and his own sentence with his own stimulations. Here was one perplexity resolved.

Another was a question touched on a few minutes ago: what does the assuming of objects contribute to the linking of sensory stimulation with scientific theory? I concluded that it serves to tighten those logical links by reinforcing truth functions with quantifiers. I explained this in the volume *Action and Events* edited by Ernest Lepore and B.P. McLaughlin.

A third quandary concerned empirically equivalent but conflicting systems of the world. Davidson showed how to resolve their logical conflicts. Should we then reckon both as true? At last I have seen my way to doing so, by relating truth to an inclusive language rather than to either system exclusively.

A fourth insight has to do with empirically equivalent but conflicting manuals of translation. Both can be reckoned true by reckoning them as specifying two senses of 'translation'.

Cogito: Finally, tell us something about your origins. Your ancestors, I believe, came from the Isle of Man?

Quine: My father's father was born in the Isle of Man. The name 'Quine' is Manx. He went to sea as a sailor in 1866 at the age of sixteen, and plied the seas under sail for a year or more, from the Faeroes in the north to the Falklands in the south. My father's mother emigrated with her parents from Germany to Ohio. My grandfather met and married her there, and there both of my parents grew up, as did my brother and I. My mother's father, named Van Orman, came of Dutch stock some generations removed, and her mother came of British stock aged in New England.

4

ROGER SCRUTON

Art, education and politics

Roger Scruton has been Professor of Aesthetics at Birkbeck
College, University of London, since 1985. He has published
widely on aesthetics, the history of philosophy, political
theory, education and sexual desire. He has also written a
novel, *Fortnight's Anger*.

Roger Scruton (interview 1988) remains one of the most colourful and
controversial of British philosophers. Since our interview, he has been
extremely productive, publishing a steady stream of books and articles on
a wide variety of topics. The collection of essays, *The Philosopher on
Dover Beach* (1990) was followed by *Conservative Texts: An Anthology*
(1992) and *Modern Philosophy: An Introduction and Survey* (1995). More
recently still, we have seen *A Short History of Modern Philosophy: From
Descartes to Wittgenstein* (1996), *The Aesthetics of Music* (1997), *Edmund
Burke: A Genius Reconsidered* (1997) and *An Intelligent Person's Guide
to Philosophy* (1998).

Cogito: You have written on a lot of subjects: the philosophy of politics,
the philosophy of culture, the history of philosophy and aesthetics. Which
of all these things is your central concern?

Scruton: I regard myself as a 'man of letters' rather than a philosopher.
In so far as philosophy is central to my thought and literary practice, it
is because of the type of philosophy it is: not the straight analytical philosophy of the kind that one is used to at universities here.

Cogito: Many academic philosophers would associate you with your
contributions to aesthetics.

Scruton: Aesthetics has been the principal field of research over the first
ten or twenty years of my teaching career, but aesthetics is a subject which

forces you over the boundary of philosophy into neighbouring areas. In particular I have been very interested in philosophical problems that arise in the discussion of literature, music and especially architecture, which, it seems to me, have had deleterious effects on the practice of those arts.

Cogito: Could you give an example of this?

Scruton: In the case of architecture, much of the rhetoric of the modern movement, which has had enormous impact stylistically, stems from a false essentialism about building: a failure to see that the essence of any art lies in the appearance, and the desire to find something else which is the true essence. This is based on entirely false philosophical premisses, but it has had enormous impact. The over-emphasis on form and neglect of detail in the modern movement comes again from philosophical errors about the nature of aesthetic interest.

Cogito: In one of your essays on Philosophy and literature, you try to disentangle scientific or philosophical truth and literary truth. Could this be a reason for saying that we will never be able to do without art?

Scruton: That is an interesting way of putting it. It is obviously true that Newtonian physics is over because what it had to say, so far as it was true, has been absorbed into subsequent theories, and so far as it was false has been rejected. Literature does not have the same aim at an independent set of truths that science has and for that very reason does not have the same kind of expendability. What is said by a work of literature therefore, if it is a genuine and original one, is something not only which has not been said before, but which can justify itself irrespective of what has been said before. I think this touches on a very important question which is: just what is it that we learn from literature? It is not a body of propositions, not a set of truths that could be conveyed in some other way; obviously there is some integral connection between what we learn and the way in which it is presented, but at the same time our interest is not merely formal. It has some important impact on our lives.

Cogito: Could you explain why it is important for us to attend to books and plays?

Scruton: You are really asking what transformation of the individual is achieved by a high culture. It is not a matter of acquiring expertise or a full catalogue of published works; literary scholarship is independent of culture. But it is a matter of being able to see connections that are made more vividly and completely in works of poetry and imaginative prose, and to transfer those connections into the quality of one's daily life so that things, as it were, resonate. In their resonance they also enable you to evaluate them. For example, one of the most important things is to distinguish the true and false in one's own emotions. Which emotion is simply a momentary self-excitement, on which one could not build a life, and which involves that element of real commitment to something other than oneself? This is something people have rightly seen literature as providing us with the education to cope with.

Cogito: What about the visual arts and music?

Scruton: Visual art is very similar to literature in one way in that it, being a representational art, is presenting objects other than itself for our attention. It is inviting us to distinguish between those objects which are worthy of our attention and those which are not, and to try to see the emotional and moral meaning of particular episodes.

Cogito: Is there emotional and moral meaning within objects?

Scruton: Of course. We find the meaning of our lives outside ourselves and to the extent that we try and look for it inside ourselves, we lose it. There is nothing inside ourselves. Music is the great problem case in that it is not a representational art and yet its emotional impact is undeniable.

Cogito: There are theories that music acquaints us with pure emotion untainted by objects.

Scruton: There are such theories, but unfortunately they are based on quite naïve views about the nature of the emotions; they neglect the whole phenomenon of intentionality which is at the heart of emotional experience.

Cogito: 'Intentionality' being the direction of attention towards a specific goal or object?

Scruton: Yes. I think there has not been a successful theory of musical expression or musical understanding that has really come to grips with this problem of the moral reality of music; yet it is obvious that in music, more than in any other art, the distinction between good and bad taste can be drawn, and that bad taste contains enormous dangers. These are the dangers that Plato recognised in *The Republic* and which we would recognise in the Dionysiac frenzy of the discotheque.

Cogito: Do you regard the discotheque as an evil?

Scruton: Yes. I regard that form of dancing and that form of music as a decline from a use of music, a use of dancing, which create genuine moral relations between people.

Cogito: Would folk dancing be an example of this?

Scruton: We are now off the subject of music, but I think it is through the idea of dancing that a lot of the sense of the morality of music can be obtained. The dance in the modern world is first of all narcissistic; it is self-directed, it is undisciplined, it does not involve learning a disciplined order or step. It also is purely sexual in so far as it relates to another person; that other person with whom you are dancing is your sexual partner. If not, that is only an accident; whereas the traditional social dance could be done with anybody. It had a distant sexual meaning, but it was so filtered through ceremony that it was transformed into something else and it was a way in which whole communities could relate to each other, not through speech but through participation in a disciplined order other than themselves.

Cogito: Does your view on disco dancing stem from your philosophical objections to the doctrines of individualism?

Scruton: What I said about dancing is fairly abstract and does not particularly depend on any theory. You might say this is simply repudiating the individualistic approach to human contact. But if I were to address myself to your philosophical reflection – Is there underlying this a repudiation of individualistic modes of philosophising? – then I would want to say it depends what you mean. I would certainly not wish to reject the Cartesian inheritance in epistemology: the view that ultimately epistemological questions are about what I can know, and similarly, moral questions are about what I can know about my duties. In the end, the first person case does have a certain authority in defining philosophical problems; but when it comes to social philosophy then I would repudiate the philosophically interesting kind of liberalism which is associated with liberal political theory. I put my position in the following way: I believe, with Kant, that the individual is the ultimate source of all value and the ultimate object of all evaluations. Yet I also believe that he is also, in a very important respect, a social artifact. So I would like to keep one half of the liberal view, with its emphasis on the irreplaceable value of the individual, but also modify it in a Hegelian direction, recognising that what it is to be this kind of rational, choosing individual is not to be fully understood outside the context of social interaction and custom.

Cogito: The politics of liberalism stem from liberal individualism. What politics could stem from your philosophical view?

Scruton: In our time the options in political philosophy have been horribly under-described. On the one hand, there is the liberal individualist position, which has a metaphysics of the human individual lying at the heart of it, never fully explained; on the other one has the socialist collectivist, with an idea of the overall good for society, whether it is social justice, equality or whatever; I hold neither of those positions.

Cogito: Would your politics give rise to no plan for human society?

Scruton: In so far as there is such a thing as political conservatism, it consists precisely in the repudiation of the idea of a plan, and a recognition that rational conduct in society comes through the adoption of forms, customs and traditions which are not of one's own devising.

Cogito: To a lot of people tradition implies the oppression of the individual.

Scruton: Yes, but then that is where it is necessary to be more subtle about this question about what the individual is. For the old-fashioned Millian liberal, that is right. Mill talked of the 'despotism of custom', and thinks of custom as on the side of oppression of the individual who is trying to release himself from bondage. I think that the matter is far more subtle. If one can be forgiven for using Hegelian language, I think there is a dialectical relation between an individual and the community of which he is a part.

Cogito: Does talk of tradition not sound reactionary given the current British government's support of free-market liberalism?

Scruton: I do not know if your interpretation of the *realpolitik* of the Conservative party is right. Its actual appeal is the idea of the continuity of the British nation and of British sovereignty, the idea of law and order.

Cogito: Are you then well disposed towards the current movement of neo-Aristotelianism?

Scruton: Aristotle's vision of what man is, and particularly his philosophy of virtue, has got much in it that is of use to us and I think his idea of what a moral education is, is right.

Cogito: What consequences do his ideas have?

Scruton: That happiness consists in self-discipline, in acquiring habits that mediate between excess and deficiency. As I argue in my book on sexual desire, you cannot be an Aristotelian without seeing a lot of the point of traditional sexual morality. You cannot be a sexual libertarian and an Aristotelian.

Cogito: Aristotle believed that virtue could be acquired through habit. What do you therefore think of proposals to teach philosophy in schools, a subject in which critical thinking rather than factual retention is important?

Scruton: I am against teaching philosophy in schools for the reasons you are suggesting. It is fine to teach people to question, but first you must give them some certainties. Without certainties the whole point of intellectual endeavour would never be grasped. Unfortunately, and in our time increasingly, school subjects are not being taught as hard fact, but as areas of discussion and opinionated vagueness: that is to say, introducing into the classroom issues which can only be understood properly at the level of postgraduate research.

Cogito: Teachers might argue that the uncritical frame of mind encouraged by rote learning is a bad thing, it being better to encourage critical thinking in children to make them more inquisitive and searching.

Scruton: I know that is what teachers say, and I think they are wrong. They are wrong for the reasons that Aristotle gives, that we enter the palace of Reason through the Courtyard of Habit, and habit means learning things by rote, doing things without knowing the reason why, so that you will have the moral equipment to learn that reason later.

Cogito: Do you think, then, that most people are incapable of reaching the level of critical thought that you, for example, have reached, and should remain at the level of prejudice?

Scruton: If you count among prejudices such things as those intuitions that Kant tried to rationalise through the theory of the Categorical Imperative, it seems to me far better that they are accepted unquestioningly than that people learn to think critically about them and lose themselves in a wilderness of doubt and uncertainty.

Cogito: Is it all right for some people to think critically about them though?

Scruton: I think there is an enormous responsibility laid on everyone who does, not to be a corrupter of youth. To introduce critical thinking to people who first of all may not be capable of it, and second, who do not know how to use it responsibly, could be a bad thing. We have seen a growing relativisation of the values of ordinary people who are left rather bewildered not being given the sort of moral leadership they were once given by the Church.

Cogito: Do you believe that tradition, rather than critical thought, should have authority in our society?

Scruton: One should never make a god out of anything human, and tradition is only something human and therefore suffers from all the imperfections of everything else that we do. It does not have any absolute authority over us, it simply is a source of authority. It is interesting because it is a source of authority which comes from what has been rather than from what will be. Its advantage therefore is that you can know about it, unlike the future. The future has exerted too great a fascination over Western Man since the Age of the Enlightenment, and the past has been insufficiently attended to, despite the fact that it is epistemologically superior. One of the problems is understanding what we mean by tradition. My paradigm of tradition is Common Law, a continuously developing system of authority.

Cogito: Does our traditional moral view, embracing Kant, not demand some kind of equality of moral status for everyone? You cannot just claim autonomy or critical thinking for yourself according to this.

Scruton: It is part of what Western civilisation means, and what Christianity has meant from the beginning, that in some sense in the eyes of God we are all of equal value. That has been translated into the secular morality of Kant, in the terms of the Categorical Imperative: its logical structure is dictated by the attempt to eliminate the distinctions between people. At the same time, however, as Kant himself recognised, we cannot weigh one individual against another, put aside some individual for the sake of some goal. Therefore these plans to equalise people, in respect of their wealth or whatever, which involve riding roughshod over human arrangements or agreements, get ruled out by the same underlying egalitarian metaphysic which required them, and this has led to a tension within the whole European conception.

Cogito: How would you characterise this equality then?

Scruton: This equality is an equality at so deep a level that it does not actually emerge as a social prescription. The kind of equality one has in mind is best exemplified in a court of law: equality before the law, whereby each person, no matter what his social standing and so on, is to be judged by what he did and punished for that action, or compensated for that injury. That is the sort of equality that is built into our moral system. Some people argue that equality of respect between people stems from this.

Cogito: But is what is taken to be respectful itself not governed strongly by tradition?

Scruton: People's expectations determine exactly what equality of respect amounts to, and it is impossible to disentangle it from the historical given.

Cogito: Is a good person, in the Kantian sense, almost debarred from being a good politician?

Scruton: One's life as a moral being is well lived to the extent that one discharges one's responsibilities, and the responsibilities of the politician are different from those of a private individual. Moral virtue can be exemplified just as much in discharging one's political responsibilities as in discharging one's responsibilities towards the individuals one encounters in one's private life. There will always be different responsibilities and there is always the possibility of a clash. But the possibility of moral dilemmas is part of our condition.

Cogito: Would you say that Utilitarianism best suits the needs of politics, and Kantianism the needs of the individual?

Scruton: I would put it like this: it only seems that Utilitarianism is the scheme that governs the political sphere because the responsibilities of the politician are drawn so widely. What he is doing has a different description from what he does in the private sphere. His duty as a moral being is to discharge his responsibilities, not to try to remedy the human condition, or even increase the sum of happiness overall. One can reasonably argue, then, that as a moral being he is compelled not to reason in a utilitarian way. The standard conservative view makes a lot of use of the image of the 'ship of state'. This thing has been set in motion by someone else; you have been given the steering wheel. It is going nowhere in particular and the safety of everybody on board is your concern.

Cogito: Philosophy's tool is Dialogue, its task is Truth; Politics' tool is Rhetoric, its task is steering the Ship. Must this not make them stand opposed?

Scruton: Plato regarded himself as defending philosophy against rhetoric in much of his work. In the course of doing so he advocates a state constructed on philosophical principles with the philosopher as king. It is the most famous justification of the 'Holy Lie' in all history. He says that for a philosopher to rule, he must be prepared to countenance untruth told to the people. And sometimes I think rhetoric, which does not aim specifically at truth, might be a better way to ensure that truth does prevail than philosophy. The attempt to construct a state on philosophical principles, which we see in Leninism, leads to far greater institutionalised untruth than the to-ing and fro-ing of rhetoric. Attempting to impose a truth you yourself have not fully grasped is a recipe for disaster.

Cogito: Why do we not drop the whole philosophical project then?

Scruton: It is not a political project. It is a personal project, just as religion is; it is something which occupies our private hours, and maybe our happiness and salvation are in some deep way tied up with it.

Cogito: Do these reflections upon a midnight hour make you a better person in society?

Scruton: I am not sure about that. That is to go against the Burkean conception of how men live; men live well if they live by sound prejudice, and prejudices become weakened by this habit of too much reflection.

Cogito: You would not agree with the claim made by some philosophers that their philosophy leads them to a higher state of being?

Scruton: Somebody who is a philosopher, but who has not got some basic humility about his own activity, who thinks he makes himself superior to the ordinary man, is somebody who is deceiving himself, to say the least. Fortunately, analytical philosophy, as it now is, is something that nobody in his right mind could think made him morally superior to anyone. On the other hand, philosophy should involve the search for wisdom, and it is one of the catastrophes of our time that that whole philosophical enterprise has been set to one side. But wisdom is not a question of knowing a body of theoretical truths; it does involve the Aristotelian virtues and having some order in one's sentiments.

Cogito: For many people today philosophy still means a wisdom or a plan of life. Have we moved away from this in academic philosophy?

Scruton: Academic philosophy, as it now is, does address itself to the traditional idea of philosophy. It seems to me that all the questions surrounding self-knowledge and the first person and his relation to his world, as explored in Kant, are absolutely integral to having a conception of a starting point for morality constructed at the level of reflection, rather than at the level of prejudice. For example Wittgenstein's Private Language Argument, one of the most abstruse and difficult of all philosophical arguments, has enormous implications for the enterprise of creating a philosophy of life in our time. There are epistemological and metaphysical questions which have to be solved along the way of finding the path to wisdom.

Cogito: What are you working on at present?

Scruton: I am writing a novel at the moment and also preparing a study of the meaning of Wagner's Ring.

5

PETER STRAWSON

Sir Peter Frederick Strawson (1919–) is a leading figure in the post-war British philosophical scene. Following his war service (1940–6) he was appointed Assistant Lecturer in Philosophy at the University College of North Wales. A year later he moved to University College, Oxford, and in 1968 he succeeded Gilbert Ryle as Waynflete Professor of Metaphysical Philosophy, a succession that involved a move to Magdalen College. He was knighted in the Queen's Jubilee year 1977. Many of the major moves in the philosophy of the last forty years were initiated by his writings. His books include *An Introduction to Logical Theory* (1956), *Individuals: An Essay in Descriptive Metaphysics* (1959), *The Bounds of Sense* (1966), *Freedom and Resentment and Other Essays* (1974), and *Subject and Predicate in Logic and Grammar* (1974).

Professor Strawson (interview 1989) is another elder statesman of Oxford philosophy. Since our interview, he has published *Analysis and Metaphysics: An Introduction to Philosophy* (1992) and *Entity and Identity and Other Essays* (1997). He has also become the subject of a volume in the Library of Living Philosophers series, edited by Lewis Hahn under the title *The Philosophy of P.F. Strawson* (1998).

Cogito: This occasion is evocative for me of a philosophical baptism of fire I had to submit myself to some thirty years ago. In the autumn of 1959 I presented my very first seminar paper in English. At the time, in Freddie Ayer's Senior Seminar at University College London we were discussing your book *Individuals* which had just come out, and I was asked to report on one of the chapters. It was a tall order for anyone, let alone for a novice who had crossed the Channel for the first time only a year previously and was still none too surely feeling his way in the alleys and byways of analytical philosophy as well as fighting a fierce war of attrition with the English idiom. Freddie Ayer had a weird sense of humour in those days. Still, I am glad to say the book has survived my exegetic efforts, and has indeed gone from strength to strength to become something of a landmark in modern philosophy in the English-speaking world. What in your view has made it so spectacularly successful?

Strawson: I think a number of factors contributed to such effect as it had. The book was wider in scope – more ambitious, if you like – than most of the work published in the immediately preceding period. It made a quite unapologetic use of the word 'metaphysics' – which was overdue for revival anyway. It linked a number of central ontological or metaphysical issues with issues in the philosophy of logic and language, and unified them around a few crucial notions – those of identity and existence, on the one hand, and reference and predication on the other. It had a certain originality. The chapter in which I explored the fantasy of a purely auditory world was imaginatively appealing; and the one on 'Persons' seemed to many – and still does to me – to get close to the heart of the matter on a subject which is bound to be of intimate concern to everybody. This is beginning to sound like giving my own book a puff – so I'll stop there.

Cogito: Did you work to a plan from the beginning, or was the book – as often happens – the result of welding together different and independently written pieces of earlier work that seemed to arrange themselves around a single unifying theme?

Strawson: Like all my books, it emerged from lectures which I had given and developed over a number of years. I first gave the relevant lectures in this case in the year 1954–5, and the book appeared, as you say, in 1959. Since I always lecture from a full text, the actual writing up, in its final form, did not take more than about six months.

Cogito: May I ask you how you write? Some people agonise over every sentence. Do you revise a great deal, or do you commit your ideas to paper only after they have acquired more or less a final shape inside your head? Do you find writing philosophy difficult?

Strawson: Well, of course I find writing philosophy difficult, as everyone must do. On the other hand, I don't re-write a great deal. I have, before I begin, a pretty fair idea of the general line I am going to follow, and then I write each sentence with some care, thinking as I do so. At the end, I correct some sentences or improve them, even paragraphs, but large-scale re-writing – many drafts – is not something I go in for at all.

Cogito: I'd like us to return to *Individuals* again for a moment, if I may. In this book, in effect, you come down on the side of common sense, endorsing (I am quoting your own words) 'what we believe on instinct', viz. that things which exist in a fundamental sense – what Russell would have called the 'basic furniture of the world' – are material bodies and persons. Why, as philosophers, should we trust common sense?

Strawson: I wasn't concerned to defend common sense as such. I was concerned, rather, to elucidate the general structure of our conceptual scheme, i.e. the most general structural features of our thought and talk about the world and ourselves. This work of conceptual elucidation – whether undertaken in limited areas or, as in this case, more generally – seems to me the essential philosophical task. The aim is to achieve a kind of reflective conceptual self-consciousness. And, of course, the achievement of the aim – if it is achieved – isn't going to result in any radical change or *revision* of the scheme – merely a clearer understanding of it. But I agree, of course, also that many philosophers have thought that deep enough reflection should compel just such a radical revision. So my view has not been universally shared – though I think it might be said to have prevailed in our current tradition.

Cogito: I take your point about your book not being specifically intended as a defence of common sense. Nevertheless I take it that in essence you still subscribe to the thesis of the fundamentality of material bodies and persons?

Strawson: Well, that's difficult. I think if you take the criterion of being objects of reference as a criterion of existence, as Quine would do. I would agree that material objects and persons are basic objects of reference; and this is explicably so. One can argue as to why this is the case, why particulars in general are basic objects of reference, and why among them, material bodies and persons are fundamental; but I would think it a mistake to be restrictive about this and would add, and have argued, that abstract objects and other kinds of particulars should also be admitted to the domain of existents.

Cogito: As a comparatively young man you were involved in an intellectual exchange with Russell, which caused a considerable stir at the time. At the centre of the dispute was Russell's interpretation of the referential phrases beginning with a definite article – the so-and-so type of phrase – or 'definite descriptions', as they are called. How did the dispute come about, and what was so earth-shakingly important about such phrases?

Strawson: My disagreement with Russell, as you say, concerned phrases of the form 'the so-and-so' in the grammatical singular. Russell produced a solution of certain problems about such phrases by representing what he thought was their real logical form or character in what is now the accepted notation of modern formal logic. The solution – his 'Theory of Descriptions' – was ingenious and elegant. It was described by Frank Ramsey as a 'paradigm of philosophy'. But it seemed to me then – in 1950 – and still does, that the theory, though it may fit some cases, misrepresented the true character and function of these phrases, these expressions, as we actually use and understand them – at least for the most part; and that it did so by neglecting pragmatic, contextual and communicative aspects of their use. The issue was, and is, controversial. But I think the linguists would be mostly on my side. Not that there weren't faults of presentation on both sides in the original controversy.

Cogito: Russell, of course, replied to your criticism of his theory. Coming to think of it, you never commented publicly on his reply. Why not?

Strawson: It is perfectly correct that I didn't reply publicly to his reply. I thought that reply of his was unworthy of him, and didn't wish to show a degree of disrespect I would have had to show if I had replied candidly.

Cogito: Taking this disagreement to one side, how do you view Russell as a philosopher?

Strawson: Russell as a philosopher? I think one needs to make a sharp distinction between his work in logic and the philosophy of logic on the one hand, and his work in general metaphysics and epistemology on the other. As far as the first half of this division is concerned, Russell is a figure of quite major importance, who made perhaps more of a difference in the field of logic than anybody else in this century or, indeed, in any of the preceding centuries back to Aristotle. It is true that this logical revolution, so to call it, was largely anticipated by Frege, whose work became known to Russell in the early years of this century; but it was Russell, working in collaboration with Whitehead, who really carried the revolution to fruition and who, incidentally, found a devastating contradiction in Frege's own work. As regards the other half of the division – general metaphysics and epistemology – I think a different judgement is called for. Here Russell wrote much – in the empiricist tradition – and wrote with characteristic clarity and grace, but his particular views (which anyway changed from time to time) had neither the originality nor the lasting influence of his work in logic and the philosophy of logic.

Cogito: Did you feel any affinity with Russell's social and political views?

Strawson: I have a natural sympathy with Russell's Whiggish liberalism – though I think he was inclined to underestimate the complexity of social and political questions.

Cogito: Another target of your philosophical criticism was of course Austin, in particular Austin's version of the correspondence theory of truth. I have heard it said that Austin never quite managed to live down your onslaught on his correspondence theory. What was wrong with his theory, and have your own views changed in any way since then?

Strawson: I think Austin did not clearly distinguish the question of what it is for certain words, as uttered on a certain occasion, to constitute the utterance of a certain proposition or statement from the question what it is for that proposition or statement to be true. Of course the questions are connected, but not identical. Austin's remarks about semantical conventions bear on the first question rather than the second. On the second question I think Ramsey had it right: for a proposition to be true is for things to be as someone who utters that proposition thereby says they are. Of course this is a correspondence account in a sense, but I would call it a correspondence platitude or truism rather than a correspondence theory. I mention in passing that in my original (1950) criticism of Austin I made a mistake which I excluded from the subsequent ones. The mistake arose from confining my attention to positive assertions that some proposition was true and thus being trapped into declaring that all uses of 'is true' were cases of confirming or endorsing; and this is clearly incorrect, since 'is true' can also occur, without change of sense, in e.g. a conditional clause.

Cogito: Austin was of course your colleague at Oxford. What was he like as a man?

Strawson: He was very original, clever, witty and in many ways kind. It was always stimulating to be in his presence and sometimes a little alarming; for he was somewhat aloof – didn't go in for the ordinary amiable banalities – and could be devastatingly severe with whatever was muddled or pretentious.

Cogito: By contrast to Austin you seemed – philosophically, at any rate – to have been much more circumspect about Ryle; or am I misreading your own position? What is your own personal recollection of Ryle?

Strawson: I think of Ryle as the brilliant and benevolent leader of Oxford philosophy in the post-war period. The development and flourishing of the subject here owed an immense amount to his vision and his enterprise. Not that he was in the least autocratic. He shared Austin's dislike of personal gossip; but he was extremely good company, and an excellent and amusing conversationalist. I don't think I was particularly circumspect about him; indeed, I went so far as to criticise his accounts of his central, cherished notion of a type- or category-mistake.

Cogito: Ryle's 'magnum opus' was of course his *Concept of Mind*. What is your opinion of this book? Was Ryle right in thinking that the Cartesian dualism, ultimately, can be traced to a logical error?

Strawson: *The Concept of Mind*, though open to criticism, shows Ryle's characteristic combination of brilliance and insight. I don't think it would be quite right to suggest that Cartesian-type dualism was based on *a* – i.e. just one single – logical error; but I think it is quite right to say that it is in the end conceptually – or, in a broad sense logically – incoherent.

Cogito: Let us now talk about Kant. You have devoted to Kant a fine and much quoted book. Clearly Kant is your philosopher. Yet you reject Kant's doctrine of the 'Thing-in-itself', which many philosophers, including Kant himself, would regard as absolutely fundamental to his whole system. Notoriously this doctrine is a cornerstone of Kant's *Critique of Pure Reason*. Why do you think that this doctrine represents an aberration and that Kant needs to be rescued from himself, as it were?

Strawson: Well, anyone who reads *Critique of Pure Reason* must be aware of three features: first, that the work is extremely difficult; second, that it contains a uniquely ambitious attempt to describe and establish by argument the general structure, even the necessary structure, of our thought about the world of our experience; and third, that the explanation given of the supposed success of that attempt involves a contrast between the world of our experience, things of which we can have knowledge, on the one hand, and things including ourselves, as they *unknowably* are in themselves, on the other. The first feature – the difficulty – constitutes a challenge; the second – the attempt at an argued description of structure – seems to me the central purpose of philosophy; the third, the *soi-disant* explanation of the possibility and success of that attempt seems to me gratuitous, and even, by Kant's own best lights, dubiously intelligible or coherent. I hope that answers your question.

Cogito: Nevertheless one might interpret Kant's doctrine of the Thing-in-itself as a sort of insurance policy against idealism. For, once it is accepted (as Kant insisted it should be) that the world is knowable only as processed by our receptive mechanism of sense and reason, how can we be sure that there can exist such a thing as an 'unprocessed' reality at all? But leaving this aside, Kant of course had another reason for postulating the Thing-in-itself. He thought that whereas the phenomenal world was subject to strict causal laws, freedom must have a trans-phenomenal source.

Strawson: My answer to that is that such freedom as we enjoy requires no such transcendent source. We make decisions and choices in the light of our desires and beliefs, and if nothing prevents our acting in accordance with those choices and decisions, that is all the freedom it makes sense to want. I realise that many philosophers would be dissatisfied with this conventional answer – including Kant. But I cannot understand *his* answer and neither, to do him credit, did Kant claim to understand it himself. The most he claimed was that we could comprehend its incomprehensibility.

Cogito: Another philosopher whom I know you admire is Wittgenstein. I remember one occasion when I made a somewhat disparaging remark about Wittgenstein you voiced a strong disagreement, saying that in your view he was unquestionably a genius. He was also in many ways disastrously wrong. Why do you regard him as a genius?

Strawson: Perhaps I can begin to answer that question by saying that when, in the early 1950s, I first saw a typescript of Wittgenstein's *Blue Book* I felt that I was, for the first time, seeing thought *naked*, as it were. And this sense of his quality stays with one – or stays with me – as one reads more of the work of his later period. He has an extraordinary, almost unique, power of dispelling philosophical illusion, of helping us to get a clear view of how our language, and hence our thought, *actually works*. Mind you, he shows some traits I dislike: I don't care for the moral arrogance or for the refusal to engage in systematic and orderly exposition. But I'm inclined to see these as the *défauts de ses qualités*. In any case, it would be hard to mention another twentieth-century philosopher who is likely to have such a profound and lasting influence.

Cogito: Do I take it that you subscribe to Wittgensteinian doctrine that the way to find out about the structure of the world is to analyse the structure of the language in which we talk about the world, and hence that philosophy inevitably reduces to language analysis?

Strawson: I don't think that was Wittgenstein's doctrine at all – at least not in the work of his later period. He thought, rather, that we are apt to be led into philosophical error by failing to see clearly how our use of language is embedded in our 'forms of life', our practical activities. He aimed to dispel philosophical illusions by helping us to a clearer view of this. I myself think that a more systematic account of conceptual structures is possible than he ever sought, or wished, to produce.

Cogito: As far as I know, you have not published a great deal on ethical issues. I wonder whether something you said in an article called 'Social Morality and Individual Ideal' might provide a clue to this. There you wrote that 'the region of the ethical is the region where there are truths but no truth'. Could you explain this a little?

Strawson: I meant that we all have had the experience of encountering general statements about life – statements embodying some ethical attitude or reflecting some ethical ideal – with which we feel an immediate imaginative sympathy so that we may be prompted to say, or think, 'How true!'. But such statements, and the attitudes and ideals they embody, may be, and usually are, quite incompatible with one another. And one thing we do know is that incompatible propositions cannot be jointly true. I suggested that we should, within limits, welcome this variety of conflicting ideals or visions of the true ends of life, but resist the idea that any one such vision embodies the ethical truth. At the same time I contrasted this region of ethical ideals with what I called the common social morality. Which – among other things – should be such as to make room for the relatively harmonious co-existence and pursuit of different ideals.

Cogito: You are clearly strongly committed to the traditional liberal outlook on life; very much, I'd say, in the tradition of J.S. Mill. I wonder whether there is some sort of family history behind this. Was your father a dominant influence on you in your formative years?

Strawson: Well, no doubt genetic inheritance is partly responsible for anyone's outlook and views. As for my father's influence in my formative years – well, there might be said to have been a certain negative influence in that. His health having been ruined, and his temper impaired, in the First World War, he became somewhat intolerant and authoritarian – and those are attitudes I reacted, and react, against. So that might well be part of the explanation of what you refer to as my liberal outlook.

Cogito: Incidentally, what was your father's profession?

Strawson: He was a schoolmaster, indeed later in life headmaster of a London school. Both my parents were teachers.

Cogito: Might I end by asking you another personal question? I know you have a keen interest in literature, especially French literature. Moreover I have it on good authority that you write poetry. What motivates you to write verse? Is your poetry in any way philosophically inspired?

Strawson: I don't know how good your authority is. I write less poetry now than I did when younger. Such poetry as I do write is not in the least philosophical. It reflects personal concerns or is often quite frivolous light verse. If I could have chosen my talents, then I would have chosen to be a poet, but alas, I am not talented enough in that sphere.

6

HILARY PUTNAM

The vision and arguments of a famous Harvard philosopher

Professor **Hilary Putnam** teaches philosophy at Harvard University. His work, which spans and inter-relates the area of logic, mind, language and mathematics has exercised a great influence on contemporary philosophy. The three *Volumes* of his papers are required reading for students and teachers of philosophy. Others of his books, which contain clear and arresting discussions of themes central to modern philosophy, are *Reason, Truth and History, Meaning and the Moral Sciences* and, most recently, *Representation and Reality* (1988).

Professor Putnam (interview 1989) is now the Cogan University Professor in the philosophy department at the University of Harvard. Since our interview, he has published *Realism with a Human Face* (1990) and *Pragmatism: An Open Question* (1995), which indicate a further shift in his position away from the scientific realism of his earlier work and towards more pragmatist accounts of meaning and truth.

Cogito: Professor Putnam, what makes a good philosopher?

Putnam: No one thing. Just as there are different sorts of poet and different sorts of scientist, there are different sorts of philosopher. What made Kierkegaard a great philosopher was not the same thing that made Carnap a great philosopher. If one has to generalize, I would agree with Myles Burnyeat who once said that philosophy needs vision *and* arguments. Burnyeat's point was that there is something disappointing about a philosophical work that contains arguments, however good, which are not inspired by some genuine vision, and something disappointing about philosophical work that contains a vision, however inspiring, which is unsupported by arguments. But 'vision', 'argument', and 'support' can mean many different things.

44

Cogito: But on what grounds, then, can one criticize a philosophical theory? If, as you say, 'vision', 'argument' and 'support' can have different meaning, what distinguishes rational criticism from a mere expression of personal bias?

Putnam: We can and do criticize philosophical visions on a variety of different grounds – sometimes by criticizing their presuppositions, some-times by criticizing their feasibility, sometimes by criticizing their compatibility with other ends we are not willing to give up, and so on. As far as 'argument' and 'support' are concerned, there are very different senses of those notions, ranging from the strong deductive sense (deduc-tive proof), through various senses of 'inductive' argument and support, to what one might call 'pedagogical' arguments – the giving of examples and hints which are designed to get the reader to do the real work of figuring something out for himself, or to see that his perceptions have been biased. No one has given a formal criterion for the validity of an argument except in the first sense (the deductive sense), although episte-mologists have tried for centuries to state the principles which determine when a non-deductive argument is sound. But it doesn't follow that the distinction between a sound and an unsound non-deductive argument is non-existent or 'subjective', unless one is prepared to give in to scepti-cism completely. I don't have a 'proof' that scepticism is wrong, but I am certainly not a sceptic.

Cogito: Let us now turn to your own work. Your name is associated most frequently with a theory in the philosophy of mind known as 'function-alism'. Could you explain briefly what this theory is all about? Some people argue that functionalism really is just a refined form of materi-alism. What is your view on this?

Putnam: I no longer believe in functionalism – I say this, in case it was a presupposition of your question that I do. My new book, *Representation and Reality* (MIT Press, 1988) explains why I have given the position up. But I would still say that my functionalism was *neutral* with respect to the issue of materialism. The leading idea of functionalism – and I still accept this leading idea – goes back to Aristotle. It is simply the idea that we are not bodies *plus* immaterial souls, but things-that-think. (And not just 'think', but also things-that-desire, things-that-feel, and things-that-act-on-thoughts, feelings, and desires.) In other words – words Aristotle virtually used – our 'souls', properly conceived, are not separate substances but simply our organization-to-think, feel, desire, need and act on our thoughts, feelings, desires and needs. The 'soul' of a living organism is that organism's 'way of working', its effective capacities. Obviously, this view is completely neutral with respect to the question whether that 'way of working' is totally explainable in physical terms (which is one form of 'materialism'). And I always rejected the view that our mental predicates are *reducible* to our physical ones – which is another meaning of the word 'materialism'. So in one sense I was neutral with respect to the question of materialism, and in another sense I was anti-materialist.

What my functionalism added to Aristotle's theory was the idea that our 'way of working' at the psychological level, our mental states, could be described in the language one uses to describe a digital computer. This language is neutral with respect to the question 'What *stuff* does the computer consist of?', and indifferent to the question, 'Does the computer, as a whole, obey the laws of physics or does it obey different laws?' Thus my functionalism, like Aristotelian proto-functionalism, was neutral with respect to the question of materialism. (By the way, *that* question only arose millennia after Aristotle lived, since the notion of 'physical law' involved in *our* debates about materialism did not exist until Galileo.) My former position could be described as *computer-ism*, perhaps, but not as materialism.

Cogito: What you say about functionalism being 'neutral' with regard to materialism is evocative of Gilbert Ryle's 'logical behaviourism' which equally pursued the policy of neutrality with regard to materialism/anti-materialism in its analysis of mental phenomena. Leaving the analogy with computers to one side, in what way does functionalism represent an advance as compared to logical behaviourism?

Putnam: In the first place, functionalism did not depend on the dubious notion of 'analyticity' (or 'conceptual necessity') that logical behaviourism relied on. Functionalism was a thesis about what mental states *are*, not a thesis about what psychological predicates *mean*. I would say that, in that respect, it was more sophisticated than logical behaviourism. (I know that what I've just said runs counter to the view – still popular in some versions of analytic philosophy – that it is always more sophisticated to formulate philosophical questions as questions about 'concepts' rather than about things.) In the second place, functionalism recognized that mental states are *explanatory* – to say that someone is angry is to explain why he behaves in certain ways, not just to say that he is disposed to behave in those ways. And of course the connection with computer science was not just incidental; by exploiting that connection, functionalism opened up a host of new questions for philosophers and cognitive scientists, questions which it is apparent will be argued about for years.

Cogito: Why have you abandoned functionalism? It might be useful at this point, I think, especially for those who have not had a chance to read your book, if you sketched out briefly your present position.

Putnam: Functionalism was itself a reaction against the idea that our matter is more important than our function, that our *substance* is more important than our *activity*. My functionalism argued that, in principle, a machine (say, one of Isaac Asimov's robots), a human being, a creature with a silicon chemistry, and a being with an ectoplasmic body could all work much the same way when described at the relevant level of abstraction, and they would all be conscious, all have feelings, etc. That much I have not given up. Functionalism argued that mental states cannot simply *be* physical–chemical states, although they are emergent from and supervenient on physical–chemical states; I now argue that mental states also cannot be computational states, although they are emergent from and may be supervenient on our computational states. I do this by showing that the way in which mental states are individuated is enormously different from the way in which computational states are individuated – so different, that a one-to-one correspondence is impossible.

Cogito: I now wish to ask you about the conditions of meaningful ascription of certain mental states to animals and humans. Is it merely a prejudice rooted in the way our civilization has evolved that prevents us from ascribing to animals, even those that are close to us in evolutionary terms, the kinds of feelings that we ascribe to humans? If an animal can feel pain, why can't it feel remorse?

Putnam: First of all, some animals do feel remorse: human beings are animals, and human beings feel remorse. But I take it that the question is, why can't a non-languaged animal feel remorse? And the answer is that, as a point of conceptual analysis, to feel remorse one has to feel that one has failed to do what one ought to do, not just that one has failed to do what one *wanted* to do – there is a difference between regret and remorse. (Remorse also involves the idea that someone has suffered as the result of one's failure to do what one ought.) The notion that one ought to do something in turn depends on other notions   the notion of an obligation, for example, and the various notions that we use to describe faults of character – ingratitude, unkindness, and so on. Typically, I am remorseful if I feel my action not only hurt someone else, but that it manifested 'selfishness', or 'injustice', or 'insensitivity', or the like. In short, 'remorse' is a *post-language* emotion. Does this mean that only humans can feel remorse? Not necessarily. Chimpanzees have learned some language. Whether they can learn enough to make it appropriate to say they have acquired notions like 'ought' and feelings like 'remorse' is an empirical question. But it is an empirical question which is surrounded by conceptual confusions (such as failure to appreciate the difference between a concept like 'feeling sorry' and a concept like 'feeling remorse').

Cogito: Would you go as far as saying that remorse *in principle* could be meaningfully attributed to computers too, provided their language was rich enough?

Putnam: I already said that I still think that Isaac Asimov's wonderful robots would be conscious! But the robot's language isn't what would have to be rich: the robot *life* would have to be rich as well. Unless the robot behaved in a way that led us to attribute a *life* to it, and not just 'performance', there would be no sense in ascribing emotions to it.

Cogito: In connection with this, could you perhaps comment on the work that is going on in the field of 'artificial intelligence'? What precisely does the term mean?

Putnam: The term 'artificial intelligence' is one I don't like. Supposedly, 'artificial intelligence' researchers are trying to make computers that 'think', computers that are (at least in certain respects) as intelligent as (or more intelligent than) a human being. In reality, they are simply software designers. That some software designers call their work 'artificial intelligence' does not, in my view, mean very much. Nothing that has so far been done really deserves the name 'artificial intelligence'. But it is understandable that philosophers are interested in discussing the *possibility* of machines that think.

Cogito: Do you subscribe to the view that it is, in principle, possible to construct machines that will be capable of highly abstract thought, including philosophical thought, similar to human beings? Does the idea of a 'robot philosopher' make sense?

Putnam: I said that my view – both my former view and my present view – is neutral with respect to the question whether human beings are completely subject to the laws of physics, which is one form of the question of 'materialism'. But in fact I believe that they are; so in that sense I am a 'materialist'. But so was G.E. Moore, who believed that there are properties that things have – value properties, in particular – which are completely 'non-natural' (i.e. non-physical). Moore did not doubt that everything *obeys* the laws of physics; he doubted that all the properties of things are reducible to physical properties. And so do I. So, in what I think of as the important sense, I am not a materialist. But that doesn't mean that I deny that a physical system – even, perhaps, an artificial one – can be the seat of mental, emotional, value, etc., *properties*. Our bodies are, at least metaphorically, 'machines'. And our bodies are the seat of mental, emotional, and value properties. The idea of a 'robot philosopher' makes complete sense to me. The question is, whether such a thing is actually possible, not whether it involves a conceptual absurdity. With respect to that question – the question of actual possibility – I am extremely sceptical. Our mental working is, in my view, probably not something that we can describe well enough to succeed in simulating it in a computer. But that is an empirical question. What I do think is that, if we ever succeeded in constructing 'robots that think', we would find their thoughts – and their emotions – as unpredictable as those of human beings. If that seems strange – the idea of a computer that humans build, but whose behaviour humans cannot predict – reflect on the fact that there already exist complex programs whose working cannot be predicted except by actually running them and seeing what happens!

Cogito: Is there any difference between philosophy of mind and theoretical psychology?

Putnam: Here is an example of a proposition in philosophy of mind that I believe to be true: even if we succeeded in describing the working of our brains completely in cause–effect terms, such a success could not and would not answer the question: what makes some of the things that go on in our brains or minds *thoughts*, i.e. what makes them *about* something other than themselves, what makes them *true* or *false*? These properties – 'aboutness', truth-value (and one could add such epistemological properties as being confirmed or warranted) – are not causal-descriptive properties. They are properties of another kind altogether. Many philosophical discussions have been relevant to the nature of these properties (among recent discussions, I think of discussions by Wittgenstein, Davidson, and Quine). But *scientific* discoveries, while not irrelevant to philosophy, do not answer questions which are not requests for a causal explanation, but rather attempts to know 'how things hang together'.

Of course, conceptual questions and scientific questions interpenetrate. Einstein had to do conceptual work on the notion of 'simultaneity' to clear the way for a new empirical theory, and some conceptual analyses become obsolete because the concepts in question turn out to be bad concepts for empirical reasons. (The idea that conceptual truths are totally 'necessary' has been shattered by Wittgenstein and Quine.) But there is still a difference between conceptual inquiries and empirical ones. One of the central conceptual questions that philosophers are discussing today is the question whether the nature of 'meaning' is really a question for *psychology* at all. The radical alternative – this has been defended by the young American philosopher Tyler Burge – is that 'meaning' is a *social* phenomenon. If Burge is right, then theories of the nature of meaning which simply assume the answer must be found at the level of individual psychology, or individual neurology, or even 'artificial intelligence', are badly confused. This connects with a previous question: if animals don't feel remorse, Burge would say it is because they don't have the right sorts of *social* interactions. Actually, I think he is right.

Cogito: Let us now turn to another issue that has been the subject of much debate recently, that of realism. Common sense urges on us the belief in a world that exists independently of anyone's perception, or even thought; an entirely objective world 'out there'. Are you a realist in this sense?

Putnam: I don't at all agree with your claim about 'common sense'. I don't think 'common sense' has any view at all on philosophical questions about things existing 'independently' of our perceptions, because I think the notion of 'independence' is a metaphysical one, one that has no place in common sense, and, in fact, I think the notion is hopelessly confused. Of course, the moon exists 'independently' of my perceptions in the sense of having existed *before* there were perceptions. Its existence was not *caused* by perceptions. But no philosopher *says* it was caused by perceptions. To pretend that critics of 'realist' metaphysics deny the *causal* independence of the moon, or the solar system, etc., from human thought and perception is to misdescribe the issue. The first problem, in trying to get any clarity on these debates, is to see how obscure questions about the 'independence' of the objects of perception and thought really are, not to simply treat them as clear questions.

If I had to give a very rough sketch of my own picture, I would say that there is an 'objective' world in the sense that there are states of affairs which obtain whether we believe they do or not, but that those states of affairs do not force one unique description upon us. Thus the world is both 'objective' and not 'objective'; we cannot ask what is the case without choosing some system of concepts (and no one system is uniquely fitted to describe 'the world'); but once we have a system of concepts in place, what is true or false is not simply a matter of what we *think*. Again, I have to emphasize that these are difficult philosophical questions, and the pretence that 'common sense' has any view about them at all seems to me just that – a pretence.

Cogito: Some argue that the thesis that there is something existing independently – logically independently – of whether it is thought or talked about, some kind of 'thing in itself', strictly cannot even be intelligibly *asserted*. What is your view on this?

Putnam: I notice that now you have given 'independently' the sense of 'logically independently'. Well, there is a famous paradox about saying that there is a natural number that no one ever talks about; for if there is such a number, then there is such a number as *the smallest natural number that no one ever talks about*; and, in using this phrase, haven't I just talked about it? Similarly, there is a paradox about saying there is a bird, or a hill, or anything else that no one ever talks about.

The solution is to distinguish levels of language: is there any contradiction in saying that there is a thing – say a hill – that no one ever describes without using any 'higher order' expressions (without using 'semantical' terms like 'talks about')? No there isn't. And no philosopher *says* there is any contradiction. Every philosopher thinks there can be things which exist 'logically independently' of whether they are ever talked about (in first-order language). Again, the position of philosophers like me – critics of stock 'realist' views – is being caricatured.

The hard question – and the real question – is whether there can be things that exist in such a way that we *couldn't* verify that they exist. Of course there can be things that we don't learn of, things that no one ever verifies the existence of; but as long as they *could* be learned of, described, and so on, they aren't what Kant called 'things in themselves'. The notion of a 'thing in itself' is the notion of something whose properties couldn't be described, verified, by sentient beings like ourselves. (So a hill couldn't be a 'thing in itself'.) With respect to this question, the hard question, I would say that the notion of a 'thing in itself' in this sense is hopelessly confused for two reasons. First reason: because the word 'thing' (or 'object') has not one use, but an enormous variety of alternative uses. (Are *numbers* 'things'? Are *points* in space (*or* space-time) 'things'?) The idea that reality itself fixes the use of the word 'thing' is a hangover from pre-scientific metaphysics. But this metaphysical idea is presupposed by the question, 'Are there things in themselves?' Second reason: truth, in my view, is tied to the use of words. The meaning of the words we use does not somehow establish itself, it does not outrun the way we use our words. The notion that something we say might be 'true' although nothing could license our *calling* it true is just the myth of a meaning that transcends use. Rejecting that myth isn't in any way denying that there is a world (cf. my answer to the previous question), or saying that there is only perception and thought; rather, what I am saying is that language is a *human* instrument, and what we can *say* about the world depends on the ways we use that instrument.

Some philosophers who have seen that the notion of a 'thing in itself' is confused, have, none the less, defended the idea of a reality which is 'independent' in the sense that all scientific investigation of it is destined to converge to one single theory, one single picture. But this too is confused; for every major physical theory has a variety of radically different formulations. Quantum mechanics, famously, can be presented as a description of the behaviour of particles (no 'waves') *or* as a description of the behaviour of fields ('waves'). It's the same theory, presented either

51

way, and it describes the same states of affairs. Does it describe the same 'objects'? Not in any sense I can understand. 'Objects', in quantum mechanics, arise within the particular scheme that we use to describe the 'objective' reality. The reality is objective, but the 'objects' aren't! Perhaps this *is* a shocker to 'common sense'; if so, common sense will have to change, as it has changed in the past.

Cogito: What, in your view, are the most important tasks that philosophy should try to accomplish?

Putnam: A currently popular description of the task of philosophy is due to Wilfrid Sellars – 'To say how things, in the widest sense of "things", hang together, in the widest sense of "hang together".' Broad as that task is – and I agree that it is a task that philosophers have always taken on – it is not the whole task of philosophy. Speculating about how things hang together requires knowledge, sophistication, imagination, the ability to draw out conceptual distinctions and connections, and the ability to argue. The activity appeals to our curiosity, our daring, our delight in intellectual keenness. But speculative views, however interesting, or well supported by argument, or insightful, are not all we need. We also need what Burnyeat called 'vision' – and I take that to mean vision as to how to live our lives, and how to order our societies. Philosophers have a double task: to integrate our various views of our world and ourselves (and we are bombarded with a greater number of such views today than ever in history, in part because all the views that have been produced in history are available to us today), and to help us find a meaningful orientation in life. Finding a meaningful orientation in life is not, I think, a matter of finding a set of doctrines to live by, although it certainly includes having views; it is much more a matter of developing a *sensibility*. Philosophy is not only concerned with changing our views, but also with changing our sensibility, our ability to perceive and react to nuances. Philosophers are, ideally, *educators* – not just educators of youth, but of themselves and their peers. Stanley Cavell once suggested that as the definition of philosophy – 'education for grown-ups'. I think that is the definition I like best.

Cogito: Who, among philosophers past or present, do you admire most?

Putnam: Let me confine myself to philosophers since the eighteenth century, since they are the ones most relevant to the situation we ourselves are in: I admire Kant, not just for his undoubted genius, but for his breadth of vision – his concern with religious and social as well as theoretical epistemological and metaphysical questions, and his ability to integrate all of those concerns. I admire Kierkegaard, for his insistence on the priority of the question, 'How shall I live?'. In our own century, I admire Russell, for his unbelievable logico-philosophical gifts, James – who badly needs to be rehabilitated and reinterpreted – for his unique combination of epistemological and moral ideas, Peirce for his originality and fertility – many of Peirce's ideas are only really beginning to be 'mined' now, Dewey for his epistemological and ethical holism and fallibilism, and for his combination of philosophy with social and educational activism, and Wittgenstein for sheer *depth*. In my view, Wittgenstein was simply the *deepest* philosopher of the century (and, unfortunately, the most misunderstood, with the possible exception of James). Of my own acquaintances, I most admire W.V. Quine and Nelson Goodman – two philosophers of genius, and two wonderful people.

Cogito: What arguments would you use to try to persuade the business community to help keep in existence philosophy departments within universities? Or would you rather philosophers received their money from the government?

Putnam: In my country, I am happy to say, the business community has continued to understand that you cannot have flourishing 'applied' knowledge, unless you support 'basic' research, including philosophical research. I know that this is a fact which has been currently forgotten in many countries; I am sure that the countries that have forgotten it will learn to their sorrow that this is a disastrous error. At a more fundamental level, I would simply say that we need a sense of direction more than we ever have. In a democracy, a direction cannot be imposed; it will either come from a surge of emotion – and that leads to disaster – or it will come from reflective discussion. Philosophy does not provide 'answers', but it is still the best model we have of informed reflective discussion. Government support helps when it is available, but I think the independence of philosophy, and of the university in general, requires strong support from the private sector.

Cogito: Returning now to your own work, people have been impressed not only by the wealth and novelty of your ideas, but also by your highly readable prose. Do you have an interest in literature as well as philosophy? What do you read?

Putnam: Thank you for the compliment! I do love literature – my father, Samuel Putnam, was a writer, in fact – and my reading is wide and unpredictable. George Eliot, Henry James, the Austrian novelist Robert Musil, and the Israeli writer S.J. Agnon (whom I read in Hebrew) are among my favourites in recent years. Part of Wittgenstein's appeal to me is that he is a writer as much as a philosopher.

Cogito: What are you working on now, and what are your plans for the future?

Putnam: I am beginning to work on an interpretation of the philosophy of William James. That is my next big project. After that – we'll see!

7

STEPHAN KÖRNER

Stephan Körner, JurDr, PhD, FBA was born in Czecho-
slovakia and was educated at Charles' University, Prague and
Trinity Hall, Cambridge. He was Professor of Philosophy at
Bristol University 1952–79 and at Yale University 1970–84.
His interests in, and contributions to, philosophy are wide-
ranging. Few students of philosophy will have missed his
celebrated study of *Kant* (Penguin Books, 1955). Amongst his
many other distinguished writings are *The Philosophy of
Mathematics, Experience and Theory, Experience and
Conduct, Metaphysics: Its Structure and Function. Who's Who*
lists Stephan Körner's recreation as 'walking'. Readers of the
following interview will discover that he has vigorously tra-
versed an extensive and fascinating philosophical landscape.

Stephan Körner (interview 1990) is still a familiar figure to members of
the University of Bristol, and a welcome visitor to the philosophy department. Meanwhile many of his ideas, e.g. on the logic of imprecise or 'fuzzy'
concepts, and on the role of categorial frameworks in our ordering of
experience, are being taken up by a new generation of philosophers.

Cogito: We are pleased to be sitting in a drawing room with Professor
Körner, whom we have known for many years. Although during the last
fifteen years of your academic career you have divided your time between
Bristol, Yale and Graz universities, you have always regarded Bristol as
your home. It is a great pleasure to interview you, Professor Körner. You
were born in Czechoslovakia and as a student you studied, and then briefly
practised, the law there. What influence did your legal studies have on
your philosophy?

Körner: I was from the very beginning greatly impressed by the contrast
between legal thinking, on the one hand, and mathematical thinking on
the other. That impression has stayed with me. If you look at mathematical

thinking and at scientific thinking, in so far as it is embedded in mathematics, you can hardly fail to note that mathematical thinking is governed by the Fregean requirement that the definition of every concept determine for every object once and for all whether or not it falls under it. In legal thinking the situation is quite different, as already the Roman lawyers clearly saw. For many legal concepts are not exact, but admit of borderline cases and their meaning is partly determined in the course of their application. When a judge comes across a borderline case, he can't just say, 'Sorry, this is a borderline case.' He must decide whether it is to be turned into a positive or negative case and his decision can, and often does, become a precedent for the future application of this concept. Now this inexactness is characteristic not only of legal thought but also of ordinary thinking. This feature of ordinary language has been emphasized by Wittgenstein, although, so far as I know, he was not aware that its recognition was commonplace among lawyers.

Cogito: Philosophy, it is said, is commonly, at least to some extent, pursued by means of analysis. But analysis is a very broad term and presumably there are different forms of analysis, let us say in history, that are not philosophical. Just what kinds of analysis are the proper preoccupations of philosophers?

Körner: I agree with your statement that the concept of philosophical analysis stands itself in need of clarification, and I've pointed that out quite often. I find it especially useful to distinguish between two kinds of analysis which I respectively call 'exhibition-analysis' and 'replacement-analysis'. Exhibition-analysis does nothing else but make explicit the rules which we use in our thinking. For exhibition-analysis it does not matter if these rules turn out to be inconsistent with each other or defective in some other sense, because its aim is to exhibit the rules as they are. As against this, replacement-analysis is concerned with replacing defective concepts (or, more precisely, concept-governing rules) by sound concepts. The fulfilment of this task presupposes the adoption of some criteria of soundness. Among them are not only the principle of non-contradiction and other logical principles, but also non-logical principles. An example of such a non-logical, 'supreme' principle is the principle that *natura non facit saltus*, which was accepted by Leibniz and Einstein among others. Replacement-analysis consists in replacing concepts which are defective in the sense of being inconsistent with a person's logical or non-logical supreme principles by concepts which are consistent with these principles and serve the purposes which the replaced concepts were meant to serve.

Cogito: So then I think we should ask you, is philosophical analysis an autonomous activity?

Körner: I would say that exhibition-analysis is autonomous. But replacement-analysis goes beyond the mere exhibition of defects by stating the conditions for their removal and by trying to satisfy these conditions. In so far as replacement-analysis depends on criteria of soundness, it depends on wider philosophical assumptions.

Cogito: But I think you are critical of at least one school of analysis which presumably fails to meet the requirement you have just stated – Oxford ordinary language analysis as practised in the 1950s and 1960s.

Körner: Yes, Oxford ordinary language analysis as practised by some people seemed to me to be rather superficial and strange. It seemed to me to be based on a principle which I found to be unacceptable. The principle could be formulated in a somewhat exaggerated way as follows: If it sounds odd it can't be true.

Cogito: I assume that of all philosophers Kant has had the greatest influence upon you. Your book on Kant in the Penguin Philosophy Series must now have been read by generations of undergraduates. Which philosophers, however, had the earliest influence upon you?

Körner: The philosophers who had the earliest influence upon me were Schopenhauer, whom I came across by accident and whose style, especially in the original German, I still greatly admire, and Spinoza; later came Leibniz and Kant, and to some extent also Plato.

Cogito: That seems a fine list of philosophers to have been influenced by.

Körner: Yes, but I would say, Leibniz and Kant have become most important to me.

Cogito: You were a postgraduate student at Cambridge from 1939 to 1943 with the support of the Czechoslovak government in exile. Could you tell us what philosophical life was like at Cambridge at that time? Was it very different from what it now is?

Körner: I do not know very much about present philosophical life in Cambridge, but when I was there it was very exciting. First of all I learnt a very great deal from my supervisor, Richard Braithwaite, and I also enjoyed Wittgenstein's, Broad's and Ewing's lectures, as well as the meetings of the Moral Sciences Club at which they expressed their often fierce disagreements with each other. Braithwaite convinced me, among other things, that contemporary philosophers should not ignore mathematical logic. For even if you condemn it as philosophically irrelevant, as I don't, it is important that you should know what it is that you so condemn.

Cogito: You developed an account of the nature of scientific theories in your book, *Experience and Theory*. May I ask you now a rather large question, but a direct one. How do your own views differ from those of Kuhn and Popper?

Körner: I would say that I make a distinction which, I think, they also make between scientific information and scientific explanation. But I make this distinction differently. If I may give an example: it very often happens that scientists who deny the explanatory power of a scientific theory yet appreciate its predictive power. Thus Einstein, who rejected orthodox quantum mechanics as lacking explanatory power, made contributions to the theory because of its predictive power. The same applies to Leibniz who made, as he points out, contributions to a 'Democritean' theory to which he denies explanatory power. Now Kuhn tries to account for this explanatory power by his theory of paradigms. And he distinguishes between revolutionary science and normal science. As an example of revolutionary science he gives general relativity theory. And here it is rather interesting to note that Einstein disagrees with him and thinks that the theory is not revolutionary. So what is revolutionary science for one person can be normal science for another. I think that Kuhn's notion of paradigm is not clear enough to account for this fact. Instead of the notion of paradigm I have introduced the notion of a categorial framework, which bears some analogy to a country's constitution, since an action which is constitutional in one country, may be revolutionary in another. A person's categorial framework consists of his logical principles, as well as a certain class of his other supreme principles which, though they may differ from person to person, have some important features in common. (I have discussed this, in detail, in *Metaphysics: Its Structure and Function*.) It is because the categorial frameworks of Kuhn and Einstein are different that the theory of general relativity constitutes a scientific revolution for Kuhn and a normal development for Einstein.

Cogito: And Popper?

Körner: What I mainly object to in Popper's theory is that he does not consider sufficiently the difference between what is formulated in ordinary language and what is formulated in scientific theories. That is to say, he seems to me to overlook the role of idealization in science. In my view the application of a scientific theory, especially a mathematized scientific theory, is dependent upon an idealizing transition from ordinary language to the language of the theory. The steps are the following: description in ordinary language which everybody understands; idealization, i.e. translation into the theory; intra-theoretical deduction; and then de-idealization of the conclusion back into ordinary language. This way of accounting for scientific information explains *inter alia* why even incompatible scientific theories can together give more information than they do separately.

Cogito: Is the idea of idealization connected to another very arresting thing that you say about science, and that is that it is a Procrustean activity?

Körner: I do not recall having said that, but I would say that idealization involves a modification of ordinary experience, as described in ordinary language. A simple example is the relation between an empirical triangle and a Euclidean triangle. An empirical triangle (say a triangle drawn on a blackboard or a triangular fence) differs from a Euclidean triangle in many obvious ways. For instance, a Euclidean triangle has sides which are one-dimensional, whereas the sides of an empirical triangle are three-dimensional. Unlike the empirical triangle's sides the Euclidean triangle's sides consist of a non-denumerable infinity of dimensionless points. So it is obvious that the concept of an empirical triangle and the concept of an Euclidean triangle are quite different. Yet they are conditionally identifiable. That is to say that for certain purposes and in certain contexts one can treat them *as if* they were the same and this is characteristic of all mathematical idealizations. Idealizations are not limited to mathematical thinking. Yet what is peculiar to it is the employment of highly comprehensive idealizations, in particular idealizations which affect the whole of mathematics or of some branch of it. The foremost example is, of course, 'exactification', i.e. the satisfaction of the requirement that all mathematical concepts be exact. Another important example is 'infinitization', i.e. the introduction of the concepts of the infinitely great and the infinitely small.

Cogito: Picking up this point, Professor Körner, about idealization, you remark in *Categorial Frameworks* that there are some disciplines where this idealization has not taken place – and you give history as an example; whereas physics, as you say, is a double-layered discipline, history is single-layered because idealization does not take place in historical thinking. Now in *Fundamental Questions of Philosophy* you discuss Collingwood's philosophy and you say, 'The historical science of ultimate presuppositions is too different from traditional metaphysics to be called by its name, yet historical dogmatics, as it might be renamed, is a perfectly feasible type of enquiry, interesting in itself and useful.' Now it strikes me that perhaps Collingwood is raising a question of understanding something like a two-layered approach to history, that is to say that history as we speak it now is in the everyday language of today, but we have to understand the historical dogmatics of another age, which is not unlike the sort of idealization you are talking about.

Körner: I would say that history is in any case free of the exactification and infinitization which are characteristic of mathematics. Moreover, in so far as it is the historian's task to describe events as they actually happened, he must avoid replacing their description by a representation which modifies them in any way. And idealization, in any sense of the term, involves such a modifying representation.

Cogito: Many years ago I was impressed by your discussion and account of the Einstein–Born correspondence and your exposition of the (perhaps for a non-scientist surprising) view that Einstein, despite being so intimately connected with the development of quantum theory, in fact held the laws of nature to be deterministic rather than probabilistic. And it was of interest, I remember, all the time to consider the sort of claim Einstein was making when he said this.

Körner: Well, in Heisenberg's introduction to that volume, he asserts that physical theory cannot be pursued except in a philosophical framework. The physicist must make certain assumptions which he accepts because of their explanatory power. For Einstein the principles of continuity and determinism were among these assumptions. So I would say that his categorial framework was different from the categorial framework of Born. And it is very interesting to see that their main disagreement is philosophical. It is a disagreement about those supreme principles which were different for Born and Einstein. And I think that not only Einstein but also Born was aware of this. In this connection it is worth noting that Einstein's answer to the question whence he got his supreme principles of determinism and continuity, amounted to the statement that he plucked them out of the air.

Cogito: We know of the considerable influence of Kant – you've already spoken of that – on your own work. May we then ask how far your own metaphysical system is similar to that of Kant's?

Körner: I find a distinction, which Kant makes, extremely useful, namely the distinction between immanent metaphysics and transcendent metaphysics, the topic of which is 'reality' or 'the world in itself'. But whereas Kant holds that both systems are unique, I reject this uniqueness claim. In fact Kant's *Critique of Pure Reason* is not only supposed to provide the immanent metaphysics, or the categorial framework, if I may use my own expression, of Newtonian physics. He also holds that Newtonian physics and, hence, its categorial framework do not admit of alternatives. That I reject the uniqueness claim for immanent metaphysics is clear from what I said about the Einstein–Born correspondence. I also consider it a mistake to think that there is only one transcendent metaphysics. In my view there are various systems of transcendent metaphysics, all of which are the result of pure speculation. But I would not reject transcendent metaphysics since it has, for example, turned out useful to science. For even if, to use Wittgenstein's terms, when you do transcendent metaphysics the engine of language idles, it can sometimes be put into gear. Consider, for example, the Democritean theory of atoms which later was woven into the science of physics and chemistry. Just as some pure mathematics can become applied mathematics, so some speculative metaphysics can find its way into science. And to reject it without qualification seems to me unreasonable.

Cogito: I think your rejection of uniqueness in metaphysics is a very valuable contribution to philosophy. And some of the most interesting things that you've written are in *Categorial Frameworks* and in your later book, *Metaphysics*, where you discuss the various kinds of immanent metaphysics and, even more interesting, how one may pass from one metaphysical system to another, or from one categorial framework to another. And you mention the concepts both of the 'corrigibility' of metaphysics, which implies an improvement in metaphysical systems, and 'progress' in metaphysics, again with the same implications of doing better. I wonder whether you would like to say any more about these concepts of corrigibility and progress in metaphysics?

Körner: I would say that while I accept the notion of metaphysical change, I do not accept the notion of metaphysical progress *per se*, because in order to speak of it one must have a criterion of such progress. Now I think that in the sciences we have a criterion of progress which is independent of their explanatory power, namely the increase in predictive power. As against this the notion of metaphysical or explanatory progress is much less clear and depends on certain convictions which cannot be conclusively justified. In this connection I may recall Einstein's acknowledgement of his inability to justify his – as opposed to Born's – notion of scientific explanation. It is also interesting that scientists sometimes feel forced to change their metaphysical assumptions, but find this very difficult. When Planck, for example, gave up the principle of continuity he said that he did so out of desperation. However, that people may have a strong emotional attachment to their metaphysical principles does not really help to clarify the notion of metaphysical or explanatory progress.

Cogito: Following up that point, it has often been remarked that European philosophy and science are still tied in some ways to the metaphysics of classical Greece, and that the metaphysics of classical Greece is distinguished by a concern for the eternal and the unchanging and, hence, people who are still influenced by Greek thought find that they expect their philosophical and scientific concepts to be universal, eternal and unchanging. Since you have explored the possibility of metaphysical change, would you agree that it is time that we sought to abandon the metaphysics of classical Greece?

Körner: This is a large question. What I would emphasize, is that, although there are different metaphysical systems, they all share certain features. I have tried to show for instance that as a matter of anthropological fact every thinker adopts certain kinds of supreme principles. Thus every thinker accepts a certain core of logic, even though the periphery may differ from one set of people to another. Every thinker distinguishes between particulars and attributes, or as Frege put it, between objects and concepts, although not all thinkers do it in the same way. Every thinker employs concepts which help him to distinguish between what seems to be the case and what is the case, for instance, by applying the concept of substance, although, for example, the Aristotelian and Kantian concepts of substance are different. So I would say that it is very important not to overlook the difference between on the one hand the *genus* 'metaphysics', in the sense in which it is unavoidable for a person to have *a* metaphysics, and on the other its various species. It may be that because I am more interested in the generic notion of metaphysics than in its specific versions, I cannot think of any clear characterization of a specifically Greek metaphysics and of any convincing reason for abandoning it in favour of some other metaphysical species.

Cogito: Many of our student readers of *Cogito* will have heard at least one thing about metaphysics, and that is Hume's famous dictum:

> When we run over libraries, persuaded of these principles, what havoc must we make? If we take in our hand any volume; of divinity or school metaphysics, for instance; let us ask, Does it contain any abstract reasoning concerning quantity or number? Does it contain any experimental reasoning concerning matter of fact and existence? No. Commit it then to the flames: for it can contain nothing but sophistry and illusion.

Körner: I think that this remark could have led to some embarrassment for Hume, because if he had looked in a library and found his own book there, he would have had to ask himself this question and commit it (or large parts of it) to the flames.

Cogito: In the introduction to your latest book (*Metaphysics*) you mention the view that the nature of transcendental reality is, at best, conveyed only through aesthetic representation. You don't say that is your view; you say this is a view. And then you go on to say that the chapter on aesthetic attitudes constitutes the sketch of a book which is unlikely to be written. While we regret that this book is unlikely to be written, may I ask whether you are here in agreement with the closing words of Wittgenstein's *Tractatus*: 'Whereof one cannot speak, thereof one must be silent.'

Körner: When I said that the book on aesthetics will not be written, I meant that it will not be written by me, but that somebody else might be able to do so. I don't think that one has to be silent about aesthetic experience. What I do think is that by now *I* have to be silent about it.

Cogito: You have written a great deal about theoretical reasoning. People, however, spend much of their lives reasoning practically. And you argue in your book *Experience and Conduct* that practical reasoning too has a certain structure. Will you tell us something of your account of this structure?

Körner: I would say that just as theoretical reasoning has a certain structure – everybody accepts a minimal logic, distinguishes between particulars and concepts, and so on – so practical reasoning has its structure. It is especially important to note that practical attitudes are stratified. I can, for example, have a practical pro-attitude towards smoking and a practical anti-attitude towards this pro-attitude. The stratification of practical attitudes is closely related to their universalizability. Thus I not only have an anti-attitude to my pro-attitude to smoking, but also an anti-attitude to my and everyone else's pro-attitude to smoking. From the stratification, the universalizability and other features of practical attitudes, it follows that since all human beings think practically, there is a *genus* of morality which comprises different *species* of morality, just as there is a *genus* of metaphysics which comprises different *species* of metaphysics. And just as having a metaphysics is unavoidable, so having a morality is unavoidable.

Cogito: Would two examples of moral species be Kant's moral philosophy and utilitarianism – both making possible different views on a particular moral question?

Körner: Yes. I think, however, that Kant thought that the Categorical Imperative, when sincerely and correctly applied, can lead only to one result. I would say that Kant's notion of the Categorical Imperative and his *Critique of Practical Reason* are very important contributions to the analysis of the *genus* of morality. He did, of course, hold that the *Critique of Practical Reason* expounds the one and only correct morality. Utilitarians usually make the same mistake.

Cogito: It follows from your view that Kant's Categorical Imperative allows for different moralities?

Körner: That's right. I can imagine an honest Moslem applying the Categorical Imperative in such a way that it does not make polygamy immoral, and an honest Christian applying it with the opposite result. Yet both apply the Categorical Imperative honestly. I would like to add that this does not lead to a boundless moral relativism because the unavoidability of having a morality is a large constraint.

Cogito: Are you any sort of relativist, then?

Körner: I am not a relativist; I am a pluralist. I try to show that it is unavoidable to have a morality, just as it is unavoidable to have a metaphysics. To exhibit the common structure of different metaphysical systems and of different moralities is not to denigrate their important roles in the life of individuals and in their social relations. It may even help to throw new light on these roles.

Cogito: You will know that one of the Cogito Society's aims is to encourage the development of philosophy teaching in schools. Do you welcome the growth of such teaching?

Körner: I remember that the grammar school in my native town offered a course in philosophy and that when I took this course, I felt, for the only time in my life, that philosophy was not for me. But I do think that such a course could be useful. What I would suggest is that philosophy be started, not out of the blue, but in connection with some other subject. For instance, let it be shown that, and how, mathematics or history or grammar all lead naturally to philosophical questions. I do not think that philosophy should be studied in isolation. Plato said that in order to do philosophy one has to know some geometry. I think, more generally, that in order to do philosophy one has to be acquainted with at least one other discipline.

Cogito: You still lead a very active philosophical life; indeed most people who walk around the precincts of Bristol University know that you lead an active life in general. Philosophers, however, must needs take some time away from philosophy, if only to refresh themselves for further philosophizing. Will you tell us how you spend your leisure time away from philosophy? What, for example, do you read?

Körner: Well, instead of doing crossword puzzles, I try to learn something new. At the moment I am in my leisure time learning a bit of physics, namely the theory of chaos. This is a new theory which I study not only because I find it interesting, but also in order to remain mentally alert. I also like to read poetry – but that is a different matter.

8

RICHARD DAWKINS

Richard Dawkins is an evolutionary biologist whose work –
as will be seen in the interview – raises fascinating philosophical questions. He was educated at Oxford University,
where he studied for his doctorate with the Nobel Prize-
winning ethologist Niko Tinbergen. After a short spell as
Assistant Professor of Zoology at the University of California
at Berkeley he returned to Oxford in 1970 where he is now
a reader in zoology and a Fellow of New College. His three
books, *The Selfish Gene* (1976, 2nd edition, 1989), *The
Extended Phenotype* (1982) and *The Blind Watchmaker*
(1986) have had a great influence on many areas of contemporary thought.

Richard Dawkins (interview 1991) is now Professor for the Public
Understanding of Science at the University of Oxford, and a prominent
spokesman for science and scientific values in public debate, where he
seems to have assumed the role of a latter-day Thomas Huxley. Since our
interview, he has published *Climbing Mount Improbable* (1996) and *River
out of Eden* (1996) in the *Science Masters* series.

Cogito: You're best known for your book *The Selfish Gene*, but a lot
of people got quite upset by the title, saying genes couldn't possibly be
selfish.

Dawkins: Well, one person said that! I don't think it is a serious matter.
A philosopher should know that when I speak of a 'selfish gene' I do not
mean that a gene has motives. I think it is safer to talk about a 'selfish
gene' than it is to talk about, for example, a 'selfish elephant'. There is
real doubt about how many animals can have motives, including selfish
ones. But no sane person could think that a DNA molecule has motives.
I had thought I was safe, therefore, in using that phrase.

Cogito: So what do you mean, then, when you say that a gene is selfish?

Dawkins: You have to see it in the context of the debates that were going on in evolutionary biology: the group selection, species selection, individual selection debates. One way of putting it is to say that, at some level, we are talking about a selfish entity that works to preserve and propagate itself. In an unplanned, unforeseeing, automatic way, a Darwinian entity takes whatever steps are necessary to preserve itself through time. That is the sense in which a gene is selfish. In that sense, neither groups, nor species nor individuals are the Darwinian, selfish entities. It has to be a self-replicating entity that is selfish: hence the phrase, 'the selfish gene'.

Cogito: So the groups, species and individuals do not have an identity through time?

Dawkins: That's right. They do not make copies of themselves. David Hull and I agree over most things, but he is wrong over this. He thinks that an individual organism is a replicator – but a very bad one. A goose makes more geese and, in a way, that is making copies of itself – it is just a bad replicator since each goose gets only half its genes from each parent. But I say that a goose is not a replicator in any sense whatsoever, not even a bad one. Even an identically-cloning asexual organism such as a stick-insect is not a replicator; its genome (the set of all its genes) is a replicator, but the stick-insect itself is not. To say the opposite is tantamount to committing the Lamarckian heresy.

Cogito: One of the more arresting concepts in *The Selfish Gene* was that of memes, mental constructs which are to mind and culture what genes are to anatomy and behaviour. We don't hear that much about memes these days. Was 'memes' an unfit meme?

Dawkins: Not at all. There is even a new journal devoted to the study of memes! But there are problems with trying to apply Darwinian ideas to culture. For Darwinism to work, it seems that one has to have something equivalent to Mendelian genetics: a very high stability of the intrinsic units, a fidelity of copying such as is possessed by DNA molecules. Genetic mutations are extremely rare. It is a digital system: the genes do not blend or merge in a quantitative way. So, if cultural Darwinism is to work there are certain conditions that have to be met that may not be very plausible. On the other hand, there are things that do make memes look plausible. The current epidemic of computer viruses sets up a new analogy. These are programmes written by malicious people which spread themselves around in a genetic, epidemic way. They are, in one way or another, self-propagating, and are obeyed by any computer they get into. The epidemiology of these things looks identical to the epidemiology of measles or whooping cough. They are DNA-like and extremely meme-like.

I have toyed with the idea of a community of brains being susceptible to a virus of this kind. What would it feel like if you were the victim of a mental virus? You could well find yourself possessed of a mysterious but deep inner conviction, which you might describe as 'faith'. It might even sound like a 'still small voice'. If you ask yourself why you hold this particular faith rather than another of the hundreds of available faiths, you'd notice that it had more to do with epidemiology than with evidence: it is exactly the same faith as your parents'! If a virus of this kind has been around for some centuries it might have evolved to take effective action for its own survival. It might even drive you to kill people who had an alternative faith.

So, I think there possibly is a science of 'memetics' waiting to be developed. I should, however, say that when I first used the word in *The Selfish Gene* I was not trying to make a point about human culture, but rather an anti-gene point. I was really saying that you can do Darwinism without DNA. Darwinism is much more than just a DNA-based theory. It is the only theory we have that can account for the increase in organized complexity which is life, anywhere in the universe.

Cogito: Much of your writing is, you say, advocacy. And the ideas you advocate are often most clearly expressed mathematically. Can your verbal expositions, eloquent and powerful though they are, ever have the persuasive power of a mathematical model?

Dawkins: John Maynard Smith once wrote that he does not understand why I don't use mathematics since clearly the ideas are mathematical; I obviously think in words, he wrote, and yet I get it right! There are important truths that you cannot get without mathematics, for example the outcome of the Fisher theory of sexual selection. You can explain it in words, but you don't know whether it will work until you do the mathematics. I would not wish to be associated with those – and there are many – who are proud of being non-mathematical, but I am gratified to be able to go quite a long way using words, believing that there is much that is mathematical behind the words.

Cogito: You often use very concrete metaphors when explaining why an animal behaves as it does; for example the idea that it weighs up the costs and benefits of some course of action and then decides on the basis of that calculation. You justify the approach by saying it doesn't matter what the animal is actually doing; it behaves *as if* it were weighing costs and benefits. But are you interested in mechanisms?

Dawkins: 'As if consciously calculating' could be said of any computer programme which behaved as if it were weighing up costs and benefits. Yet we do not have to think that the computer is conscious. The question of the mechanics of an animal's 'rules of thumb' is an interesting and important question but we can do our Darwinism without bothering with it. It is a matter for neurobiology.

Cogito: You also make a great deal of use of computers, both as metaphors and as aids to your thinking and advocacy. Do you regard organisms as computers?

Dawkins: I do think that organisms and computers are the same kind of thing – neither of them are mystical objects. The laws of physics must be applied to in order to explain both. On the other hand the statement that organisms are computers could be mistaken to mean that organisms work like computers in some more detailed sense, e.g. that they use binary, digital codes, that they are serial processing devices with huge, infallible memories, and so on.

Cogito: So here is another 'as if'?

Dawkins: Sort of. But I would prefer to say that if you look into the future technology of computers, there may be computers that are a lot more like brains than the present ones are. Parallel computers are becoming prominent already.

Cogito: Are computers capable of thought?

Dawkins: Not yet. I can see no reason, in principle, why they shouldn't be. I am persuaded by well-known thought experiments such as progressively replacing an entire brain, neurone by neurone, with silicon equivalents: presumably there would be no particular moment when the consciousness disappeared. Such arguments seem to me persuasive; I do not think that conscious thought is ruled out for machines of the future.

Cogito: You began your biological career as an ethologist, studying the natural behaviour of animals. Why?

Dawkins: I suppose I was inspired by Niko Tinbergen who was my tutor. I wanted to work with him, and did.

Cogito: Niko Tinbergen, one of the founding fathers of ethology, must have been an important influence at Oxford. What was it about his approach that attracted you to work with him?

Dawkins: Much of it was his personal kindness. I characterize his approach somewhat differently from the way it normally is. He is seen as the great field experimenter – which of course he was – and a great naturalist. But what I most recall from his lectures was the idea I was to later dub the 'survival machine'. He did not call it that. This is the idea that the organism, including its behaviour, is a machine for surviving and reproducing. He talked of the nervous system as 'behaviour machinery'. I found those images inspiring.

Cogito: Tinbergen, like Konrad Lorenz and Karl von Frisch, was, in the title of one of his books, a curious naturalist. Do you see yourself as a naturalist? What are your earliest recollections of the natural world?

Dawkins: I am sorry to say that I am not a naturalist. My father is a naturalist, but I was never any good at learning the names of birds and flowers. I never collected anything. So my interest in biology was not that of a naturalist. I got into biology more for its philosophic interest. I saw Darwinism as providing answers to deep problems about existence and purpose.

Cogito: You spent some time at the University of California at Berkeley in the heady days of 1968. What was it like, and did the experience have any effect on your academic development?

Dawkins: I was very involved in the politics of the time. I went on marches. My involvement was if anything a distraction from what you have called my academic development. Perhaps it did make me iconoclastic. But that puts me in mind of the fact that in the field of Darwinism there is a good living to be made by people pretending to be more iconoclastic than they are. I am anxious not to be associated with that. I think I am an orthodox neo-Darwinist, although I express it in an unorthodox way which I hope is illuminating and which may even help Darwinians to have new thoughts, for instance the idea of the 'extended phenotype'.

Cogito: Having pursued an analytical approach to the mechanisms of animal behaviour, always bearing in mind that it had been shaped by natural selection, what prompted you to switch course and take such an interest in the explanation of evolution?

Dawkins: That switch came about during the winter of power failures – 1973, I think. I couldn't continue with my research. I was using Skinner boxes and other electrical apparatus when the power went off. I switched to writing. I was impressed by the pervasiveness of the group-selection fallacy in the popular view of Darwin. I decided to write a book – I called it my 'best seller' – which would be a reply to people like Robert Ardrey who implied that modern Darwinism was group-selectionist. I wrote one chapter of *The Selfish Gene*, and then went back to research when the power came on; but on sabbatical leave in 1975 I returned to the book and worked seriously and fast. That is a good way to write a book; otherwise, if you spin it out, you are a different person when you finish.

Cogito: You have argued that natural selection is an inevitable consequence of life forms that reproduce; that you would expect it wherever we might find life. Does natural selection, in a sense, define life?

Dawkins: 'Define' is perhaps too strong, but I would put my shirt on the bet that wherever there is life, anywhere in the universe, it will be Darwinian life.

Cogito: Would you believe someone who said 'X is alive' if you did not think X had evolved?

Dawkins: No. I would suspect there was some trickery; if that were ruled out I would have to be forced by the facts. Another possibility is that it was made by something that had evolved.

Cogito: You are associated very much with the idea that natural selection is a slow, gradual process, in contrast to Stephen Jay Gould's ideas of punctuated equilibria, described by John Turner, another gradualist, as 'the theory of evolution by jerks'. Is there really such a profound difference between the two schools of thought?

Dawkins: I don't think that there is. I believe that Darwinism has always left plenty of room for the idea that evolution goes at different rates and might even stop for long periods of time. I think that the only sort of punctuationism that will work is one in which evolution, when it happens, is still gradual, though it may be rapid. During those periods of rapid evolution it still must be gradual otherwise you have the problem, which Darwin encountered, of accounting for spontaneous adaptation by luck. Gradualistic evolution is the answer to how you can build up to complex adaptations which are otherwise statistically too improbable to contemplate. So if there is punctuationism what it amounts to is rapid, spasmodic, gradualism.

Cogito: What do you think when you see critics of the whole idea of natural selection latching onto these arcane internal arguments?

Dawkins: I think it is a form of opportunism. There are people, such as creationists, who desperately want evolution as a whole to be untrue. So when they see internal arguments, such as those we have just been discussing, they will seize upon them to suggest that there is something fundamentally wrong with Darwinism.

Cogito: Many people bridle at the suggestion that studies of animals can have anything to say about the human condition. What is the relevance of animal studies to modern humans?

Dawkins: Speaking taxonomically, human beings are just one of ten million species; we are just a tiny twig on an enormous bush. Our closest relatives, the chimpanzees, are extremely close and extremely recently branched off. It would be a singular anomaly if we could learn nothing from the rest of the bush.

Having said that, every species has its unique characteristics. Our own uniquenesses are very particular, and to force a naïve Darwinian interpretation on everything we do in our everyday lives would be an error. Most of us, while writing our books or whatever it is that we do, are not thereby advancing our Darwinian fitness. The correct way for a Darwinian to interpret the behaviour of any animal which is no longer living in the natural environment where its genes were selected, is to say something like the following. This brain and body were shaped by natural selection in one environment. It is now living in another environment, so you cannot interpret its behaviour naïvely as increasing its genetic fitness. Moths fly into candle flames not from some urge to commit suicide but because candle flames are not a salient part of the environment in which their genes were naturally selected. The world in which we live is a great forest of candle flames of one sort and another. We can go back to the moths and say they are probably using candle flames as a light-compass. In nature, bright sources of light at night are always at optical infinity and can be so used. As soon as the world contains candles which are not optical infinity, we must re-write the question. We ask, not 'Why is the moth committing suicide?' or 'What is the survival-value of suicide behaviour?' but 'What is the survival-value of x behaviour?' where x is a rewriting of suicide behaviour into something that makes sense, like light-compass behaviour. We cannot give a sensible interpretation of human behaviour unless we re-write our questions in moth-like ways.

We can further say that the forest of candles in which we live is a particularly complicated one because cultural evolution – a quasi-Darwinian process perhaps – has led to an especially rapid change in the environment. We are totally surrounded by artefacts of our own civilization. The environment in which we now live has especially little to do with that in which we were naturally selected. We can still make a simple Darwinian interpretation of things like hunger and the sexual drive, but for most of our questions we have to employ re-writing rules.

Cogito: On the other hand, your work has also been adopted by those who see evolution and natural selection as an 'excuse' for certain sorts of human behaviour. I'm thinking of racism and xenophobia, and even sexual double standards. Again, what do you see as the real relevance of studies of animals to human behaviour?

Dawkins: It unfortunately still needs to be said that just because something is natural it does not follow that we should do it. If it did, we ought not to wear clothes. Suppose I were to provide a Darwinian explanation of racism and say that it's a hangover from a time when we needed to be reproductively isolated from Neanderthalers. The fallacy is to say, 'Oh well, if it's Darwinian then that's that – it's inevitable so we can't help it' or 'It's natural and therefore good'. On the contrary, it is very easy to undo, by learning, the impulses of our genetic programming. We need to understand the evolutionary bases of our unpleasant impulses in order to fight against them.

Cogito: Your book *The Blind Watchmaker* is a direct challenge, to William Paley's argument from design in his *Natural Theology*. Aren't you in danger of replacing Paley's Deity with your own version, Natural Selection?

Dawkins: The problem with that is the implication that they are both equally good. We want to know what is true. Paley thought he knew; he was wrong. All the evidence suggests that Darwinism is true. It remains open that someone could come along and show us that it is not. I don't think anyone will. Simply because I believe in Darwinism and Paley believed in God doesn't put the two beliefs on the same footing. Some beliefs are supported by evidence and some aren't!

Cogito: Humans, as a species, seem to have an innate capacity for language: not English, nor Chinese, but language. Do you think there could be a similar innate capacity for religion: not Christianity, or Sufism, but some sort of satisfying belief system?

Dawkins: I think there could, but it would be a lot less interesting than the innate capacity for language that Chomsky claims. Language is such a complicated and detailed faculty, and, if he is right, it is unique to our species. It really seems to need a special kind of explanation. Whereas it is very easy to think why one might have an innate capacity to find religion satisfying. You only have to have a (very understandable) fear of death to be drawn towards any doctrine that tells you, in an authoritative way when you are an impressionable child, perhaps, that you won't have to die. You could call that an innate capacity for religion, but it is about as interesting as an innate capacity to enjoy being warm and comfortable.

Cogito: Natural selection, notwithstanding its scientific truth, is, for those who accept it, a very satisfying answer to the question 'Why are we here?'. Are the critics correct, then, when they say that evolutionary biologists treat Darwinism as a religion?

Dawkins: I would prefer not to put it that way. It is true that anybody who professes anything academic or intellectual will be satisfied by good reasoning. If she finds an argument which helps everything fall into place that will be a deeply satisfying experience. But I find it unilluminating to speak of that as religion, merely because religion also may be satisfying. Many things are satisfying – strawberries and cream, for example – without being a religion. Religion has other defining properties which neither science nor strawberries have. For example, it is justified not by evidence but by faith.

Cogito: You said, in the introduction to *The Blind Watchmaker*: 'For reasons that are not entirely clear to me, Darwinism seems more in need of advocacy than similarly established truths in other branches of science.' Are the reasons really not entirely clear to you?

Dawkins: I went on to offer one or two. There is the fact that in order to understand it you need to steep yourself in the vastness of geological time, which our brains find very difficult. There is the fact that it is unpalatable to people who can't tell the difference between what is and what they would like there to be. Bernard Shaw said that when you contemplate Darwinism your heart sinks into a heap of sand within you. It is a deeply disturbing idea if you want the universe to have purpose, beauty, elegance and so on. But of course a thing can be both disturbing and true. What I had in mind in the passage that you quote is that it is not clear why Darwinism, as opposed, say, to physics, has to put up with such charges. You don't find television evangelists denouncing Newton and Einstein.

Cogito: Is it possible to reconcile evolution, in which change is essentially the outcome of random processes given direction by selection, and free will?

Dawkins: I find it difficult to contribute to this ancient philosophical discussion. There is, I think, nothing that is added to the debate specifically by evolution.

Cogito: I think Darwinism does add something in that if you are having a debate without Darwinism you can say that something is guiding everything and therefore what you consider your free will is merely being guided. If you are having a debate with Darwinism, the Darwinist would say that there is no guidance, only selection. Therefore, as there is no guidance, your actions are free.

Dawkins: I think that if Darwinists have an attitude to free will it is probably that the matter is one for physics – the physics of the nervous system. If you really want to know my attitude to determinism, I take refuge in *complexity*. In view of the huge complexity of events in the nervous system it probably doesn't matter whether there is free will or not.

Cogito: There is a great deal of concern today about the destruction of the environment. How far does this concern you *qua* Darwinist? Do you think that the kind of biology you do can help us to deal with acute problems of the environment?

Dawkins: I am deeply concerned as a citizen. As an evolutionary biologist I don't think I have very much to say. Great catastrophes in the conditions of life have happened before. The origin of oxygen in the atmosphere, vital to us now, was originally a monstrous piece of pollution. Natural selection favoured those organisms that could survive in spite of it. There have been other major catastrophes in which most of life has been wiped out. Evolution happens in the intervals between these catastrophes and catastrophes have a place in the history of evolution. But I now speak just as a citizen and want us to do everything we can to avert a catastrophe. When I think about the loss of whales and the loss of rain forests I am apt to become angry beyond the sort of reason that is suitable for a philosophical journal, so I think I had better shut up about it!

9

ALASDAIR MACINTYRE

Alasdair MacIntyre is the McMahon/Hank Professor of Philosophy at the University of Notre Dame, Indiana, USA. His writings in ethics, social and political philosophy, sociology, the philosophy of mind and the philosophy of religion are known to, and discussed by, an international audience. Many of his books are mentioned in the interview that follows; few readers of *Cogito* will have failed to read *A Short History of Ethics*, a book that has influenced a whole generation of students of moral philosophy. He has, remarkably, held appointments at the Universities of Manchester, Leeds, Oxford (Nuffield and University colleges), Essex, Princeton, Branders, Boston, Vanderbilt and Wellesley College before his present post at Notre Dame. His views stimulate and provoke; his ideas are widely discussed. We are pleased to welcome him to the columns of *Cogito*.

Professor MacIntyre (interview 1991) published the third volume of his 'interminably long History of Ethics', the *Three Rival Versions of Moral Enquiry: Encyclopaedia, Genealogy, and Tradition* in 1991. He became Arts and Sciences Professor at Duke University in 1995. In the past few years, he has been much cited as an important source for the communitarian critique of liberalism, and a small 'MacIntyre industry' seems to be emerging in the philosophical literature, with books such as J. Horton and S. Mendus (eds), *After MacIntyre: Critical Perspectives on the Work of Alasdair MacIntyre* (1994), Peter McMylor, *Alasdair MacIntyre: Critic of Modernity* (1994), and Michael Fuller, *Making Sense of MacIntyre* (1998).

Cogito: We usually begin with a biographical question, and perhaps this is especially appropriate in your case, since *After Virtue* is so concerned with ideas of a quest and of a narrative of a life. What would you emphasize in your own 'narrative'?

MacIntyre: Any adequate narrative of my life would have to emphasize a radical change in it around 1971. Before then I had had a number of disparate and sometimes conflicting sets of concerns and beliefs, and I was unable to move decisively towards any resolution either of the problems internal to each particular set of concerns or beliefs or of those which arose from the tensions between them. Both in political philosophy and in political practice I had learned, from Marxism, how to identify the moral impoverishment and the ideological function of liberalism. I had also learned, partly from Marxism and partly from non-Marxist sociology and anthropology, that certain older types of teleologically ordered community were incompatible with the dominant economic and social forms of modernity. But I did not as yet know how to disengage what I had learned from the erroneous and distorting theoretical frameworks, Marxist or Durkheimian, in terms of which I had formulated what I had learned. The work which issued in *Secularization and Moral Change* [Oxford University Press: London, 1967] had taught me that the moral presuppositions of liberal modernity, whether in its theory or in its social institutions, are inescapably hostile to Christianity and that all attempts to adapt Christianity to liberal modernity are bound to fail. But I did not as yet understand either the philosophical presuppositions of a biblical theism – bound up with the claim that this is a teleologically ordered universe – or the resources that the Catholic Church has for sustaining its own form of life in antagonistic social environments. Consequently I then believed that the only versions of Christianity in which it retained its theological and religious integrity, that of Kierkegaard, for example, or Karl Barth, were philosophically indefensible.

In philosophy I had had to recognize very early that Frege and Wittgenstein had transformed our conception of what is problematic. Although I thought that I had already appreciated the truth in Professor Anscombe's remark that investigations prompted by Frege's and Wittgenstein's questions 'are more akin to ancient than to more modern philosophy' [*An Introduction to Wittgenstein's Tractatus*, Hutchinson: London, 1959, p. 13], I was only much later beginning to understand the extent to which the inadequacies of my reading of Aristotle, inadequacies brought home to me by subsequent reflection on what I had written about ancient ethics in *A Short History of Ethics* [Macmillan: New York, 1966], arose from my failure to bring Aristotle's answers into relationship to modern questions and modern answers to Aristotle's *aporiai*.

Critical reflection on the *Short History* also provided a better focused view of the difficulties involved in giving a philosophical account of evaluative and normative concepts and judgements which was genuinely informed by an understanding of the range and variety of moral differences between different cultural and social orders, an account which therefore does not confuse the idiosyncratic local moral idioms of modern liberal individualism with '*the*' language of moral evaluation.

The essays collected in *Against the Self-Images of the Age* [Duckworth: London, 1971] brought this period to a close. I set out to rethink the problems of ethics in a systematic way, taking seriously for the first time the possibility that the history both of modern morality and of modern moral philosophy could only be written adequately from an Aristotelian point of view. In the same period, after 1971, I had occasion to rethink the problems of rational theology, taking seriously the possibility that the history of modern secularization can only be written adequately from the standpoint of Christian theism, rather than vice versa. It was not until quite some time after I had completed *After Virtue* [University of Notre Dame Press: Notre Dame, 1981] that these two lines of enquiry finally coincided in a realization that it is from the standpoint of a Thomistic Aristotelianism which is also able to learn from modern philosophy – especially from Frege, Husserl, Wittgenstein and their critics – that the problems of philosophy, and more particularly of moral philosophy, can best be articulated. But already by 1977, when I began to write the final draft of *After Virtue*, I had identified in main outline the framework and central theses of my subsequent enquiries.

So my life as an academic philosopher falls into three parts. The twenty-two years from 1949, when I became a graduate student of philosophy at Manchester University, until 1971 were a period, as it now appears retrospectively, of heterogeneous, badly organized, sometimes fragmented and often frustrating and messy enquiries, from which none the less in the end I learned a lot. From 1971, shortly after I emigrated to the United States, until 1977 was an interim period of sometimes painfully self-critical reflection, strengthened by coming to critical terms with such very different perspectives on moral philosophy as those afforded by Davidson in one way and by Gadamer in quite another. From 1977 onwards I have been engaged in a single project to which *After Virtue, Whose Justice? Which Rationality?* [Notre Dame University Press: Notre Dame, 1988] and *Three Rival Versions of Moral Enquiry* [Notre Dame University Press: Notre Dame, 1990] are central, a project described by one of my colleagues as that of writing *An Interminably Long History of Ethics*.

Cogito: In fact, have you any plans to write an autobiography?

MacIntyre: Answering the previous question has already stretched my autobiographical powers to their limit. To write a worthwhile autobiography you need either the wisdom of an Augustine or the shamelessness of a Rousseau or the confidence in one's own self-knowledge of a Collingwood. I fail in all three respects.

Cogito: *After Virtue* is also very much concerned with the idea of a 'tradition' and you tackled this again in the Gifford Lectures you gave at the University of Edinburgh in 1987–8. Why is it so important?

MacIntyre: The concept of 'tradition' has at least three different kinds of importance. Concepts are embodied in and draw their lives from forms of social practice. To understand how a particular concept is used it has to be located in terms of the activities and norms of some form of established practice. But any practice of any importance has a history. Practices come to be, are sustained and transformed, and sometimes perish as parts of the histories of particular societies. Within such societies the normative and evaluative modes of judgement and action which inform both activity within practices and attitudes to practices have to be handed on from one generation to another. And one aspect of the social embodiment of concepts is their transmission in this way. So to abstract any type of concept, but notably moral concepts, from the contexts of the traditions which they inform and through which they are transmitted is to risk damaging misunderstandings.

Second, a shared ability to ask and answer together such questions as 'What is our common inheritance from our common past?' 'What should we have learned from our shared experience to value it?' and 'What in it is open to criticism and requires remaking?' is one prerequisite for the kind of social life in which the rational discussion of both ends and means, by its continuing elaboration and reformulation of some conception of a common good, provides an alternative both to the mindless conservatism of hierarchies of established power and to fragmentation through the conflicts of group interests and individual preferences, defined without reference to a common good.

Third, rational enquiry is itself always tradition-dependent. The best established theories – those which it is rational to accept – in contemporary natural science are not worthy of acceptance because they conform to some timeless set of canons for scientific theories, positivist or otherwise. Rather they are worthy of acceptance because of their superiority to their immediate predecessors, in respect of providing resources for the solution of certain types of problem and remedying certain types of incoherence, in the light of some particular conception of what it would be to perfect theory in this or that area. And those predecessors in turn were related, although not in precisely the same ways, to their predecessors, and so on. The vindication of contemporary natural science turns out to be the history of that science, the retrospectively constructed history of a prospectively oriented tradition of enquiry, within which the development of the standards by which incoherence and resourcelessness are judged itself has a history. Of course traditions of rational enquiry may, like other traditions, be disrupted or fail or be displaced in various ways, as I believe the Aristotelian tradition of the virtues was.

Cogito: In the course of the Gifford Lectures you asked if the modern revival of Thomism had resulted in 'too many Thomisms'. How can we distinguish controversy within a tradition from confusion and disputes not rooted in any tradition?

MacIntyre: Any tradition depends for its survival on retaining shared beliefs and practices sufficient for identifying common ends and for making and recognizing progress towards achieving those ends. Where there is not agreement in such identification and recognition, there may of course be forms of *ad hoc* cooperation, intellectual, social or whatever, derived from longer or shorter term coincidence of interests, but the necessary conditions for the survival, let alone the flourishing of a tradition will be absent. But when I raised the question 'Too many Thomisms?' about the multiplicity of standpoints within Neo-Thomism, it was not because I believed that in its case these necessary conditions were lacking. What afflicted Neo-Thomism was much more mundane: too many different tasks were imposed upon it in too short a time. So at a very early stage in the Thomistic revival, Thomists were called upon to enter into a variety of philosophical and theological conflicts with different opposing views, while at the same time devising systems of instruction for a number of very different types of institution and student; yet the reappropriation of Aquinas's work was itself still at a relatively early stage. So different and rival perspectives appeared all too soon. And it may be that in order for Thomism to recover adequately from these afflictions it had to go out of fashion for a time, so that what has proved to be a continually deepening scholarly understanding of Aquinas could be dissociated from a variety of distorting educational tasks and polemical engagements. What has survived as a result of this respite is recognizably a tradition which is in its own terms flourishing.

Cogito: Both in *After Virtue* and the Gifford Lectures one of your main complaints about modern secular liberal ethics seems to be that it does not constitute a tradition. But in *Whose Justice? Which Rationality?* you discuss the transformation of liberalism into a 'tradition'. Can you clear this up?

MacIntyre: We need to distinguish the culture of liberal individualist modernity at large from liberalism as a changing body of theory, expressing the practice of a set of theorists who have handed on, while reformulating, the doctrines of liberalism from the eighteenth century to the present. There has of course always been a close, if complex, relationship between these two, but they are not the same. Earlier liberal thinkers were avowed enemies of tradition. In 1865 Sidgwick declared to Oscar Browning, 'History will have in the future less and less influence on Politics in the most advanced countries. Principles will soon be everything and tradition nothing, except as regards its influence on the form.' This earlier liberal theorizing was the expression of modes of social, political and economic practice which in what Sedgwick called 'the most advanced countries' often enough dissolved tradition and deprived many ordinary people of its possibilities. But at the same time liberalism as theory embodied itself in a continuing and now often dominant tradition of enquiry, and recent liberal thinkers have to some degree recognized this. So there is no basic incompatibility between the account of the anti-traditional character of liberal culture in *After Virtue* and in my Gifford Lectures and the account of the development and nature of the liberal intellectual tradition as a tradition in *Whose Justice? Which Rationality?* But I would have done better to make clear the relationship between these.

Cogito: In your work you very much weave philosophy, sociology, history and literature together. Indeed, another of your basic complaints about modern ethics seems to be that it is so relentlessly abstract, as if philosophy can declare its independence from the world and get to and from first principles in a realm of pure, universal reason. But if there is a liberalism, that you criticize, of this highly rationalist, Kantian kind, do you not tend to overlook (like modern 'rationalists') a liberal tradition in which philosophy, sociology and history are interwoven? As, for example, in the Scottish Enlightenment, or in the work of Montesquieu, Tocqueville, Durkheim.

MacIntyre: The problem with trying to combine a sociological understanding of modernity with liberalism is that what the modern world has realized are the worst fears of the Scottish Enlightenment rather than its best hopes. What we confront in advanced societies is the conjunction of an excluded and dependent cultural proletariat with a set of overlapping élites who control the presentation of political choice, the manipulation of economic organization, the legal structures and the flow of information. Instead of that ever widening educated public of the democratic intellect, who were the intended beneficiaries of those who understood the distinctive merits of the Scottish universities in the eighteenth and nineteenth centuries – George Elder Davie has written their history in *The Democratic Intellect* [Edinburgh University Press: Edinburgh, 1961] and *The Crisis of the Democratic Intellect* [Polygon Books: Edinburgh, 1986], two books which should be compulsory reading for every newly appointed university teacher in Britain – we have the mass semi-literacy of television audiences.

Adam Ferguson and Adam Smith both had their apprehensions about the moral effects of modern social and economic modes. Both also thought, however, that there were stronger grounds for optimism than for pessimism. But their pessimism – limited in Smith's case, less limited in Ferguson's – has turned out to be foresight.

Cogito: You argue that philosophical and ethical inquiry must be within a tradition. Many worry that this is a receipt for relativism, and you devote the last three chapters of *Whose Justice? Which Rationality?* to explaining why it is not. Is it possible for you to sum up here what is so wrong with relativism and why your view of philosophical and ethical inquiry does not lead to it?

MacIntyre: Those who impute relativism to me have, I suspect, both misunderstood my position and misunderstood relativism. Let me begin with the latter. The mistake in many versions of relativism is to take the argument one or two steps beyond what the relativist needs to make her or his crucial point. That crucial point is that there exist a number of culturally embodied systems of thought and action, each with its own standards of practical reasoning and evaluation. Some of these are such that not only do their adherents arrive at evaluative and normative conclusions which are incompatible with those of the adherents of some other such systems, but their standards of reasoning are such that from the standpoint of each contending party the reasoning of the other must be judged unsound. The relativist then further observes that in relation to some of these rival contending systems the system of thought and action which she or he espouses is in no different a position. It is up to this point that I agree with the relativist. Where then do I disagree?

Relativists universally proceed one stage in the argument beyond this and characteristically two stages. In neither do I accompany them. The first stage is that of supposing that somehow or other those conclusions about the multiplicity of concrete modes of reasoning and of modes of justification for evaluative and normative conclusions provide grounds for putting in question and altering one's view of the justification of one's own reasoning and conclusions. The second is that of supposing that the same considerations should lead to a rejection of the claims of any substantive conception of truth. Neither of these stages in the relativist argument is justified and it is of course only by having pursued the argument to this unwarranted point that the relativist lays her or himself open to those types of self-referential refutation which have so often been deployed against relativism.

Cogito: There are so many other questions we could ask about your work, whether relatively detailed and concerning, e.g. your interesting idea of a practice, or more general and concerning, e.g. your contribution to the revival of Aristotle and 'virtue ethics'. Can you offer a question of your own and answer it?

MacIntyre: The question which is perhaps the most important that you could put to me is that of how the concept of a practice must be further developed, if it is to be as philosophically fruitful as I hope that it may be. In *After Virtue* I provided a general characterization of practices and

I gestured towards some examples. But a great deal more needs to be said, more particularly in order to throw light on how evaluative concepts and normative concepts have application. Consider how, within the context of at least certain types of practice, shared standards of success and failure make the application of such concepts relatively unproblematic, as, for example, among the crews of a fishing fleet. Their standards of success and failure are set by shared goals: to secure a large enough catch between spring and fall to ensure a reasonable income for the whole year; not to overfish the accessible fishing grounds, so as to deprive themselves of their livelihood; not to lose their lives or their boats or their nets; to be able by doing these things to sustain the lives of their families.

Two kinds of shared achievement provide the goods internal to this type of practice; that which belongs to the attainment of excellence in the cooperative activity of fishing, the excellence or lack of it of each crew member in playing her or his part contributing to the excellence or lack of it of the whole crew, and that which belongs to the excellence attained in sustaining the lives of the households from which the crew members came and to which they return. The range of uses of 'good' and cognate expressions will be intelligible in terms of the structures of activity of the crew and the household. To be good at this or that aspect of the tasks of fishing requires skills whose utility depends on qualities of character and mind in those who use them, qualities which generally and characteristically enable their possessor, by doing what is required of them on the right occasions, to achieve the goods of both crew and household, for the sake of which all else is done. So 'good at', 'good for', the virtue words, the expressions which appraise performance of duty, and 'good for its own sake' are at once socially and semantically ordered. And the next philosophical task is to spell out these related orderings.

When 'good' and its cognates are used intelligibly outside the context of particular practices, it is a presupposition of their use – an Aristotelian presupposition – that human societies as wholes are ordered as practices, wholes of which particular practices, such as fishing or philosophy or cricket, are constituent parts. And here again the ordering of the uses of 'good', as these are socially and semantically structured, is a philosophically urgent task. When by contrast 'good' and its cognates are abstracted from any such context, either theoretically or practically, characteristically in social orders in which practice-based relationships have been marginalized, so that the use of such expressions has to change, they inevitably degenerate into what appear to some as no more than generalized expressions of approval, voicing either what we feel or what we want to feel, and to others as naming peculiar properties, perhaps in virtue of some relationship of supervenience. So philosophical controversies between moral realists and moral anti-realists are themselves perhaps symptomatic of a particular type of social condition.

To have understood this, of course, is no more than to have learned how to go back to the beginning in enquiries about good and 'good'.

Cogito: *Cogito* has a special interest in the development of philosophy teaching in schools. American schools seem, in this matter, to be much further forward than those in the United Kingdom. Do you think there is a strong case to be made for teaching philosophy in schools? How would you state it?

MacIntyre: Introducing philosophy into schools will certainly do no more harm that has been done by introducing sociology or economics or other subjects with which the curriculum has been burdened. But what we need in schools are fewer subjects not more, so that far greater depth can be acquired. And philosophical depth depends in key part on having learned a great deal in other disciplines. What *every* child needs is a lot of history and a lot of mathematics, including both the calculus and statistics, some experimental physics and observational astronomy, a reading knowledge of Greek, sufficient to read Homer or the New Testament, and if English-speaking, a speaking knowledge of a modern language other than English, and great quantities of English literature, especially Shakespeare. Time also has to be there for music and art. Philosophy should only be introduced at the undergraduate level. And then at least one philosophy course and, more adequately two, should be required of every undergraduate. Of course an education of this kind would require a major shift in our resources and priorities, and, if successful, it would produce in our students habits of mind which would unfit them for the contemporary world. But to unfit our students for the contemporary world ought in any case to be one of our educational aims.

Cogito: When, perhaps in rare moments, you are away from philosophy, which books do you read? Could you tell us of some books that have been/are of importance to you?

MacIntyre: It is not always as easy as one might think to tell the difference between when in one's reading one is reading philosophy and when one is not. So I leave out the clearly borderline cases, such as Dante, Jane Austen, Dostoevsky, Kafka and Borges, including only among books that I have read every twenty years or so: *Redgauntlet, Women in Love, To the Lighthouse*, among books that I have read more often: *Ulysses, Finnegans Wake*, Flann O'Brien's *At Swim-Too-Birds*, short stories by Flannery O'Connor, Peter Taylor and Máirtín O'Cadhain; among books without which I might well not have lasted out the last twenty years: Saichi Maruya's *Singular Rebellion*, Randal Jarrell's *Pictures from an Institution*, Robertson Davies's *Rebel Angels*, Patrick McGinley's *Bogmail*; among what I hope still to be reading twenty years from now: *The Táin Bó Cuailnge*, Eileen O'Connell's lament for Art O'Leary, Akhmatova's 'Poem without a Hero', the poetry of George Campbell Hay, Sorley MacLean, Iain Crichton Smith and Máirtín O'Direáin; and of course a perpetual low-life diet of Raymond Chandler, Philip K. Dick, etc, etc, although perhaps reading *them* is still reading philosophy.

10

DAN DENNETT

Daniel C. Dennett is Director of the Center for Cognitive Studies at Tufts University, Massachusetts, and a philosopher of mind of international standing. His books include *Content and Consciousness* (1969), *Brainstorms* (1978), *Elbow Room* (1984), and *The Intentional Stance* (1985). He was also joint editor, with Douglas Hofstadter, of the popular collection, *The Mind's I* (1981). His most recent book, *Consciousness Explained* (1991) features in the following interview.

Dan Dennett (interview 1992) is still Professor of Philosophy and Director of the Center for Cognitive Studies at Tufts University. Since our interview, he has published *Darwin's Dangerous Idea: Evolution and the Meanings of Life* (1996), *Kinds of Minds* (1997), another volume in the *Science Masters* series, and *Brainchildren: Essays on Designing Minds, 1984–1996* (1998).

Cogito: Where did you study philosophy, and what were the main formative influences that shaped your philosophical views?

Dennett: I started off by going to Wesleyan University in Middletown, Connecticut. I was originally going to go there for four years. I took a course in logic in my first term. My teachers were under the mistaken impression that I was a budding mathematician, so they put me into a high-powered logic tutorial. Instead of doing a regular logic course, we read Quine's *Mathematical Logic*, and some other books which were much too hard for me. Almost out of despair, one night in the math library, I came across another book by Quine, *From a Logical Point of View*. I read it gratefully, and was fascinated. I thought, 'I'm going to be a philosopher, and go to Harvard and tell this man Quine why he is wrong.' So I transferred to Harvard with it in my head to set Quine straight about various things I thought he was wrong about, as only a freshman could.

And in fact I did work on that throughout my undergraduate career. By the time I left Harvard I thought I was one of the great anti-Quineans of the age. I then went to Oxford to do my DPhil (under the supervision of Gilbert Ryle), and discovered within a few weeks that I was the village Quinean, that I accepted much more of Quine than anyone else in Oxford did. It's clear to me now that both Ryle and Quine had an enormous influence on my work. Maybe I'm what you get when you cross Ryle with Quine and add a little neuroscience.

Cogito: You mentioned Gilbert Ryle, whose famous book *The Concept of Mind* (1949) was so influential in the 1950s and 1960s. Yet it is hard to get the students of today to see 'what all the fuss was about'. How much, in your opinion, of Ryle's work is still alive today?

Dennett: One of the facts about philosophy is that it is much more seasonal than students and professors realize. Ryle's work was extremely import-ant at the time in getting people out of a certain slumber they were in. But he succeeded so well that you don't have to read him any more for that purpose. Now, when we read Ryle, we tend to see the parts he was wrong about, and take the parts he was right about for granted, because everybody thinks that way these days. *The Concept of Mind* was certainly a very exciting book to me when I read it as an undergraduate. That's why I went to Oxford: I thought, 'This is the next step for me – I've got to work with Ryle.' At the same time, I went, once again, in a spirit of controversy, determined to show Ryle what he was wrong about. At first I found him a very frustrating person to work with, because he never fought back. I would try so hard to get him provoked into a disagree-ment, but he was always so bland and agreeable in response that I thought, 'This is terrible. It's like punching a pillow. I'm just not getting anywhere with this man.' I didn't think I was learning anything from him. Then at the time I submitted my DPhil dissertation, which was done under his supervision, I happened to go through an early draft and compared 'before' and 'after' to see the difference. Ryle's hand was just all over it – by some strange osmotic process I wasn't even aware of. I wish that Ryle had had more of an influence on the field in one regard, and that is that he was very much opposed to the sort of gamesmanship and one-upmanship that was prevalent in Oxford at the time and is still very much a part of philoso-phy. I wish that Ryle's spirit of constructive criticism was a little more widespread than it is.

Cogito: Many contemporary philosophers of mind are hostile to the analytic philosophy of the past generation, often dismissing it as a sort of sterile or reactionary scholasticism. You, by contrast, still seem to have considerable respect for the work of Ryle, Anscombe, and others. How do you see the relation between analytic philosophy, on the one hand, and the new empirical work in cognitive psychology and artificial intelligence on the other?

Dennett: When I was a graduate student at Oxford, I was appalled by the way ordinary language philosophy was proceeding in one regard. It was as if you could get a good theory of horses by just studying how ordinary people used the word 'horse', never bothering even to enquire of somebody who might own a horse. That struck me as risky at best. I thought that it might help to see what people knew about horses – or about minds. But what I found when I looked at some empirical psychology was that, once you got used to the technicalities, the very same problems that were addressed at the ordinary language level were addressable there, only *better*, because it was a richer workshop of tools and ideas. There were more data around, but all the interesting philosophical issues had their homes there as well, and some of the methods and techniques of ordinary language philosophy played a good role. So it seemed to me then – and still seems to me today – that ordinary language philosophy taken neat is hopeless; it gives you very modest results of minor (but not quite zero) significance. But if it is coupled with an enquiry into the theoretical presuppositions of the latest empirical work, then you get a much more potent application.

Cogito: Until quite recently, accounts of mental processes (perception, say, or memory) that involved a reference – explicit or implicit – to a *homunculus* (a 'little man' sitting in front of an 'inner' video screen; or a little 'librarian' hunting through the archives) were dismissed as *obviously* non-explanatory. You defend (some) homuncular theories against this objection. Can you explain how?

Dennett: The fundamental homunculus objection, which has been around for a long time, foresees an infinite regress. If the little man in your head looking at the little screen is using the full powers of human vision, then we have to look at the even smaller man in *his* head looking at a still smaller screen, and so on *ad infinitum*. That's what's wrong with the little man in the head. However, if you make a simple step, if you break that little man down into a committee of specialists, each of which does less than the full job, has less than the full competence you are trying to explain, now you face the prospect of a finite regress that will bottom out in something purely mechanical. We start with specialist homunculi, no one of which has the full mentality we are trying to explain, and we gradually break these down into simpler functional units, which only by courtesy are called homunculi, and finally we get down to things that are so simple you could replace them with a machine, i.e. with a neurone, or a flip-flop in a computer that only has to remember 0 or 1 as its only expertise.

This idea of avoiding the quandary of an infinite regress with a finite regress seems to me to be actually a much more valuable lesson in philosophy than just this application. The homuncular breakdown is one application, but I think there are others. For instance, consider the idea of an ultimate value. One thinks, 'All values cannot be instrumental, because then we'd have an infinite regress of instrumental values; so there must be a *summum bonum* which is intrinsically valuable.' No: I think there are other ways of looking at the matter which involve the same sort of move. When you reach a phenomenon with a certain sort of complexity, you see that the notion of value doesn't need a foundation in this way. It can peter out in a finite regress without anything that has to count as a *summum bonum*.

One of my favourite examples is the following, which I owe to David Sanford. Consider the following paradox. 'Every mammal has a mammal for its mother. There have not been an infinite number of mammals. Therefore, there have not been any.' The way to break this regress is not to find the 'Prime Mammal' from which all others have been born, but to recognize that the boundary between non-mammals and mammals has been gradually passed. The security and reality of today's mammals do not depend on there being a first one, nor on the existence of necessary and sufficient conditions, in the philosopher's sense, for being a mammal. We can let 'mammalhood' trail off indefinitely – but not infinitely – in a finite regress.

Cogito: In your paper, 'Brain Writing and Mind Reading' in *Brainstorms* you attack the notion of a 'language of thought', the idea that our thoughts might be literally inscribed in our brains. It is not wholly clear, though, whether your objections are empirical, *a priori*, or both. If you were to return to this question today, how would you reformulate your arguments?

Dennett: You notice correctly that this argument sits on the cusp between *a priori* and empirical – and for a good reason, because people aren't sure what they mean by 'language'. If they mean something quite literal, then as a matter of empirical fact we know there's no such thing as brain-language. If we then ask, 'What must there be?' or 'Could there be a system with some of the important, perhaps defining, features of a language, that is involved in the organization of our cognitive lives?' then that becomes many different questions depending on how we cash out the relevant features. One crucial feature that just about everybody hits on is generativity – the fact that an infinity of different contents can be represented very efficiently. That seems to be a feature of human cognition; we, but perhaps no other animals, seem to have a sort of generative cognitive capacity. A question we might ask is, 'Does any system of representation that has generativity count as a language?' Some people might just answer yes, but I think they are missing some possibilities. Consider the following bizarre theory, which as a matter of empirical fact we know to be false. I call it the theory of mental clay. According to this theory, our brains contain a special substance called mental clay, which we use to form little mental clay replicas of all the things in the world that we have a model of. Everyone agrees that we have a model of our world in our brains; this theory just takes that idea literally in supposing that it's a model made of mental clay. So that when grandma dies, you take your mental clay model of grandma, 'kill' it, and put it in a mental clay coffin. It's pretty clear that mental clay is a generative system of representation. But is it a language? If so, if those complexes of mental clay models count as *sentences*, then *anything* surely counts as a language. Now that's a daft theory of mental representation, but there are other possibilities, perhaps at this time still fuzzily conceived, where it's just not clear whether they count as languages. In 'Brain-Writing and Mind-Reading' I was arguing against the over-casual assumption that any system of representation had to be language-like in the way that was assumed. It seemed to me that this involved a failure of imagination on the part of those who were arguing that way.

Cogito: Philosophers of Mind often seem to find themselves debating – ahead of the empirical evidence – what computers can and can't do. Do such debates serve any useful purpose?

Dennett: Well, they sell a lot of books, and permit some people to become famous. Do they serve any other purpose? I suppose they do. Let's look, for instance, at the contributions of Hubert Dreyfus. His book, or manifesto, *What Computers Can't Do*, was roundly criticized by the AI community when it came out, and I think it's fair to say that the fate of the ideas in it over the years has been roughly as follows. It is now granted, even by some of his harshest critics, that Dreyfus, although he overstated his case right down the line, identified the hard problems, the really deep difficulties facing AI. He didn't have the right language, and he misdescribed some of the problems he saw, but he didn't do a bad job of pointing to where the truly troubling issues were. So one might say that he did some good. Or one might say that he didn't really, because they were finding those hard spots anyway and all he did was misdescribe them enough so that he got everybody's blood boiling and created a lot of heat and not very much light. But I would think that, still, history's verdict on Dreyfus is on the positive side, and that his contribution to the debate has been significant. I don't think that anybody else has made a significant contribution with an argument about what computers can and can't do; and I would include in that regard the most recent argument put forward by Roger Penrose, which is simply based on a factual misunderstanding of what AI is about.

Cogito: In your paper, 'Cognitive Wheels', you discuss the so-called 'frame problem' facing workers in the field of Artificial Intelligence (AI). The problem, roughly speaking, is that of how our mass of *background knowledge* is to be represented, and made accessible to the system as and when required. Opponents of AI such as Hubert Dreyfus make a great deal of this objection. Have the defenders of AI made any progress towards its solution?

Dennett: I think in fact that the people working in AI have made some progress on a number of fronts. There's a new volume entitled *The Robot's Dilemma Revisited*, which is the proceedings of a conference held in Florida a year or so ago where a number of the leaders in the field discussed the frame problem and various approaches to it. My impression from that meeting was that there were a number of very interesting avenues being explored, as well as some dead ends. I think that one of the ways that people have begun thinking about the problem differently – very differently – is by abandoning some of the arch-computationalist ideas (what I call 'High-Church Computationalism') in their setting of the problem. They are taking a more biological approach to thinking about the organization of cognitive systems. I have in mind people like Rodney Brooks at MIT. Now you might say that their work is not even approaching the frame problem yet, because they're trying to model simple insects. But at least they are trying to model creatures that can get through their whole lives without falling off most cliffs.

The problem with the frame problem is that it started by assuming that the right underlying model for a cognitive agent acting in the world is the *walking encyclopedia*: you've got a big batch of facts, indexed and organized somehow, and an inference-engine that generates the right inferences from your core set of facts in order to illuminate and guide your current behaviour. Now that's not an inevitable model. There are other models which suppose that there is in fact a division of labour, where you've got one system which is responsible for keeping track of locomotion, for keeping you from bumping into things and looking out, in real time, for the sort of contingencies of that sort which matter; and then you've got another system which can take its time and operate more or less off-line, secure in the knowledge that the 'pilot' is taking care of 'the cliff problem'. Once you have made that division of labour then you can begin to conceive of different ways of making headway on the frame problem.

My own suggestion at that meeting was to take seriously the idea of some anthropologists, that basically, what you have in your head is a whole lot of stories trying to happen. There's 'Three little pigs', and 'Goldilocks', and every folk-tale that you grew up learning, plus lots of things you've seen subsequently. This is the stock-in-trade of simple narratives, which actually have a lot in common from culture to culture. Suppose that the way you're organized is that all of these narrative fragments are sitting there, in parallel, trying to be the truth about the world that you are inhabiting. So you meet somebody new, and one story is saying, 'I bet that's the tin woodman'; another is saying, 'No, it's the big bad wolf', and so on. They are all making tentative assignments of their characters to the people that you meet. This has the effect of getting you to ask roughly the right questions at the right times.

This idea, that you've got all these stories in your head trying to happen, is actually a nice way of designing a system which will not be at a loss for questions to ask itself. The system will tend to ask the questions that are relevant; but only based on what has proven relevant in the past. We are always susceptible to making an entirely novel blunder. But in fact human beings aren't very good at escaping entirely novel blunders. The main reason we don't paint ourselves into corners more often is that we have heard – and remembered – stories about people painting themselves into corners!

Cogito: In 'Why You Can't Make A Computer That Feels Pain' (in *Brainstorms*) you set out to write a 'Pain-Program'. The exercise reveals that what seems, at the phenomenological level, to be a single simple *quale*, may turn out, at the sub-personal level, to be an extremely complex functional state. What does this reveal about the amount and quality of the self-knowledge that we can obtain through introspection?

Dennett: I think that introspection is a remarkably unreliable source, that our access to our own mental states is not only in most regards not privileged; it is also, as Keith Gunderson once marvellously said, actually under-privileged. We are designed to have pretty good ideas about what's going on in us, but they tend to be couched in metaphors and subject to systematic distortion, so that our authority is limited and in the end vanishing. Wittgenstein once gave the example of a man who says, 'I know how tall I am – I'm *this* tall', placing his hand on the top of his head. Well, there's a person who is not wrong, but only because he's not right about very much. He has reduced his claim to a logical minimum. And if we do this we can arrive at something that no one would be able to show to be wrong, but such claims have lost all interest.

Cogito: At the heart of your philosophy of mind is the notion of an *Intentional System*, a system (animal, robot, human, or whatever) to which we *attribute* beliefs and desires as part of an explanatory theory by which we attempt to understand the system's behaviour. This theory has laid you open to accusations of two sorts of anti-realism: (1) that there is no *real* (i.e. objective) distinction between systems that are, and those that are not, Intentional Systems; and (2) that even for a system that we have agreed to regard as an Intentional System, there may be no *right* answer to the question of what it 'really' believes or desires. How do you answer these objections?

Dennett: The first of these objections is one I think I've already addressed in talking about the breakdown of homunculi. The question, 'At what point do we stop having *real* intentionality and have mere *as if* intentionality?' is like the question, 'At what point do proto-mammals give way to mammals?' The question doesn't have to have a principled answer for it to be true that human beings, and some of their sub-parts, are real intentional systems.

Now what about the other question, as to whether or not there's a fact of the matter? Here I claim that, since at the heart of any system of intentional attribution there is an idealizing assumption of rationality – ultimately a normative assumption – it follows that in those cases where there is a falling short from optimal rationality, there's just no fact of the matter at all about what the truth is. I don't view this as a surprising, or metaphysically extravagant or unsettling result. It seems to me to fall into a rather ordinary variety of facts – where the conditions that are presupposed for the proper application of some term lapse, there is no fact of the matter about what the proper application of the term is.

Cogito: In regarding another person as an Intentional System, i.e. ascribing to him or her beliefs and desires, we are committed, in your view, to interpreting most of those beliefs as *true* (or at last rational). Many students find this claim quite incredible. Have you found any way of convincing such doubters?

Dennett: I've found a way that convinces *some* of them. I don't know what I can do about the residual doubters, except throw up my hands and wish them well. I think that the source of this doubt is their acceptance of a familiar philosophical bit of misdirection. They think of beliefs as sentences deemed true; and moreover they think of beliefs as a rather special sort of these, i.e. the ones considered, reflected on, and asserted. In fact, these are the states I would call *opinions*, and they represent a vanishingly small proportion of our beliefs. They are not themselves, I want to say, beliefs; they are, as it were, the offspring of beliefs. Right now, you have extraordinarily many beliefs about the room you're in and about what's happening in front of you. These are beliefs that are produced by your eyes, ears, and other sense organs. You have lots and lots of beliefs about where you were born, what you have done today, and so on. When we are talking about the majority of your beliefs being true we have to include all those. Your beliefs about physics, about philosophy, about the nature of truth – your theoretical beliefs – are not even close to being one millionth of one per cent of the information that you have and rely on. Now when students and other sceptics say, 'I can imagine a creature most of whose beliefs are false', I just don't think they can. They haven't done the job of imagining right. They can't coherently describe an agent, most of whose beliefs are false, that can be treated as a believer at all.

There's a certain cartoon character who comes close – the nearsighted Mr Magoo. Mr Magoo informs us by his almost continuous monologue of how he takes the world to be, and he's always dead wrong, and at great risk because he's misinterpreting everything because of his colossal near-sightedness. But of course the joke is that it always works out; that is, the crocodile never quite closes its jaw on Mr Magoo; and he ends up back safe and sound in his own bed at the end of the day. It's a wonderful comic conceit, and I think it proves my point. One recognizes that the world *cannot* be this way, not for more than a few minutes. The near-sighted Mr Magoo is impossible for a fairly deep reason. You can't survive to adulthood unless most of your beliefs are true.

Cogito: Well, that both leads us to our next question and, I think, ties up neatly with what has gone before, namely your attack on Cartesian assumptions in general. It is surely easier for me to think of the possibility of most of my beliefs being false if I think of myself as a sort of disembodied spirit, than if I think of myself as a biological organism and a product of evolution by natural selection. Now in your later book, *The Intentional Stance* (1987) you seek to 'ground' your philosophy of mind in a philosophy of biology. How much support do you think Darwinism gives to your particular views about the mind?

Dennett: I haven't a settled opinion about this, because my estimate keeps growing. That is to say, the extent to which I think the theory of evolution by natural selection is necessarily implicated in any sound philosophy of mind keeps growing. In a recent article called 'The Interpretation of Texts, People, and Other Artifacts' [in *Philosophy and Phenomenological Research*, Supplement, 1990] I make the claim that interpretation, whether it is of texts, as in hermeneutics or literary criticism; or of people, as in folk-psychology; or of artifacts in general, is always the same game – that is, there is one exercise that's going on, and it's grounded, all of it, in evolutionary considerations. The principles of reverse engineering that one must apply in order to make sense of minds, or of their products, turn out to be the very same principles that are used by biologists to make sense of organisms, and ultimately it's all grounded in the theory of natural selection. That's why my next book is going to be on Darwin – it's called *Darwin's Dangerous Idea*.

Cogito: In your current book, *Consciousness Explained* [In the USA, Little, Brown, & Co, 1991; in the UK, Allen Lane, 1992] you propose a 'Multiple Drafts Model' of consciousness. Your theory is extremely subtle and complex. It is probably unfair to ask you to summarize such a rich book in an interview, but perhaps you could give us a rough idea of the key features of the theory?

Dennett: I would say that my view involves a family of the theories, rather than a single theory. The alternative is the view that I call 'Cartesian materialism', or 'the Cartesian Theatre'. The Cartesian materialist says, 'Everything Descartes said about the mind was true, *except* of course the claim that it's immaterial. The mind is just the brain, but there has to be a material place in the brain where the contents of consciousness are presented.' To whom? To the inner witness. We seem to be right back where we started from, with a presentation and appreciation process happening somewhere in some special inner sanctum in the brain. Now we know there's no place in the brain where it all comes together. Yet we find it very hard to conceive of how consciousness could exist if that were not the case.

I'm trying to sketch, in effect, a family of alternative theories. That's why it has to be, in some regards, very metaphorical, because I want to be neutral with regard to some possibilities I am in no position yet to resolve. The main point of my alternative is that the appreciation, the 'taking' of the 'given', has to be broken down, fragmented, distributed around in space and time in the brain. This has implications that are far from obvious; indeed, some of them are profoundly counterintuitive. My task in *Consciousness Explained* is to make the theoretical world safe for these alternatives, so that they no longer seem so profoundly counterintuitive, so that we can begin to think positively about their details.

Cogito: One of the main misconceptions that you attack is the idea that there is a single point or centre in the brain which is the seat of consciousness, the 'place where it all comes together'. You go on to argue: 'Since cognition and control – and hence consciousness – is distributed around in the brain, no moment can count as the precise moment at which each conscious event happens' (p. 169). But surely the brain-events which underpin conscious experiences must occur at definite times, even if they occupy different places in the brain?

Dennett: Sure. The individual brain-events are clockable down to the millisecond, if you have the right equipment, but my claim is a conceptual point about what does not and cannot follow from that. There is a nice analogy. Let's consider the British Empire, which was distributed all over the world in the nineteenth century. Now let's consider the notorious case of the battle of New Orleans, which was fought fifteen days *after* the truce was signed in Belgium, ending the war of 1812. The battle of New Orleans was an intentional action of the British Empire. So was the signing of the truce. Yet they happened in an unfortunate and anomalous order. Now suppose somebody asks, 'When did the British Empire learn of the signing of the truce?'. Suppose we can tell when the ambassador in Belgium knew it, or the commander of the British forces in New Orleans, or Parliament, or the monarch, or the Governor-General in Calcutta. Each of *those* questions can be answered to the second, or at least to the day. But if you ask, 'When did the British Empire learn of the truce?', the question is ill-formed. We can reply, 'Oh, sometime in early 1815', but that's as close as you can get.

Now compare that question to this one. The subject asks, 'When did I become aware of the red disc turning green in Kolers' phi-phenomenon? Don't tell me what happened on my retina; don't tell me what happened in my vocal apparatus at the output end; don't tell me what happened in area V1 in my brain; I want to know when *I* became conscious of it.' Same answer. *You* are not located in any one place in your brain. So, just like the British Empire, the question of when you first learned this fact has no determinate answer.

It's interesting that when I ask the first question, about the British Empire, a lot of people initially think, 'Well, we'll have to find out when *the King* learned.' Fine. Maybe a case can be made for: 'the Empire, *c'est moi*', in the case of the king. But there isn't any king-homunculus in your brain; there just isn't any one place in the brain where the message has to get through so that that's when *I* learn about it. So this idea that there isn't any way of determining, to the millisecond, when *a person* is conscious of something, is simply the same conceptual point at a different time-scale.

Cogito: May we pursue the relation between time and consciousness a bit further? In chapter six, which begins with a quotation from Kant, you make several Kantian-sounding points. For example, you say (p. 148) that the representing by the brain of *A before B* does not have to be accomplished by, first, a representing of A, and then, a representing of B. You point out that a person can judge, in a single momentary act, a proposition about a temporal sequence. Suppose, however, that we consider, not a person judging that A occurred before B, but rather a person actually *experiencing*, in real time, a process in which A occurs then B occurs. Doesn't this person *have* to experience A first, and then experience B?

Dennett: The way you have worded the question, the answer may well be yes. But consider a slightly different case. Consider a man experiencing something illusory. There isn't an A first, followed by a B; but nevertheless there is an experience of A-followed-by-B. Now here you're suggesting a distinction between experiencing and judging that I want to combat. Let's take a very simple case of perceived motion. You see an arrow move where no arrow moves – there are just two separate flashes of light. Now it's tempting to think that for you to see the arrow move, if the arrow out there doesn't move, then the brain has to make an arrow, make it move, and let you look at it. But that's a fallacy. You can see the arrow move without the brain having to construct a moving arrow for you to look at. It can be the case that you see the arrow move even though the arrow 'out there' doesn't move, and no arrow 'in here' moves either.

I never know whether that point is just obvious, or whether it's really counterintuitive, but I think it's a truth that can be arrived at by many different paths. For example, V.S. Ramachandran has a wonderful experiment in which subjects look at a TV set on which there is just snow, twinkling little spots of light randomly distributed. You now draw a little X in the centre and ask the subject to fixate on X. To the side of the X, you then fix a little piece of grey cardboard. If the subject continues to fixate on X, the grey cardboard will gradually be filled in with twinkle and will disappear. Then, marvel of marvels, if you arrange suddenly for the background to become uniform (without twinkle), there will be, for a brief period of time, some twinkle left over in the square. A stunning and surprising experimental result. This is twinkling that isn't in the world, and never was in the world. Here is the relevant philosophical question. Can the brain represent twinkling without representing lots of individual twinkles? Does the brain's representation of twinkling *have* to consist in its representation of a lot of individual twinkles? The answer is no. The brain does not have to represent all the individual twinkles for you to *perceive* twinkling. Perception does not involve the presentation of a display in a Cartesian Theatre.

Cogito: You claim that 'there are no fixed facts about the stream of consciousness independent of particular probes'. Scientists in many fields encounter the practical difficulty that their attempts to measure something inside a system *interfere* with the system, and consequently affect the properties of the thing they are trying to measure. So they never obtain data that are interference-free. But you seem to be making a much stronger claim here. Could you please elucidate further?

Dennett: I am making a stronger claim, because the phenomenon we are talking about is a phenomenon which is, if you like, by definition a matter of probing. That is to say, to talk about a conscious phenomenon that exists unperceived or unobserved is to talk apparent nonsense. Curiously enough, some attempts to account for consciousness have the feature of trying to establish the category of the objectively subjective, which is, I think, just a covert contradiction. There is no such thing. Here is the one place where verification reigns, and obviously *should* reign. The astronomers' rule of thumb, 'If you didn't write it down, it didn't happen', nicely overstates the verificationist thesis, but when it comes to consciousness, that's just the truth. 'If you didn't experience it, it didn't happen (in experience)' – that's just a tautology. But to say that you experienced it either means that in some sense you 'wrote it down', that it was a probe that led to further effects, or it doesn't mean anything.

This is particularly clear, I think in the case of meta-contrast, or backward masking. If you are shown a flashing red disc on a screen, you have no problem at all in seeing it and in counting the flashes. But if, very briefly after the disc flashes on, a 'doughnut' shape is flashed, so that the disc would have been, as it were, in the 'hole' of the doughnut, then you get a sequence of flashes, disc-doughnut, disc-doughnut, disc-doughnut, etc. However, all that you will then see – all that you will report seeing – is the doughnut. It is as if the disc were not there at all. How do we explain this fascinating result? There seem, at first sight, to be two possibilities. The standard explanation in the literature is what we might call the ambush theory. This says that the disc-stimulus is on its way up to consciousness; when somehow the doughnut-stimulus overtakes it and ambushes it on its way, so that all that ever gets into the door of consciousness is the doughnut. But notice that there might be another explanation, i.e. that you do become aware of the disc in consciousness, but that immediately afterwards the doughnut rushes through the gate of consciousness and not only impinges itself on your memory but also erases your memory of the disc having been there a moment before.

Now we seem to have two distinct theories. One of them says that there's a post-experiential tampering with memory by a sort of Orwellian Ministry of Truth. The other says that there's a pre-experiential expunging of the stimulus on its way up to the Theatre of consciousness. I argue that this is an illusory disagreement. There can't be any fact of the matter as to which side of the Theatre the interference occurs, because there isn't any Theatre. Manifestly, the second stimulus interferes with the processing of the first stimulus, but if we ask ourselves whether this is post-experiential memory processing or pre-experiential presentation processing, there just is no answer to that question.

Cogito: Your colleague Douglas Hofstadter remarks, on the dust-jacket of the book, 'While *Consciousness Explained* is certainly not the ultimate explanation of consciousness, I believe it will long be remembered as a major step along the way to unraveling its mystery.' Do you agree with the first bit? And if so, what, in your view, are some of the mysteries that still remain?

Dennett: Oh, I agree with the first bit in this sense. I think that the hard empirical work remains to be done. I said before that my theory is a sketch. It is deliberately neutral with regard to some big puzzles. But they are puzzles, not mysteries. The difference is that with a mystery you don't know how to proceed, whereas with a puzzle you have a good idea about what the ground rules are and about what constitutes progress. In my braver moments I think I've turned the mysteries of consciousness into a series of puzzles. But that still leaves a lot of work to do.

Cogito: So turning mysteries into puzzles is a legitimate aspiration for the philosopher in general, and the philosopher of mind in particular?

Dennett: I think so, yes. In fact, I think that's an ancient and well-regarded tradition in philosophy, the idea that philosophy starts with the mysteries, and when it can turn a mystery into a puzzle it gives birth to a new science. Of course we already had the sciences of psychology and neuroscience, but they were, in a sense, prematurely born, so there's still work for the philosopher to do before they can simply proceed with their puzzles.

Cogito: Perhaps we could end this interview with one or two questions of a less technical nature. Within psychology, there has long been a tension between so-called 'scientific' and 'humanistic' approaches to the subject. Scientific psychologists have often argued that humanistic psychology just perpetuates confusion, falsehood, and wishful thinking. The challenge may come from Skinner's behaviourism, or from the eliminative materialism of Paul and Patricia Churchland, but the message is that our 'folk-psychology' is under threat from the advance of science. How do you regard this debate? Are scientific understanding and human dignity compatible?

Dennett: I think there are several issues wrapped up in your question. The question of whether folk-psychology has a future can be split into two. One might ask, 'Does it have a role in scientific psychology?', which is really what the debate between humanistic psychologists and Skinnerians was about. There, I think, the answer is that it does, but not the role that someone might think. It's analogous to setting the specifications for an engineering problem, rather than being a description of the solution. We use folk-psychology to partially characterize the nature of a competence to be implemented; and once the implementation has been created, we may see that the traditional folk-psychological way of talking about it no longer has application. That's not a negligible role at all for folk-psychology within scientific psychology – in fact, I think it's an exalted and very important role.

But that's quite distinct from the question of whether, as materialistic neuroscience marches on, there is going to be room for our notion of human dignity. I think the answer there is manifestly *yes*, but with different foundations. Anybody who supposes that our vision of ourselves as moral agents, or as lovable, or as having dignity, depends on a certain dualistic conception of ourselves as harbouring a special sort of spirit, seems to me to hold a remarkably trivial and trivializing notion of the source of human dignity. It's as if we each carried a special gold coin without which we were trash – a stupid idea when you look at it that way. Our appropriateness as objects to love, respect, admire, or care for, is much more a function of our complexity, and of the kind of complexity that we manage to have. If anything, the account of our worthiness that one gets from a mature cognitive science is vastly preferable to the one that you get from the traditional vision. And this is not just a theoretical issue – it's also a practical one. Ethical issues regarding abortion, or prolonging the lives of brain-damaged patients, for instance, require informed moral decisions. At the moment I think that the traditional moral categories are just getting in the way. They are not doing any work, and sometimes they are positively harmful. I do not believe that progress is made on the abortion debate by asking, 'At what point does the soul enter the foetus?' I think that is a manifestly preposterous way to engage in the debate. Well, then, let's find some other and better terms.

Cogito: Do you see your technical work in the philosophy of mind as helping to solve such issues as those mentioned above? Might it, for example, help us to formulate a credible *moral psychology*?

Dennett: In fact, I have long aspired to extending and developing my ideas in this direction. *Elbow Room* fills part of the gap, as do the papers, 'Conditions of Personhood' and 'Mechanism and Responsibility'. I think there is a natural extension of my ideas into the area of moral psychology, and I am delighted to say that a wonderful inroad has been made by a colleague of mine, Stephen White, in his new book, *The Unity of the Self*. Although his theory of mind, in that book, is almost entirely consonant with mine, the book is far more than just an extension of some of my ideas – it also goes deep into areas which I hadn't imagined at all. The book seems to me to go a long way to demonstrate how to tie ethics and philosophy of mind together in the field of moral psychology.

Cogito: I hope you will forgive us if we end with a more personal question. Do you find that your work in the philosophy of mind helps you to gain a greater understanding of yourself and others? Are you a better husband, father, or grandfather as a result of your work? Can you think of examples where your theoretical work has guided your personal life, or *vice versa*?

Dennett: Actually, when I think about this I realize that the task of parenting, for instance, has got to go on in real time, and under such tremendous emotional pressures that it would be very unlikely for anybody's theory to play more than a passing role. There's very little evidence of a positive correlation between anybody's psychological or philosophical theories and their capacity as a parent. Not because their theories are good or bad, but just because parenting is such a difficult task.

I can think of some trivial – or perhaps not so trivial – cases from my own experience. One that I'm rather proud of occurred when my daughter was a little girl of about five. She was doing acrobatics on the piano stool, and it fell and crushed some of her fingers. She was not only in great pain but terrified, almost hysterical. I realized I had to do something to calm her down. I'd just finished my research on pain (for 'Why You Can't Make A Computer That Feels Pain'), and had an idea that I thought might work. So I tried it. I said to her, holding her crushed fingers close to the palm of my hand, 'Andrea, here's a secret. Push the pain into my hand! Quick! You can do it!' And immediately she stopped crying, and a smile formed on her face. She had 'pushed the pain into my hand'. This was a sort of impromptu hypnotic suggestion on my part that worked remarkably well. I told her, 'If the pain starts coming back, push it back into my hand again', which she did. Later, we left the pain on a wall. 'We'll leave it there', I told her, 'and go to the hospital.' She was quite content to accept the theory. In her distraught state she wasn't being very critical. But it does show that sometimes all it takes is a new theory to alter your consciousness quite dramatically. This seems to me to be a pretty good instance of it.

11

HUGH MELLOR

Hugh Mellor is Professor of Philosophy at the University of Cambridge. His works include *The Matter of Chance* (1971), *Real Time* (1981) and *Matters of Metaphysics* (1991).

Hugh Mellor (interview 1993) is still Professor of Philosophy at Cambridge. Since our interview he has published *The Facts of Causation* (1995) and *Real Time II* (1998), and has edited a volume of papers on *Properties* (1997) for the Oxford Readings in Philosophy series.

Cogito: I understand that you studied chemical engineering at Cambridge. What was it that converted you to the study of philosophy?

Mellor: I went to America to do graduate work in chemical engineering, and took a master's degree at the University of Minnesota. I had to take a subsidiary subject, and discovered that Minnesota had an excellent philosophy department, run by Herbert Feigl, who had been a member of the Vienna Circle and was a friend of Einstein and Popper. I took a course with him. That was what really led, in the end, to my becoming a philosopher.

Cogito: So you came back to Cambridge to pursue studies in philosophy?

Mellor: No, I came back to England to become a chemical engineer working for ICI. But I found I'd been bitten by the bug, and although I enjoyed myself at ICI, they weren't going to pay me to do philosophy, so I took a chance and came back as a research student to Cambridge.

Cogito: Do you think that your early training as an engineer has left any lasting influence on your philosophical work?

Mellor: Yes, I think so. An engineer, as opposed to a scientist, has to tackle situations as they are out in the world, not trimmed to test a theory;

and the engineer's problem is always to find a language, a way of describing the situation, which is simple enough to yield a solution, but complex enough to be reasonably realistic. That seems to me much more like a philosophical problem than most of those that scientists face.

Cogito: I think of you as very much a Cambridge philosopher. Do you think that there is a recognizably 'Cambridge' style or tradition of philosophy? If so, could you characterize some of its main features?

Mellor: I think there are two traditions of Cambridge philosophy. One is what you might call an ordinary language tradition, associated with G.E. Moore and then later Wittgenstein. But there is also a more mathematically based, scientifically oriented tradition of philosophy which I got from Richard Braithwaite, but which goes back through Russell and Ramsey and Broad. I feel myself as belonging to this tradition. Its main characteristic is that, although it doesn't worship science, it tries to keep its philosophy informed by relevant facts about science.

Cogito: In this century, many of the major studies on probability have come out of Cambridge – Broad, Ramsey, Russell, Keynes, Jeffreys, Braithwaite, Hacking, and your own book, *The Matter of Choice*. Do you think that has anything to do with the way philosophy was done in Cambridge?

Mellor: I think it's a special case of what we were just talking about. To understand probability philosophically you do need a certain amount of mathematics, but that's not the most important thing. More important still is an understanding of how concepts of probability are used in the sciences, for example in the assessment of scientific hypotheses. Now in Cambridge serious statisticians were also concerned with the foundations of statistics – people like R.A. Fisher. I think it was their interaction with ex-mathematicians like Braithwaite which prompted much of the philosophical work on probability in Cambridge.

Cogito: You recently edited the *Philosophical Papers* of Frank Plumpton Ramsey, the brilliant Cambridge mathematician–philosopher who died so tragically young in 1930. What particular parts or aspects of Ramsey's work were you trying to bring to the attention of modern philosophers?

Mellor: Part of what I wanted to do was simply to keep some important works of Ramsey's, which modern philosophers were well aware of, in print, and in particular to make them available in paperback so that students could get their hands on them. But there were other parts of Ramsey's work which I didn't think had received enough attention, so I was trying to bring them to the attention of philosophers. In particular, I'm thinking of his work on the nature of universals. Another such work was his article 'Facts and Propositions'. This contains a theory of truth which modern philosophers are familiar with, but that's only a small part of it; and I think the rest hasn't had enough attention, in particular the parts that deal with how linguistic meaning depends upon how the mind thinks.

Cogito: If Ramsey had lived to the ripe old age of his friend Richard Braithwaite, how might this have affected the course of twentieth-century philosophy, in Cambridge in particular and in the wider academic community?

Mellor: I think it would have affected the course of twentieth-century philosophy simply because Ramsey was so good, that he would have done a lot more good philosophy in a number of fields. In logic, for example, Ramsey would have done invaluable work on the discoveries of Gödel (made the year after Ramsey died). In Cambridge, I think Ramsey would have continued to influence Wittgenstein and the way Wittgenstein's work was received. I think he might have prevented Wittgenstein having such a mesmerizing effect on his colleagues and being made a guru in a way that was not helpful either to Wittgenstein or to philosophy in general.

Cogito: One noteworthy feature of your own philosophy is that you don't seem particularly concerned with the philosophy of language. Apart from a commendable concern for *clarity* (keeping the tools sharp, as it were), questions of language and meaning seem to have no special interest for you. Do you think that the so-called 'linguistic turn' in modern philosophy has been a mistake?

Mellor: It's true that I'm not especially concerned with the philosophy of language, *not* because I don't think it's important but because I don't have anything special to contribute to it. I have done some work on indexicals like 'now' and 'I' because mistakes about their meaning have encouraged mistakes about time and the self; but not much else. What I do jib at, however, is the idea that metaphysics depends on the philosophy of language and needs to be based on semantics. I think the 'linguistic turn' in modern philosophy has greatly exaggerated the importance of language for philosophy. That has had a very bad effect, especially on metaphysics but also on the philosophy of mind, which has also needed to be rescued from its subservience to the philosophy of language.

Cogito: You clearly believe that there are substantial philosophical questions, since you spend considerable amounts of time and labour trying to answer them. How do you respond to the Wittgenstein claim that meta-physics is just a product of the misuse of language?

Mellor: My response to that is that it just isn't true, and you can see it isn't true by looking at real issues of metaphysics. It's true that you can unearth serious metaphysical assumptions hidden in our language, and it's important to do that. But the most important issues – for example in the metaphysics of time – do not arise just because language has been misused, and cannot be settled just by not misusing it. Whether time really flows, for example, is a serious question, which cannot be settled that way. Ordinary language presupposes that it does, but that can be shown to be a mistake. The metaphysical assumptions of ordinary language are no more infallible than the Pope is.

Cogito: Time is of course a subject on which you have done a lot of meta-physical work. In *Real Time* (1981) you revive an argument of another Cambridge philosopher, McTaggart, for the unreality of *tenses*, i.e. of our past/present/future distinctions. He thought he had proved the unreality of time itself; you argue for the weaker conclusion that time is real but tenses are not. What is the philosophical motivation for this argument? Do you share the 'Spinozist' view of Jack Smart that all real (i.e. objective) facts can and should be viewed *sub specie aeternitatis*?

Mellor: I have no prior motivation here: I just follow the argument. It's demonstrable that tenses are not real, but it doesn't follow from this that time is unreal. In particular, one can still draw all the fundamental distinc-tions between time and the dimensions of space. But this talk of 'viewing' facts from the standpoint of eternity is very misleading. It's just a metaphor for expressing facts in statements that are not indexical, i.e. which are true at all times and at all places, like the statement that an interview between the editor of *Cogito* and a certain philosopher takes place in Bristol on 8 August 1992. There's nothing problematic about knowing that non-indexical statement to be true. It can be known at any time: you don't have to be in eternity to know it – that's nonsense.

But stripped of this silly metaphor of 'viewing', there is still a real contrast between these non-indexical statements and indexical ones like 'I am now being interviewed', which are true only at some times. Now the idea that tense is real is the idea that there are facts corresponding to these statements, which are facts at some times and not at others. What McTaggart showed is that this makes no sense. It is reading out into the world a characteristic – admittedly an important one – of how we think and speak. We do think and speak in tensed terms, and one and the same tensed thought, such as 'I am now being interviewed', can be had by different people at different times. Sometimes the thought is true;

sometimes it is false. But what makes it true isn't that there is then a correspondingly tensed fact, that I'm now being interviewed, which doesn't exist at other times. What makes it true is the tenseless fact that the thought is being had by someone while they are being interviewed. I believe that these tenseless facts are all the facts there are. But I don't have to believe in eternity to believe that.

Cogito: I remember a talk you gave on the BBC some years ago, in which you argued that Einstein's Special Theory of Relativity (STR) can be used to refute the metaphysical claim that only the present exists. Can you sketch the argument for us?

Mellor: The STR tells us something that is initially very surprising, namely that there isn't a simple fact of the matter about what is happening in remote parts of space at the present time, i.e. simultaneously with some given event on Earth. Think of a star one hundred light years away, and ask, 'what is happening there *now*, i.e. at the same time as this interview?' The STR tells you that there is no fact of the matter about that to within two hundred years. Any event there which I could see during this interview is definitely past; and any event which could be reached by a signal emanating from here now is definitely future. But within the two hundred years between these events it's a purely conventional matter, depending on the choice of so-called reference-frame, what events are simultaneous with this interview.

   Now those who think that only the present exists think that what exists is not only what is here and now, but also what is simultaneous with that across the whole of space. But STR tells you that simultaneity with the here and now does not pick out a unique set of events across the whole of space. So if you accept STR and maintain that only the present exists, you really have to shrink what exists to what is going on now and *here*. You have to think that nothing exists outside your present spatial location as well as your temporal location. And that is really quite incredible.

Cogito: Or, I suppose, that what exists depends on some arbitrary convention of ours; and that also, I presume, you would regard as absurd?

Mellor: Yes, that's obviously absurd. You can't bring things into existence by deciding to adopt a different convention about, in effect, how fast we are moving through space.

Cogito: I suppose people are motivated to assert that only the present exists (or sometimes, that only the present and the past exist) by their objection to the notion that the future is in some sense 'already there', as real as the past and the present. Do you think that is just a confusion on their part?

Mellor: I don't think it's a confusion, though I do think it's a mistake. It's demonstrably wrong, but a very natural thing to think because people believe, quite rightly, that what happens in the future can be affected by what they will do. So, since they haven't yet decided what to do, they think that the future is open to be affected by what they decide. And that's perfectly true. Now it's quite natural to think that this requires the future not to be there yet, in order to leave open the possibility of affecting it. But the fact is that the future demonstrably *is* there, including our future decisions, and this *is* consistent with those decisions affecting other future events. But that isn't obvious to start with, which is why people think that our ability to affect what happens in the future shows that it isn't there yet.

Cogito: *Real Time* raises a number of interesting questions about the relation between metaphysics and physics. At one point (p. 120) you jestingly dismiss a sort of Aristotelian-style 'refutation' of the big bang theory. Elsewhere, however, you claim to refute time travel (an idea that some physicists take seriously) by philosophical argument, and chide philosophers for being *too* reluctant to challenge the physicists. Do you have a considered view on the role of metaphysical assumptions and arguments in physical theory?

Mellor: It's a mistake to think that there has to be a priority one way or the other, that either metaphysics must dictate to physics or vice versa. Physics does indeed show us things which contradict some metaphysical assumptions, as the example of STR shows; and then we must of course tailor our metaphysics to fit those results. But equally, there are perfectly good metaphysical arguments, like those of McTaggart against the reality of tenses, to which physics must accommodate itself. And on the whole, physics does accommodate itself to this. It's just that many physicists, when they start talking metaphysics, don't realize that there are other constraints beyond those of physics. So just as it's important to tell metaphysicians to take account of relevant physics, it's important to tell physicists to take account of the constraints of logic and metaphysics to which physics is subject.

Cogito: Another area in which the same sort of questions are going to occur is of course that of causality. In *Real Time* you defend a principle of *local* causal action. Now many physicists would say that that principle has been discredited by discoveries in quantum mechanics. How would you respond to such objections?

Mellor: Well, physicists also find the phenomenon of so-called 'non-locality' worrying, precisely because it raises questions about causation.

To see what the problem is, we have to analyse causality. We have to decide what it is we are insisting on when we say that there is direct action at a spatial distance. I think the most important thing about causation is that it provides what the philosopher Douglas Gasking many years ago called 'recipes', ways of making things happen. Now everyone agrees that non-locality does not provide a way of making things happen: that is what the so-called 'no signalling theorems' show; and that is what prevents these phenomena contradicting what I mean by local causation.

What makes these non-locality phenomena interesting to philosophers is that they do have some of the features we associate with causation, but not those features that enable us to bring one thing about by doing another one. So they force us to concentrate and clarify what it is we are insisting on when we claim that something is causal. The sense in which some physicists say that there is causation across space is an attenuated sense that doesn't entail the most important application of causation, which is that of giving us ways of getting things done.

Cogito: So you think that our most fundamental notion of causation is the 'recipe' sense, and that one can still argue *a priori* that local action is a necessary condition for causation in this sense?

Mellor: Yes. Of course it doesn't matter how you use the word 'causation', so long as you don't equivocate. You mustn't use the word in a weaker sense, then switch back to a stronger one and argue that phenomena which are only causal in the weaker sense could be used to get messages to people and influence their behaviour across space-like intervals of space-time. You can't do that and nobody thinks you can. I think we would avoid a lot of confusion if we stuck to the stronger sense of 'causation' in which it does have the 'recipe' connotation. If we did, there would be no dispute about these cases.

Cogito: Your inaugural lecture presented a resolution of the problem of induction. Can you summarize the line of argument? Can it be said to be a distinctively 'Cambridge' solution, building on the work of Ramsey, Broad, Russell and Braithwaite?

Mellor: The main idea is that induction, inferring that things that have repeatedly gone together in the past will go together in the future, is justified because it usually works. That of course is itself an inductive inference, because it says that inductive inferences will work in the future because they have worked in the past. The standard objection to this is that it begs the question, because it involves using the inductive principle to justify itself. My reply to that is to argue that knowledge-claims in general, not just inductive ones, are justified not if *we* can justify them, but if they have *in fact* been arrived at by some process which makes them very likely to be true. That's what matters, and all that matters. In particular, we don't have to know what makes our claim very likely to be true.

Now I argue for this in a general way, and then apply this argument to the special case of induction. I show that the inductive justification of induction really does not beg the question. Because all that's necessary for induction to be justified is that as a matter of fact it usually works! We needn't be able to *prove* that it usually works. That's the gist of my inaugural lecture. It's true that I derived it from earlier work by Ramsey, Russell and Braithwaite, but inductive justifications of induction are not peculiar to Cambridge, although I suppose there has been something of a tradition of them in Cambridge.

Cogito: So the basic thrust of your argument turns on this epistemological point, that we can know something (or have good grounds for believing something) without having to know, or to justify, the means by which we came to hold the particular belief. In other words, in the jargon of the epistemologists, you reject the 'KK principle', the thesis that in order to know something I must know that I know it.

Mellor: That's right. That has always seemed to me an implausible principle, because it leads to an obvious regress which is not only obviously vicious but also incredible. If, in order to know something, I have to know that I know it, then in order to know that I know it, I have to know that I know that I know it, and so on, and I'd never be able to get started. It would take a very strong argument to persuade me that this KK principle was true, given that it would leave us knowing almost nothing. But there isn't a good argument for the KK principle, and there are good counter-examples to it which have nothing to do with induction. That was another part of my inaugural lecture. I argued in general against the KK principle, and then showed how rejecting it in the special case of induction enables us to solve the problem of induction.

Cogito: In the introduction to your recent collection of essays, *Matters of Metaphysics*, you say that the whole question of physicalism is as trivial as the doctrine is false. That might seem, out of context, to give comfort to some other 'ism'. Can you explain why it doesn't?

Mellor: Physicalism is normally opposed to dualism. The dualist says that there are two fundamentally different kinds of entity in the world, minds and physical objects, or two fundamentally distinct types of property, mental and physical. The physicalists accept this *prima-facie* distinction, but say that in reality there aren't any entities (or properties) of the purely mental kind – they are all reducible to entities (or properties) of the physical kind. What I reject is this basic division into two fundamentally distinct kinds of entity or property. There is a great plurality of properties – electrical, gravitational, chemical, biological, psychological – but there is no fundamental distinction of kind amongst them. There are lots of little distinctions, and interesting questions about which are reducible to which. So my view could be called a kind of 'trivial pluralism'. What I jib at is the importance physicalists and dualists attach to the distinction between the mind and its properties on the one side, and bodies and their properties on the other. They both think that you must *either* take this distinction to be absolute and fundamental, *or* take the mental to be somehow reducible to the physical. It is these shared assumptions that I reject.

Cogito: So you see no reason to believe either, on the one hand, the dogmatic assertion of the so-called 'unity of science', that everything must reduce to physics in the long run, or, on the other hand, the dualist's dogmatic rejection of reductionism. What you see instead are a lot of local issues about the reducibility of one particular bit of science to another?

Mellor: There are a lot of sciences, and whether they can all be reduced in some non-trivial sense to one basic science seems to me to be an open question and not a very fundamental one. I share the Kantian view that all the sciences are involved with *phenomena*, in a general sense, and these phenomena can be physical, chemical, biological, psychological, or whatever. They are all studied in ways that are methodologically similar, but of course they differ in detail according to their subject-matter. You can't investigate psychological phenomena with the instruments, using the same experimental techniques, which you need to investigate the stars. But that isn't a big issue. All sciences are part of the general project of finding out what kinds of phenomena there are, what laws govern them, and how they are inter-related: that is what unites the sciences. The division of science into different subjects studied by different techniques, and in differently labelled departments of universities, is merely a division of intellectual labour. It may be essential in practice, but it has no cognitive or conceptual significance at all.

Cogito: I understand that your next book is to be on the subject of causality. Can you give us some idea of the position you are going to be expounding and defending?

Mellor: There are different aspects to it, many of which I have taken from other people. For example, I take the common view that causation depends upon laws of nature. I believe, however, that causation also relates particular events, and that this is a local matter. In that sense I oppose a tradition on causation going back to Hume, which says that whether one thing causes another isn't a local matter: it just depends on whether things of these two kinds are correlated throughout the universe. I deny that, even though I think that one thing can only cause another if it is an instance of a law of nature. I also think that causality involves probability, so I have to say how I think they are related. Similarly with the idea, which I have again taken from others, that causal claims entail something about what would have happened if the cause had not occurred. All these elements have to be pulled together, and what makes me want to write a book about it is that I want to pull them together differently from my predecessors.

One main difference of my approach is the twist I give the idea I mentioned earlier, that causation is something that gives you recipes. If two things are related as cause to effect, then it always makes sense to bring about the cause in order to get the effect. Now this idea of being a means to an end is also studied in a completely different area of philosophy, namely decision theory. And, unlike most of my colleagues, I think that decision theory can be used to show how causation depends upon probability, via this 'means–end' of 'recipe' connotation. That is one fairly original part of my work.

Another idea, which is not original, but which I've emphasized more than most others, is the fundamental connection between causation and time: in particular, how causation makes time differ from the other dimensions of spacetime. The temporal structure of spacetime depends on causation, and the direction of time depends on the direction of causation. This is something else I want to bring out in the course of the book.

Cogito: You have recently been involved in two widely publicized debates, both of which have served to focus public attention on questions about what is and is not to count as legitimate academic work. The first of these two debates concerned parapsychology. What was your objection to promoting research in this field?

Mellor: Parapsychology trades on the familiar fact that there are lots of things about the mind that we don't know, just as there are lots of things about other aspects of the universe that we don't know. Normal science concerns itself with trying to remedy our ignorance in these respects. It tries to understand phenomena by discovering the laws governing them. Sometimes it succeeds and sometimes it fails. What's wrong with parapsychologists is that they count failure as a kind of success; that is, they think that failure to understand a phenomenon bestows a kind of glamour upon it, makes it something special, a paraphenomenon. It does nothing of the sort: all it means is that there's something we still don't understand.

The only way to keep this fundamentally silly approach going is by pointing to phenomena which look as if they should be explicable by normal science but so far are not. On the one hand, they must be phenomena that aren't obvious enough to cause serious scientists to change their theories to accommodate them. On the other hand, they have to be things which serious scientists have no interest in tackling in a normal way. The only phenomena that fit this bill are things for which there is very little evidence. That is, phenomena which only appear to show up in bizarre, unrepeatable, and anecdotal situations, rather like the Loch Ness Monster. But nothing follows from this. Any serious scientist will come across anomalous experimental results, things that don't work, things which suggest something that turns out in the end not to be there. To make a kind of occult mystery out of this common-place, and out of our failure to explain everything we try to explain, is just not being intellectually serious. That's why, although I don't object to parapsychology as a spare time amusement for people with nothing better to do, I don't think a respectable academic institution should promote it.

Cogito: The second debate I had in mind was, of course, the controversy over whether to award an honorary degree to Jacques Derrida, the French philosopher (?) and *littérateur*. You were a prominent member of the opposition. You lost the vote, of course, but succeeded in making your point. What, though, is the precise nature of your objection to Derrida? Is it that what he says is false, or unintelligible? Or is it perhaps essentially a moral objection against a kind of intellectual irresponsibility?

Mellor: Some of Derrida's early work was interesting and serious. But this isn't the work he has become famous for, and which led to him being put forward for an honorary degree. That is much later work which seems to me wilfully obscure. If you spell out these later doctrines plainly, it becomes clear that most of them, if not false, are just trivial. Take the fact that the writing down of a signature must have been present at whatever time in the past it was done. Now you can make this truism sound mysterious, as Derrida does. But there's nothing mysterious about it: it's just trivially true that if an action leaves a trace, then the trace will always be of something in the past that was once present. So one objection is that Derrida goes in for mystery-mongering about trivial truisms. But he also mixes these truisms up with silly falsehoods, which, if believed and acted on, would cripple intellectual activities of all kinds. The excesses of deconstructionism have been especially unfortunate, because they imply that writings have no intrinsic meanings that are fixed or constrained in any way by the writers' intentions or the conventions of their language; that writings are open to endless and arbitrary re-interpretation by their readers. This is obviously false, and has the most absurd implications. In the law, for instance, it implies that because a

statute has no intrinsic meaning it could be re-interpreted so as to sanction, or to forbid, any course of action whatsoever. That is nonsense,
but if people really believed it, it would sanction all sorts of arbitrary
and authoritarian practices by the state. So it is either just nonsense, if
it's not believed; or it's very dangerous, if it is believed. I'm sure Derrida
himself doesn't believe most of the nonsense he is famous for, but if you
filter that out, the rest doesn't add up to anything worthy of an honorary
degree.

Cogito: I can think of an example here that might appeal to a lover of
the theatre such as yourself. In *King Lear*, when Cornwall had Gloucester's
eyes put out, he is described as being 'naughty'. Presumably, a disciple of
Derrida must believe that he is at perfect liberty to construe that word
in its late-twentieth-century sense – the sort of rebuke that a mother would
give to a child who had just stolen a biscuit.

Mellor: That's right. The fact that the word has changed its meaning since
Shakespeare's time creates a serious problem for the actor who has to
say that line. Somehow, the actor has to get the audience to take that
word in something like its original sense. That is a serious activity which,
if Derrida's doctrines were correct, would make no sense.

Cogito: One gets an impression of you, arising from these controversies,
as a sort of embattled figure, struggling to defend Enlightenment values
against a rising tide of unreason. Do you ever see yourself in this light?

Mellor: No, no. It's not a rising tide of unreason; it's just been a bad year
for bullshit in Cambridge. But two episodes, however notable, are not
statistically significant. There is a recurrent temptation, however, for academics who look too hard for excitement to find it in silly fashions. I think
this generates a permanent running battle in some arts subjects between
those who think straight about their subjects and those whom Mrs Thatcher
described, all too accurately, as 'the chattering classes'.

Cogito: One of your passions is the theatre, and I believe that you still
act. Is there any connection between that passion and your commitment
to philosophy?

Mellor: Only that they are both things that I feel quite passionately about
and want to pursue as long as I can. The only moral I would draw from
this is that it's probably bad for people to treat philosophy as an all-
consuming vocation, to which they should devote their whole lives. I think
it's healthy from time to time to get right away from a subject with the
pretensions that philosophy rightly has. That makes you see and think

about the world in a way that's fresh and independent of your philosophical ways of seeing and thinking. So the theatre is for me, perhaps, what backgammon was for Hume.

12

RICHARD SORABJI

Richard Sorabji is Professor of Philosophy at King's College, London, and Director of the Institute of Classical Studies, based in Gordon Square. His books include *Necessity, Cause, and Blame: Perspectives on Aristotle's Theory* (1980), *Time, Creation, and the Continuum: Theories in Antiquity and the Early Middle Ages* (1983), and *Matter, Space, and Motion: Theories in Antiquity and their Sequel* (1988). His next book (at press) is called *Animal Minds and Human Morals: The Origins of the Western Debate*. He is also currently organizing a major translation project, producing the first ever English translations of many of the philosophers of late antiquity.

Richard Sorabji (interview 1993) remains at King's and at the Institute of Classical Studies, where he continues to preside over a large-scale programme, producing new translations (often for the first time ever) of Simplicius, Philoponus, and other major figures in Hellenistic philosophy. He has also published his planned book on our moral responsibilities to animals: *Animal Minds and Human Morals: The Origins of the Western Debate* (1995).

Cogito: Your father, I believe, studied at Balliol College, Oxford, when the great classical scholar Jowett was Master. Can you tell us something of the history of your family that brought your father to Oxford, and of your father's influence on your own development?

Sorabji: My grandparents on the Indian side were both closely connected with England because one of them – my grandfather – converted to Christianity as a child. This was a great disgrace to the Zoroastrian family, early in the nineteenth century, and they cast him out. Indeed, they tried to murder him: they pushed him out to sea in a boat, and he was washed up and rescued by Christian missionaries, who were English. So he had an English connection; and my Indian grandmother was adopted by an English family.

So my grandparents looked towards England and wanted to send my father there for his education. Then one of his sisters, Cornelia Sorabji, passed out as the top student in Bombay University, and there was a scholarship to send the top student to England. But they said to her, 'Ah well, we hadn't foreseen that it would be a woman, so you won't get it.' For that reason, Florence Nightingale and other English ladies put together the scholarship anyhow.

Jowett was extremely interested in training people to go out to India, and took a special interest in my father, who was in Balliol, and my aunt, who was in Somerville. When the Oxford lawyers said that they wouldn't examine a woman, Jowett brought together the dons' official body under the motion that 'Oxford University shall examine Cornelia Sorabji'. The motion passed, and the examiners were forced to do so. Jowett took a special interest in them because my father and my aunt were in the first generation of Indians to take over legal functions in India. Indeed, Cornelia invented a new function. As a woman, she was the only lawyer that women in purdah could see. While still in Oxford, she became a close friend of Jowett and his confidante.

He used to send her off for weekends to stay with people in the country. Florence Nightingale was one of these people, and when she returned from this visit, she recognized the picture that Jowett kept in his study. It was in fact a picture of Florence Nightingale. She commented on this, and Jowett confessed to her that he had proposed to Florence Nightingale, and had been turned down. So my aunt was in fact the source of that particular piece of information.

Jowett was my aunt's champion, and used to take her to the Balliol Concert on his arm. Very recently, their correspondence has emerged. Jowett ordered that all his correspondence be burned, but 600 letters survived, and the correspondence with my aunt is among them. So I hope to go and look at it soon. Jowett took a special interest in my father and aunt because of his interest in India. She was the first woman lawyer, in either country, and he was one of the first generation of Indian men who began to take over British functions in the law.

I don't know that my father was a direct influence on my academic interests; that was probably my mother. She used to hold theology discussion groups in our house, and I always took part in them, from a very early age. That is, I think, part of the reason why I became interested in philosophy.

Cogito: When you began reading Ancient Philosophy at Oxford, what was the character of Oxford philosophy's interest in the subject? Has there been an important change in British and American philosophy since then, where Ancient Philosophy is concerned?

Sorabji: Yes, I think two important things have happened. Almost the first article that I wrote was about how I thought Aristotle, though very able as an ordinary language philosopher, wasn't only an ordinary language philosopher of the type that was prevalent in Oxford in the 1950s. The example I took was that, when he gives definitions of scientific terms like 'lunar eclipse', he doesn't give you an ordinary language definition. He gives you a theory, which very few people knew at that time, that a lunar eclipse is due to the Earth's shadow. Now that wasn't part of the ordinary concept, because very few people knew it. In giving you definitions of scientific terms, he was trying to give you what Locke would call a *real essence*, in other words, some very central feature of a lunar eclipse which would scientifically explain the more superficial features. That sort of definition goes far beyond the type of ordinary language definition which was prominent in Oxford in the 1950s. So I was trying to say that Aristotle did lots of other things besides what Oxford philosophy was then doing.

I had just heard a lecture by Putnam, who was urging that this was how definitions of scientific terms should be given. His example was *lemon*, another species in which scientists are interested. Later, with Putnam and subsequently Kripke coming into print, we got views about definition which were much more like Aristotle's; but when I was studying at Oxford, that hadn't been thought of except for this one lecture of Putnam's. So that's one very big change since the 1950s: philosophy has become less dominated by ordinary language, and in that respect closer to Aristotle.

The other thing is that, in the 'Greats' course, Oxford teaches its students only two Ancient Philosophy texts – Plato's *Republic* and Aristotle's *Ethics*. There is an option of taking others, but the commonest option is just those two. But the big change in Ancient Philosophy in the last twenty years or so has been that people have looked at the next 800 years of philosophy after Plato and Aristotle. Ancient Philosophy lasted for 1,100 years, from 500 BC to AD 600. This has even been reflected in the teaching curriculum in a number of places. I think this is a very important change. It often throws light even on Plato and Aristotle to see what later people made of them, how they rebelled against them, or how they took different directions from them. As well as, of course, these later people being interesting in their own right.

Cogito: How far is it possible to go in the study of Ancient Philosophy without a knowledge of Greek and Latin?

Sorabji: I think as an undergraduate, you don't have to know Greek or Latin at all. Here in London, and also at Cornell in America, I always lectured in such a way that I didn't assume that the undergraduates knew any Greek at all. At the intermediate level of MAs or MPhils, we have now set up in London a special course to teach people philosophical

Greek. We teach them Greek through Plato's *Meno, Phaedo* or *Theaetetus*, and in the second year through Aristotle. I think they pick up a great deal. Last year, for the first time, I started up a link with one of the American universities, which provides, through its philosophy department, a twelve-week crash course in Greek. One of our students went over and came back extremely good. I am also exploring, with the Open University, the possibility of spreading the teaching of Latin and Greek, including philosophical Greek, much wider than before. That could in principle be even more effective than the US crash courses.

It's only for my PhD students that I require them to have Greek. But even they, of course, strengthen their Greek as they go along – I just have to know that they'll be quite good at it by the time they finish. So I think people should start wherever they are at, and learn as they go along. It's our job to make provision for that and to help people overcome the difficulties.

Cogito: You show in your writings that you keep abreast of philosophical developments outside the area of your speciality. How do you divide your time and effort between Ancient and Modern Philosophy?

Sorabji: It's really hardly a division. I suppose more commonly I notice something in an ancient text, and realize that it connects with what people are discussing now, so that I read the modern philosophy second. But I shuttle backwards and forwards all the time. A lot of the interest of the ancient texts for me is their sheer philosophical interest, so I want to shuttle backwards and forwards.

Cogito: Your writings show clearly your conviction that Ancient Philosophy is not *merely* a matter of scholarly and antiquarian interest, that Plato and Aristotle – and, doubtless, others – might still have something to teach us. Could you perhaps give us an example or two to illustrate this claim?

Sorabji: I'm just finishing a book on our attitudes to animals. I started off by noticing that the ancient and modern debates on attitudes to animals had reached exactly the same point. The ancients started by saying that animals don't have reason: this was Aristotle's view, and the Stoics followed him. That seems an enormous difference, if it's true. The Stoics went on to draw the conclusion that, therefore, it's perfectly all right to kill them, as they are so very different from us in this extremely important respect. But under pressure, the Stoics had to retreat. At any rate, they claimed, animals don't have *syntax*. Now I notice that that's exactly the point that modern debates have reached. The followers of Chomsky, for example, claim that syntax is unique to humans. Experiments on teaching chimpanzees American sign language faced the objection that, even if animals can learn individual meaningful signs, they can't string them together with syntax. But then I noticed that what had initially seemed quite an interesting suggestion – that animals are *very* different from us because they don't have reason, therefore we can kill them – was now reduced to 'animals don't have syntax, therefore we can kill them', which quite obviously doesn't follow.

This made me realize that I really had to face the moral issues. I had no interest in the moral issues when I started: I was just interested in the philosophy of mind. When I began to face the moral issues, I realized that ancient and modern moral philosophy, in dealing with animals, seem to have the same deficiencies. It's always very one-dimensional. The ancient opponents of animals were saying, 'There's only one thing that matters: do they have reason or do they not?' The Stoics asked, 'Are they akin to us?' The Epicureans asked, 'Have we made a contract with them? Obviously not.' Modern defenders of animals are equally one-dimensional. They ask, 'What would maximize the satisfaction of preferences?' or 'What would minimize pain?' or 'Do they have intrinsically valuable qualities like beliefs or self-consciousness?', as if there were only one, or perhaps two, questions to be asked.

What then struck me was that both the ancients and the moderns had got it wrong. If you are in your car, and you run over a pheasant, and wonder if you should stop and do something about it, you don't just ask one question, such as 'Does it have reason?', 'Have you made a contract with it?', 'Does it have self-consciousness?' or 'What would maximize everybody's preference-satisfaction?'. These are just four questions, but there are hundreds of others which might arise. Isn't it your responsibility? Isn't the pheasant in need? Do you, however, have a pressing obligation at the end of your journey? There are an indefinite number of such questions. So I keep finding myself forced to address philosophical questions, but all this started simply by looking at the ancient texts on how animals differ from humans and whether they really lack reason, which initially didn't seem to be a moral question at all.

Cogito: Some years ago you delivered the Read-Tuckwell Lectures at the University of Bristol. In the course of those lectures you articulated a *cyclical* theory of time, and defended at least its logical possibility. Were you concerned to do any more than that? Are there any reasons to believe that the theory might be true?

Sorabji: No, I don't have any reason to believe that the theory might be true, but, funnily enough, it cheered me up that it was logically possible. I have a very irrational fear of death. I am convinced by reading the common interpretation of Epicurus that it is irrational. I'm thinking of the argument, perhaps wrongly ascribed to Epicurus and Lucretius, that, since I don't feel any horror at my past non-existence, I shouldn't feel any horror at my future non-existence. Now the reason why it would cheer me up if time went round in a circle is that then my birth, which obviously lies in my past, would equally lie in my future, because from any point on a circle, any other point lies both behind and in front. So funnily enough, I would find it cheering to think that my life also lay in the future. I think this is a completely barmy attitude of mine; I don't recommend it to anyone else, and I hope you are very much more sensible than I am.

Cogito: You don't think this has anything to do with your Indian ancestry? Cyclical theories seem to have been very popular in Indian philosophy.

Sorabji: That's true, but I find the Indians are very much more relaxed about death. I've talked quite a lot about it in India. It's partly that the Hindus believe in reincarnation, which veils any problem from them. But it's also partly because they practise detachment in a way that the ancient philosophical schools also practised it. Modern philosophy seems to leave this out altogether. So I find that the Indians cope with it much better.

I don't know why I should have this particular fear, but I do remember, quite vividly, the very occasion when I first felt it. I was being taunted, told that I too would die, and I replied, 'Don't be silly, only butterflies and flies die.' I went to get my mother to reinforce what I was saying, but to my absolute astonishment – I was six at the time – she said, 'Oh no, you will die.' I felt an absolute horror, from which I don't think I've ever recovered.

Cogito: You have devoted a great deal of attention to topics such as matter, space, time and motion. Many people might think that modern science and mathematics have simply superseded the work of the ancients in these areas. Is it possible to make the views of Aristotle and others on these topics interesting to modern physicists?

Sorabji: Very much so. I once gave a seminar with a physicist called David Bohm, who had a maverick physical theory. His view was that modern physics was in a state of turmoil, because of the experiments which suggest that you can change the charge on an object over here, between positive and negative, and simultaneously affect the negative or positive charge on a distant object, without there being time for a light signal to pass from one to the other. Now if that's really true, it does overthrow the foundations of modern physics. He was suggesting that time and space are some kind of illusion, while reality consists in some kind of 'implicate order', as he called it in his book. People thought that if he was right, he would be really famous. Indeed, he had been a colleague of Einstein, so he was no fool, even if his theory was rather eccentric. Now I gave this seminar with him, and in the second half of the seminar we looked at the Neoplatonists' views on space and time, and he kept clapping his hand to his forehead and saying, 'My goodness! This is what I published in the *Journal of Physics* last week!' So it is in fact very easy to interest modern physicists in the ancient theories.

Cogito: In your recent book, *Matter, Space, and Motion* (1988) you suggest that Stoic and Neoplatonic theories of matter are significantly similar to modern field-theories. How close is this resemblance? And is it merely fortuitous, or is it the result of significantly similar lines of thought?

Sorabji: I think it's fortuitous, and I think this happens very often in the history of philosophy. I have also come across another very interesting example. Berkeley's idealism was invented in the fourth century AD, for a completely different reason, not as an answer to scepticism at all. Berkeley's main motive for saying that tables were bundles of ideas was to show how we could have any knowledge of them. We didn't have to think that they were something beyond our ideas, and therefore something we were never directly familiar with. If tables were bundles of ideas, we were obviously familiar with them, because we are immediately familiar with our ideas. But in the fourth century AD, it was nothing to do with scepticism. It was a completely different problem, a problem about causation, which gave rise to idealism. The question of the Christian father, Gregory of Nyssa, was this: 'How can an immaterial God create a material world? Surely cause must be like effect?' His answer was that, actually, the world isn't quite so material as you think. The world is just a bundle of God's ideas. Gregory works it out in some detail, and even when you look at the details, there are similarities with Berkeley, especially as, for Berkeley too, a table is a bundle of God's ideas. I think this happens quite often in the history of philosophy: that remarkably similar ideas are thought of for completely different reasons. So it's impossible to argue, 'This idea couldn't have come up until so-and-so thought of such-and-such', because it might have come up for a completely different reason. The same is true of field theories of matter.

Cogito: In *Necessity, Cause, and Blame* you discuss at length Aristotle's views about causality and determinism. You seek to distinguish causation from necessitation in such a way as to permit Aristotle to say, of a human action, that it was caused, but simultaneously to deny that it was necessary. Can you explain how this distinction works?

Sorabji: The threat of causal determinism can be put as a dilemma. If what I do tomorrow has causes, and those causes have earlier causes, the chain of causes will already before my birth have necessitated or made it inevitable what I would do tomorrow. On the other hand, if tomorrow's action has no causes, it is random. Either way, how can I be praised or blamed for what I do?

What struck me as the solution was Aristotle's idea that cause is connected with explanation, not necessitation. A cause is a factor which provides an explanation. Aristotle recognized, of course, four different types of explanation. The type which we call 'cause', and which Aristotelian commentators call 'efficient cause', is just one of these four types of explanatory factor. My idea was that if an action has a cause, that doesn't imply that it was necessitated; all that it implies is that it has an explanation.

I gave an example of a student who attends nine out of a series of ten lectures, but fails to attend one of them. We are looking for the cause of the student's missing the one lecture – or, for that matter, of his or her attending the other nine lectures. Now it might be that, in a large city like London, travel can take at least an hour, cost a lot of precious time, and cause a great deal of hassle. So there's always a disincentive to go to lectures. On the other hand, there's always an incentive, if we suppose that he or she is a good student and the lectures are good lectures. So if we are asked to explain the student's staying away on one occasion, there is always an explanation, the disincentive of the long journey and the hassle.

Somebody might object here and say, 'That's not a complete explanation. You wouldn't get a complete explanation until you have shown that the staying away was actually necessitated. So you are not going to escape necessitation, and hence avoid determinism.' What I want to say in reply is that what counts as a complete explanation is relative to the question asked. Supposing that someone comes from another university, in quite a small city, and asks why your student didn't go to all ten lectures. Very often, when you ask for an explanation, you have a contrast in mind. The questioner might be thinking, 'In face of the fact that our students normally attend all ten lectures of a course, why did your student only go to nine?' Now if that was the question, it would be a complete answer to say that, 'In London, unlike in your city, travel can take over an hour.' There's nothing incomplete about that explanation.

Now admittedly there is one other question in relation to which there is no explanation at all. Suppose somebody asks, 'In face of the fact that your student went to nine of the lectures, why didn't he or she also go to the tenth?' In the story as I am envisaging it, there is no answer to this particular question, because I am supposing that there was no extra factor on this tenth occasion which added to the weight of the disincentives. I'm assuming that in all *relevant* respects, all ten occasions were the same. So I admit, but I don't think it's strange, that there are some questions for which there is no explanatory answer. But that doesn't introduce total mystery, or total randomness, into the world. The question, 'Why did the student stay away on one occasion out of ten?' has a perfectly good answer, relative to most of the questions one would want to ask. There is only one question in relation to which it doesn't have an answer. But we still don't have necessitation, because there wasn't some extra factor on the occasion the student stayed away which necessitated his or her staying away.

Cogito: Aristotle's most explicit discussion of human voluntary action occurs in the early chapters of Book 3 of the *Nicomachean Ethics*. Some commentators have blamed him for failing to address *the* free will/determinism issue; others (e.g. John Austin) praise him for the subtlety and sophistication of his approach. How do you view the matter?

Sorabji: I disagree with both these parties, of course, because I think that Aristotle does discuss the question of determinism, and not only in the context where this is usually agreed, that is his discussion of tomorrow's sea battle in *De Interpretatione*. Here the basic determinist argument is that, for example, if it was true 2,000 years ago that I'd be going to Edinburgh tomorrow; and if the past is irrevocable; then it was irrevocable 2,000 years ago that I'd be going to Edinburgh tomorrow. Most people agree that Aristotle discusses that kind of determinism.

I believe, though, that he also discusses determinism of the causal kind. By determinism, I mean the view that whatever happens has all along been necessary. The causal version of determinism says that your actions are necessary because whatever you are going to do tomorrow has causes; and those causes have causes; and this causal chain stretches back to the present and the past. What is caused, on this view, is necessitated, and is necessitated by a chain of causes whose earlier end is already irrevocable; so how can I fail to go to Edinburgh tomorrow? I seem to have no choice in the matter. That is the causal determinist's argument, and I say that Aristotle explicitly addresses it in *Metaphysics* Book 6, Chapter 3. This chapter finishes by saying that there is no cause of something or other. What I have suggested is that the 'something or other' is a *coincidence*; he is saying that coincidences don't have causes because they don't have explanations. So he has attacked the central premise used by the causal determinist, that whatever happens has a cause. I thus disagree both with those who blame him for not addressing the issue of causal determinism and with Austin, who praises him for a subtle discussion which ignores the issue. I don't think he does ignore it.

Cogito: What are your own considered opinions on such perennial philosophical topics as determinism and physicalism? To what extent have these views been formed by reflecting on the arguments of the Ancients?

Sorabji: My view of determinism was very much formed by reflecting on Aristotle. I can't disprove determinism, but I can see that the arguments for it are unfounded, and Aristotle helped me to see this. It was Aristotle who showed me how to answer the argument for causal determinism that we have just sketched. The answer was, partly, to say that it is not true that whatever happens has a cause – coincidences are among the things that don't – but, more valuably from the point of view of human moral responsibility, what I learned from Aristotle was that, even when our actions are caused, it doesn't follow that they are necessitated. This is because the notion of cause should be connected, as Aristotle connects it, with explanation rather than with necessitation. So my view on determinism was formed by Aristotle.

Interestingly enough, my views on physicalism are also related to this. I've never believed in physicalism, and was interested to find that my interpretation of Aristotle on coincidences forms the basis of an attack on physicalism that has been mounted in a recent book by David Owens [Owens, D. (1992) *Causes and Coincidences*, CUP: Cambridge]. Owens takes issue, in his book, with the very widespread view that all explanations can be reduced to explanations in terms of physical events. For example, if inflation is to be explained as due to a rise in the money supply, physicalism would say that, really, there is one set of physical events which constitute our present inflation, and another set of physical events which constitute the rise in the money supply, and the latter explain the former. The rise in the money supply might be constituted by the motions of the factory workers printing the extra bank notes; the further events constituting the inflation would be the movements of those people who go to the shops and find they can't afford what they want to buy, or who go to work and find they've been sacked because it was too expensive to employ them, and so on. What David Owens says is that, if you're going to take one enormous conjunction of physical events as the thing you're explaining, and another as the thing that does the explaining, and you refuse to describe these conjunctions of events in *economic* terms, then you've just got a higgledy-piggledy conjunction of physical events which you're artificially treating as if it were a coincidence. That is, the set of physical events that constitute the inflation appear, when described in physical terms, like a mere coincidence. But now, on the interpretation I gave of Aristotle, coincidences don't have explanations, so the physical events that constitute the rise in the money supply aren't going to supply one.

Cogito: So the physicalist is going to *lose* significant levels of explanation?

Sorabji: That's right. Now this is new work, not done by me but by David Owens, who is applying the interpretation I gave of Aristotle. So Aristotle has once again led to an attack on physicalism.

Cogito: What Aristotelian text is most urgently in need of study and commentary?

Sorabji: I think it's terribly difficult to foresee what would be the most fruitful thing to study. What I incline to suggest to students who wonder about what to do, say for a PhD, is to say, 'Why don't you take some later text which relates to Aristotle, and then you'll see Aristotle from a new angle.' Of course, if the student has already thought of a new idea about Aristotle, they should go ahead. But if they haven't, then I think my suggestion can lead to a very fruitful approach. Seeing what people later said about Aristotle, how they interpreted him, how they reacted against him, even how they misinterpreted him, often shows you new things about Aristotle himself.

Cogito: You and others have drawn attention to the quantity and quality of the philosophical work that was done after Aristotle died (322 BC) and before Descartes was born (AD 1596). Which figures in this interval strike you as particularly important?

Sorabji: I think that Aristotle's immediate successor and head of his school, Theophrastus, was extremely important. Whereas it was said in antiquity that he only crossed the t's and dotted the i's, I think perhaps he rather crossed the i's and dotted the t's, because he raised the most embarrassing questions for Aristotle. For example, he raised a question which destroyed Aristotle's whole concept of space, or rather of place.

Of course I think that some of the Neoplatonists are very important, not only the founder Plotinus, but also Porphyry – an extraordinarily original thinker. Then, as you know, I think Philoponus was extremely inventive and influential for the history of science, and so were the two great Christian thinkers who learned from these Neoplatonists, Augustine and Boethius.

I have left some important people out, because it's sometimes easier to treat the Hellenistic philosophers as schools. I'm thinking here of the Stoics, Epicureans and Sceptics. The trouble, at least with the Stoics and Epicureans, is that much of their work survives only in fragments, so one doesn't always know which philosopher one is talking about, though one knows what the doctrines of the school were. And I think these schools certainly repay study.

Cogito: To many students of the subject, 'Ancient Philosophy' still means, first and foremost, the works of Plato and Aristotle. What is the best way to overcome this over-narrow conception? Could more texts be brought into the 'canon'? Or is the idea of a short list of 'canonical' texts itself part of the problem?

124

Sorabji: That's an extremely interesting question. I'd give a different answer for the philosophers who are fragmentary, because it's quite difficult for students to study fragmentary texts. Fortunately, a very good book has recently been brought out about three of the schools – the Epicureans, Stoics, and Sceptics. It's called *The Hellenistic Philosophers*, by Long and Sedley, and it does make it much easier for students to study these three schools. They don't cover all the schools of Hellenistic philosophy, but they do give a wonderful set of important translations and brilliant commentaries. So for those three schools, I would recommend Long and Sedley's book. For the other authors I've mentioned, we fortunately have lots of their own works. Here we could read some of their own writings, starting with a selection of Plotinus' work. If I chose any Porphyry, I would choose his wonderful treatise on abstinence from animal food. It's about not killing animals, but it contains a whole Neoplatonic philosophy about the nature of gods, humans and animals, and about how we should live. It also incorporates a lot of arguments from earlier people, including a large fragment of Theophrastus, who had lived 600 years earlier. For the other Neoplatonist I mentioned, Philoponus, I think it would be desirable to have a translation of his arguments for the Christian view that the universe had a beginning. It's called, *On the Eternity of the World, Against Proclus*. There you get the arguments of the Neoplatonist Proclus for an eternal universe, and the counterarguments of Philoponus. Finally, we come to the two great Christian philosophers. For Augustine I would choose *The City of God* and the *Confessions*, his two most famous books, and for Boethius, *The Consolation of Philosophy*.

I think your question is very good, because it's good not to have a canon absolutely fossilized. I think it would be thoroughly desirable that another teacher, or myself at another time, should choose a different set of books and authors. Another problem with a canon is that you too often study great works in isolation. In the selection I've made, the philosophers were often reacting with one another: Plotinus to earlier philosophers; Porphyry to Plotinus; Augustine to Porphyry and Plotinus; Boethius to Proclus; Philoponus to Proclus; and so on. So you actually understand the context in which they were forming their views. That avoids some of the disadvantages of many canons.

Cogito: In the late Middle Ages, Aristotle was considered to be *the* philosopher, 'the master of those who know', in Dante's memorable phrase. But how did it come to pass that a philosopher who explicitly *denies* Creation and (sublunary) Providence, and – rather more controversially – seems to deny the immortality of the soul too, came to be deemed an authority by Christian philosophers? How successful, in your view, were the efforts of Thomas Aquinas and others to reconcile Aristotelian philosophy with Christian orthodoxy?

Sorabji: The extraordinary thing is that this had been done for Saint Thomas Aquinas many centuries earlier. It was done by the Neoplatonists between AD 300 and 600. Not because they loved Christianity: on the contrary, many of them were violently anti-Christian. They were trying to make Aristotle consistent with Plato. For that reason they argued that Aristotle intended his God to be a creator, just as Plato did, and that Aristotle intended the human soul to be immortal, just as Plato did. By an extraordinarily ironical accident, this made Aristotle safe for Christianity many centuries later, when, in the thirteenth century, Thomas Aquinas was reviving Aristotle's philosophy.

Cogito: But how did they evade the plain sense of the Aristotelian texts?

Sorabji: As regards the immortality of the human soul, they capitalized on the fact that Aristotle says that there is a special type of intellect which survives when the human dies. Aristotle doesn't say that it was part of the human soul. Some people have even thought that he meant that it was God resident within us while we were alive. But they took it to mean that it was the rational part of the human soul that survived.

As for God being a creator, they capitalized on an argument of Aristotle's that, because the heavens revolve for an infinite amount of time, there must be an infinitely powerful force to make that happen. But no body can house an infinitely powerful force, because all bodies are finite. So there must be an *incorporeal* infinitely powerful force to account for the infinitely long motion of the heavens. Aristotle does argue this way in the last chapter of his *Physics*. What the Neoplatonists said was that what goes for infinitely long motion must also go for infinitely long existence. According to Aristotle, the universe exists for an infinite time; so that too must be caused by an infinitely powerful force; hence by an incorporeal force; hence by God. They read all that into Aristotle, though he spoke only about motion, and never applied the argument to existence.

This is why the work of translation I spend some of my time on is important for understanding the history of Western philosophy. The books in which this transformation of Aristotle was offered were written between AD 300 and 600, and have not previously been translated into English. They are described in a book I edited called *Aristotle Transformed*. I am now spending some of my time organizing a big translation project: we have sixteen volumes completed already, and if the funding continues we'll have fifty or sixty in the end. This will be a chunk of philosophy which is a sort of missing link. If you don't know about this philosophy, you can't answer the question you have just asked me. How on earth does one get from Aristotle, who denies the immortality of the soul, and doesn't have a creator god, to Thomas Aquinas' Aristotle, who has these features and so is safe for Christianity? You can't answer unless you can read the re-interpretation of Aristotle by the Neoplatonists during this period of 300 years. So I think that the translation project is going to make a big difference to our understanding of the history of Western philosophy.

Cogito: You have written three substantial volumes on great philosophical themes: *Necessity, Cause, and Blame*; *Time, Creation, and the Continuum*; and *Matter, Space, and Motion*. In which direction is your work going now?

Sorabji: My present thoughts are on the connection between philosophy of mind and ethics. I've just completed a book on our attitudes towards animals, which I've already referred to. My next book will have something to do with the question, 'Can philosophy tell you how to live?' I shall be looking at the emotions. So many of the ancient schools of philosophy were concerned with coping with the emotions, which is a very large part of how to live. It involves philosophy of mind, because you have to analyse the emotions before you can have a theory of how you should cope with them.

Cogito: You said in your inaugural lecture that a young man of fourteen, hearing that you had been given a chair in Ancient Philosophy, commented: 'Oh well, I suppose someone has to do it.' Why does someone have to do it?'

Sorabji: The interest is partly historical, but it's also partly philosophical. Philosophy is in some ways like painting. The great painters, the ones it's most rewarding to look at, have been scattered through the ages. You would spend longer, I think, looking at a painting by Leonardo da Vinci than at one that had won the Royal Academy prize last year. You wouldn't say that the prize-winner *must* be better than Leonardo, simply because Leonardo lived so long ago. I think it's the same in philosophy. The people whom it's really stimulating to think about are the great thinkers – some of whom, fortunately, live in our own century, which I think is rather a good one – and these people are scattered through the centuries. Just reading the latest publication isn't going to give you the most rewarding stimulus. Also I think that if you do just read what has been published recently, it will be hard for your imagination to be wide enough. What reading the great philosophers of the past helps to do is to expand your imagination enormously, enabling you to see other approaches, other ways of tackling the problems. So for a philosopher, those are some of the reasons why someone has to do it; of course, there is also a historical interest, for a person like me, as well.

Cogito: What do you do to get away from philosophy? Is there any leisure activity of special importance to you?

Sorabji: At present, doing philosophy is itself a way of getting away from filling in questionnaires! But yes, I do have a number of hobbies. I used to perform in cabarets with the guitar, and I very occasionally nowadays play the guitar in a restaurant and sing funny songs. My other hobby is a more regular one. Since I was a schoolchild, I've enjoyed exploring English villages, admiring old buildings, churches, and so on. That is still a great pleasure. As many weekends as I can, I go out into the country – in the car, I'm afraid, rather than on my bicycle – just looking at buildings and villages. That is perhaps a full-time hobby for me.

13

DAVID GAUTHIER

David Gauthier is one of the most distinguished of contemporary Canadian philosophers, although he now teaches at the University of Pittsburgh in the USA. His works include *Practical Reasoning* (1962), *The Logic of Leviathan* (1969), *Morality and Rational Self-Interest* (1970) and *Morals by Agreement* (1985).

David Gauthier (interview 1993) is Distinguished Service Professor of Philosophy at the University of Pittsburgh. He is still working on the nature of practical reason, contractarian moral theory, and the political philosophy of Hobbes and Rousseau.

Cogito: One interesting fact about your life and career is that you have always been interested in public issues. It is often said that philosophers *ought* to speak to the public issues of the day, but in your case, it seems, the philosophical background has not been constant. It seems to me that, as your opinions about philosophical ethics have changed, so your general stance towards public life has changed. Am I inventing a pattern here, or do you think that there is a real connection?

Gauthier: I don't think you are inventing a pattern. I certainly think that my views about public issues have been affected by changes in my philosophical views, more particularly by my views about morals. The main philosophical question that has occupied me has been 'Why ought I to be moral? What reasons do I have for being moral?' The sort of reasons that have seemed to me to provide some answer also limit the moral sphere, in that the reasons tend to lead to an individualistically oriented morality in which one looks upon a moral framework as trying to make it possible for each person to achieve as much as possible of his or her own life plan. It has to be a morality of mutual benefit and mutual advancement. That certainly has affected my outlook on public issues. At one time in my life

I was much more sympathetic to redistributive policies, policies that take from some to give to others; whereas I came later to think that redistribution could only be justified if there was some injustice or wrongdoing in the background, and that the sorts of political policies that could be justified were ones that could be seen as being to everyone's advantage, i.e. as mutually beneficial.

Cogito: Do you not think that your way of posing the question might actually turn out to be question-begging? You ask, characteristically, 'Why should I be moral?' rather than 'Why should we be moral?'

Gauthier: I think that ultimately we make decisions and act as individuals. I have the capacity to act in certain ways, and no one else has that capacity. No one else can literally use it. You may be able to compel me in various ways to do what you want me to do, but still I'm the agent, and I'm ultimately the decision maker. So it seems to me that it is each of us who faces, individually, the question 'Why should I be moral? Why should I accept this way of behaving?' If you take the question 'Why should we be moral?', then it seems to me that you have to show why each of us should identify with the 'we' that you have in mind. A group morality has to be defended to the individual members of the group. That seems to me to be central to the moral and political thinking of the last few centuries, and it does seem to recognize the primacy of the individual agent with his or her own concerns and life plans.

Cogito: One place I see a possible influence of your philosophy on your own life is this. Twenty years ago you were quite a fervent Canadian nationalist, and an active member of the Committee for an Independent Canada, which aimed to block American influence on Canada and, in particular, to prevent American commercial domination of Canada. Now you are working in the USA, and your views on economics are basically free market, so that you don't want to see national boundaries as barriers to commerce any more. Has your philosophy dragged your personal life in this respect too?

Gauthier: Yes, I think to some extent my philosophy has dragged my personal life. But since we're talking about the Canadian situation, there are some important qualifications to be made. Free trade between equal parties may be very desirable; free trade that permits one party to further its interests at the expense of the other (which I think does sometimes happen) becomes less desirable. I'm not sure that a free-trade framework between Canada and the USA proves to be a framework of mutual benefit, as opposed to a framework within which larger, more powerful American corporations can behave in a basically exploitative way. So just because I think that national boundaries shouldn't be a barrier to genuinely free relations doesn't mean that I want to see them dissolved when the effect of dissolving them is to permit one party to gain benefits at the expense of the other. My whole moral philosophy is against the idea of any sort of redistribution, including especially that sort.

Cogito: Decisions are made by individuals, you say, and when there is a 'we', it is a 'we' that is formed by individuals. Is there a 'we' that is particularly important in your life? Do you, for example, think of yourself as a Canadian living in exile? Or is it just that you found another university and it happens to be in a different country?

Gauthier: I certainly still see myself as a Canadian. I'm not sure that I see myself as an exile – I spend a lot of time back in Canada. At the same time, I've never thought that it made much sense to try to divide philosophy along national lines, or for that matter, to be a bit more provocative, to try to divide it on lines of gender or race. I'm a partisan of the universality of reason, and I see philosophy as an exercise of that universal reason. From that point of view, it seems to me that a philosophy department in the USA is as acceptable a home as one in Canada or in Britain. Of course there are philosophical divisions that to some extent follow not so much national as linguistic lines: English-speaking philosophy has tended to differ from French-speaking or German-speaking philosophy, though perhaps those differences are now becoming less. I identify with the analytic orientation of English-speaking philosophy; but I don't see this as something that is essentially national or racial.

Cogito: You said, a moment ago, that it was 'provocative' to say that reason was not divided along gender lines. It wasn't clear to me where the provocation was here.

Gauthier: There are so many advocates of feminist epistemology and feminist ethics these days, who think that, somehow, feminism raises special philosophical issues. I'm simply not persuaded by such claims. It seems to me that knowledge is knowledge; there is no reason to think that men, or women, have any sort of privileged access to what can be known, or privileged methods of coming to know truths. But there clearly are people who think that there are significant differences here, and I was simply indicating that I myself am far from persuaded.

Cogito: I'd like to go back to the issue of redistribution, which you've touched on twice already. In your first answer, you made what I think will seem to some – particularly liberals of an egalitarian persuasion – a surprising transition. Talking about individualism, you said how important it was to you that people be given a chance to realize their plans for life.

Now a lot of the motivation for backing redistributive policies on the part of egalitarian liberals like John Rawls stems from just that kind of concern, concern to help people to realize their plans for life, whatever those plans might turn out to be.

Gauthier: I'm uncomfortable about the term 'help' here. I see society as a framework within which each person should be able to advance his or her life plan, and do so as effectively as possible. My concern about egalitarianism is that, in effect, the redistributive measures which many egalitarians favour diminish the capacity of some to advance their life plans in order to enable others to use that capacity, and I'm not convinced that that is proper. I do see each person as having a natural right to his or her own faculties, his or her own capacities, and the resources that one can acquire using those capacities, provided one is not doing so by taking advantage of others, that is, by making oneself better off in ways that make them worse off. So I don't see redistribution as in any sense necessary to provide the sort of framework in which each person is best able to further his or her own concerns. I don't think that it's the task of society to make it possible for people to further their concerns by giving them resources that have been developed by others.

Cogito: Does it make any difference here whether you are giving them resources which have been developed by others as individuals, as opposed to, say, resources that others have inherited or otherwise appropriated?

Gauthier: Yes, the manner in which people have developed resources, or come to acquire them, certainly does make a difference here. If we think of a situation in which everything is used in common, it seems to me that it would be in those circumstances advantageous for everyone to permit individuals to appropriate resources for their own exclusive use up to a point. But of course it is advantageous for everyone because it leads to a more productive use of the resources – of the various goods. It doesn't mean that if I happen to land on a large island before anyone else I would be entitled to appropriate the whole for my exclusive use. Ways in which people acquire goods, or land, must themselves work for mutual advantage. If I could appropriate the universe simply by willing it to be mine, it is hard to see how this could be mutually advantageous.

Cogito: Perhaps we should backtrack a bit at this point. You said earlier that your main concern throughout your philosophical career has been to explore the reasons there are for an individual to behave morally. But we never saw the route by which this investigation took you to the kind of analysis of social obligation that we are discussing now. Could you explain the connection?

Gauthier: Let's see. I start with the idea that morality involves constraints on persons. If we think initially of each person simply deciding for him or herself what to do, taking into account only what seems relevant to the individual in question, then there is good reason to think that we will end up in a mutually disadvantageous situation. In effect, each of us will make decisions that displace the costs of our actions onto others, when we are in a position to do so. The end result will be that we are all likely to be worse off, because we are all likely to have more costs displaced onto us than the benefits we gain from displacing some of our costs onto others. There are nice little formal models for these situations that we can talk about later if you like.

The key thought is that if, when we interact in an unconstrained way, when each person simply pursues his or her own objectives without giving any thought to the objectives of others, this leads to a situation of mutual disadvantage, then a framework that constrains us, if it's properly designed, should make it possible for each of us to do better. Each of us can gain by refraining from imposing certain costs on others if in return others refrain from imposing costs on him or her. I see morality as one of the principal devices that plays that role, that says 'no' to those actions that would, in effect, be a displacement of costs onto others, i.e. that would work to others' disadvantage. So part of the reason that each of us can have for accepting a moral system is that each of us can expect to do better under that system, accepting the constraints (given that others do so as well), than he or she could expect to do without the constraints.

Cogito: Is there an easy answer to the worry that there's an even better possibility open to everyone, namely to engineer a situation in which everyone else is good, but you can get away with not following the rules?

Gauthier: In one sense, there is no easy answer. It's obvious that not everyone can succeed at that game. Indeed, it's fairly obvious that only a few people can succeed at that game, and that the attempt to play it is likely to impose more costs than the total benefits it provides. There are a number of lines of thought that we might pursue here. The first is that, once we see what you have correctly pointed out, that some people might attempt to take advantage of others by convincing the others that they should accept constraints, while not accepting any themselves, we will then want to put emphasis on developing character traits that are basically co-operative in their orientation, that involve not a self-denying concern for others but a 'mutual benefit' concern for others. We will value those qualities in other people and thus favour methods of education and socialization that develop them. And of course, in the process, those qualities will tend to get developed in us too. When we realize the importance of a scheme of mutual constraint for mutual advantage, we will look with a special disfavour on the sort of conduct that takes advantage of others. We'll also realize, each of us, that it's important to be seen by others as someone who is genuinely co-operative, who does genuinely work for mutual advantage and doesn't seek to use mutual advantage as a smokescreen for benefiting himself at others' expense. When we understand this, I think that most of us at least will realize that being that sort of person is the most effective means to that end, that continually trying to pull the wool over other people's eyes is likely to be a costly and ineffective strategy. So that even if some aspects of socialization have failed, there can still be this ultimately self-interested argument for being a co-operative person.

Cogito: I wonder how that fits with what you said earlier about feminism. A feminist might claim that men have persuaded women to adopt an ethic of care and self-sacrifice, whereas men are socialized into a more hard-nosed, individualistic, acquisitive type of ethic. Isn't that an example of one group of individuals successfully pulling the wool over the eyes of another group, and deceiving them in a way that seems to work, at least for the deceivers?

Gauthier: Or that traditionally has worked? Yes; I don't think I have a problem with that. I'm going to put this in a way that will itself seem pejorative, but I think that, in this respect, men have been more clear-headed than women about the real nature of ethics. I don't think that this is because women have any less capacity to grasp these ideas; it may well be simply because men have, on the whole, controlled the educational system, and have found it to their advantage to socialize women in a way that has served male interests rather than female interests. But it seems to me that what is needed here is not a feminist ethics but a clear-headed understanding of what an ethics of mutual benefit really looks like. A good many feminists have been defending the idea of *care* rather than the idea of *justice*; whereas what I would argue is that selling women the idea that they are care-givers has often been a denial to those women of equal justice with men. The proper approach here is to understand the importance of equal justice for all, that is, of arrangements which each of us can see to be in his or her interests.

Cogito: Do you think that anything like the traditional family can survive that message coming home?

Gauthier: I don't know. Sometimes I have doubts about that, but I'm not sure. The family seems to be quite a flexible institution, and I'm not persuaded that it *can't* be adapted to meet the requirements of equal justice. In any complex society, different persons are going to play various different roles. Specialization is mutually beneficial, and there may be some level of specialization within most families. What will be important is that the roles be fully agreed by the role-holders, and be genuinely seen to contribute to the benefit of all parties concerned.

Cogito: I think a lot of people will be puzzled by your emphasis on morality as a system that constrains us to our mutual advantage. Many of us see as paradigm cases of moral action cases where there simply isn't any mutual advantage, where individuals engage in risky or self-sacrificing actions for the sake of others, where they could expect no recompense. Consider, say, rescuers of Jews during the Holocaust. Aren't these paradigm cases of moral action, and don't they pose a problem for your theory that bases morality on mutual advantage?

Gauthier: I guess I wouldn't think of them as paradigm cases of moral action. One might think of them rather as cases of supererogatory actions, actions that go beyond the reasonable demands of our moral framework. The willingness to sacrifice ourselves in certain circumstances may of course be mutually advantageous. When I speak of mutual advantage – and let me underline this – I'm not supposing that things will always work out in a way that actually will be advantageous to each person. Unless we are willing to run certain risks – and, of course, given that they are genuine risks, we may end up facing real and uncompensated costs – then we will fail to gain certain possible benefits. So the idea of mutual advantage should be thought of in this way: we should be able to see that the framework would give to each person the expectation of being able to live a better life (in that person's own terms) than would otherwise be possible. This is consistent with the recognition that, life being a risky business, some persons will not actually enjoy that expected benefit. But their willingness to accept risks will be part of what is necessary if everyone is to have as high an expectation as possible of a better life. Even so, there will still be acts, like those that you have mentioned, which go beyond that requirement, where people run risks that wouldn't be required in a system of rules grounded in mutual advantage. I would have to see such acts as going beyond the requirements of morality.

Cogito: But don't they go 'beyond' in a sense that makes them *better* than what morality requires? And isn't it hard, on your view, to make sense of that notion of 'better'?

Gauthier: I'm not convinced that when we talk about certain forms of self-sacrifice as 'better', we aren't deceiving ourselves in some way. For me, paradigmatically moral actions are such things as keeping one's promises, keeping faith, dealing fairly with others, not seeking more than one's share, not seeking to better oneself by using others, not denying others the fruits of their labours, etc. Most basic of all, perhaps, is not killing others: killing is of course a very effective way of preventing people pursuing their life plans. (The ban on killing won't of course rule out mercy killing, where the person whose life is being ended might reasonably be thought to prefer death to the continuation of a miserable and dwindling existence.) The guidelines I would lay down would be ones that can be seen to satisfy the mutual benefit requirement. But many of the traditional aspects of morality will be captured here.

Cogito: Suppose I know someone who is disposed to put up with whatever I throw at him, so that I, being a ruthless individual, may exploit him without cost or risk to myself. I take it that I am then unconstrained by considerations of mutual advantage, that I may, morally speaking, do with him as I will, short of killing him?

Gauthier: If the rest of us observe that sort of behaviour on your part, we are likely to think of you as someone who would be pretty suspect as a partner in co-operative activities, as someone who has his eye out to try to take advantage of others. If we had any sense, we would then try to see to it that we excluded you from many of those activities, and that would work to your disadvantage. So I would put a fair amount of emphasis here on the desirability to the individual of having the sort of character that would make him or her welcome in a co-operative community.

Cogito: I'm not sure I find that altogether convincing. Suppose we have a population divided into ruthless hard-nosed individualists like myself, and 'doormats', i.e. people who allow themselves to be exploited. In such a society, other hard-nosed individualists may well be disposed to accept constraints in their dealings with me, and they will see that I am prepared to accept those constraints in my dealings with them. But they would regard me as soft-hearted, as falling short of the hard-nosed individualist ideal, if I were anything less than ruthless in my dealings with the doormats. I don't see that that behaviour detracts from my attractiveness to other ruthless individualists in forming bargains to our mutual advantage.

Gauthier: Yes, I think that you are right. One can envisage states of affairs in which that would be a reasonable response, given your objectives and the sort of population mix you describe. Certainly it would be undesirable for anyone to have the sort of character traits the 'doormats' possess, i.e. be the sort of person who is willing to be exploited by others. Presumably none of us would want his or her children to become doormats, so we would all have an interest in raising them to take a proper concern for advancing their own lives.

Cogito: There is a line of argument which suggests that if one is too nice to doormats, that encourages 'doormathood', so that the truly moral individual, in a world of mutual advantage, or individual maximizers, will be horrible to doormats, simply as a way of making sure that this form of anti-social behaviour is discouraged.

Gauthier: One could imagine that, but I would suppose that persons who have indeed cultivated the sorts of dispositions that I'm suggesting would generally be welcomed would not find it possible to combine that with taking pleasure in trampling on doormats. I don't suppose that it makes sense to think of human beings as psychologically so fine-tuned that they could have what we would think of as highly conflicting dispositions, but differentiated by some carefully worked-out calculation.

Cogito: Something very interesting is coming in here, which is the question of what is actually possible for human beings, the species being what it is. This is something you can't deduce from very abstract models of what it is to make choices rationally. How much of a role do you think factors about human character and human choice have to play in ethics?

Gauthier: I think that empirical human psychology will have a sort of background role. I'm not sure that we need a very detailed or sophisticated psychological theory, since I'm inclined to suppose that we can operate at the level of common sense, in terms of what we take to be possible character traits, or possible combinations of character traits, for human beings. But there may be more to be learned from psychology than I am allowing.

Cogito: But there might be models or ideals of rational individual interaction which would be in some sense impossible for human beings?

Gauthier: Yes, I think that's right. It may be, for example, that we would all be better off if each of us was willing to run certain sorts of risks that psychologically we are simply not well-equipped to run. Finding ourselves in the genuinely risky situation our animal fears might very well simply take over, in a way that wouldn't be ideal for interactions among rational individuals. This might simply reflect the sort of basic motivational characteristics that we have, and aren't really within our control. So I don't want to say that we are motivationally completely plastic. I'm partly convinced by a suggestion that I found in Alan Gibbard's book, *Wise Choices, Apt Feelings*, in which he distinguishes between a sort of animal control system, a motivational system through drives, impulses, and felt desires, that we share with other animals, and a normative control system, in which we are moved by the content of our representations of states of affairs, by our beliefs about how the world is and how it would be if we were to act in one way or another. I suppose that rationality has to do with that normative control system, and with assessing the fit between our actions and our representations of the world. But I don't suppose that it's always going to be possible for that system to have its way. There will be situations in which the evolutionarily prior animal control system, with its strong drives, will simply prove effective.

Cogito: In *Morals by Agreement* you distinguish between the constrained maximizer and the person who plays the tit-for-tat strategy in an iterated prisoner's dilemma game (see box), on the grounds that whereas the person playing tit-for-tat is following a policy directly, the constrained maximizer has, as it were, chosen a bundle of dispositions to co-operate under certain circumstances. I wonder whether you weren't over-optimistic there about the capacity that human beings have to choose to acquire bundles of dispositions or character traits. After all, there are all sorts of characteristics that I wish that I had, but, frankly, am quite unable to cultivate in myself.

Gauthier: I'm not sure that the language of 'character traits' is here the best way of talking. Earlier in our discussion I did want to talk about developing co-operative traits of character, but there I was thinking more about the emotional or affective level, rather than the rational level. When one is thinking about reasons for acting, talk of character traits may well be out of place. It would be better to say that it's important to recognize that, in addition to the directly outcome-oriented reasons that we have for acting, we also have reasons that depend upon the intentional structures (promises, threats, etc.) we have created for ourselves. Indeed, conforming to the intentions that we have created can be important, not because of the benefits that we are going to get directly from conforming, but because of the importance of creating in others the expectation that when we form a certain intention we will – other things being equal – later on carry it out. I think it might be better to put some of the points that I made in *Morals by Agreement* in terms of acquiring dispositions and character-traits rather more in the language I have just been using, i.e. in terms of the reasons we have for carrying through our intentions so that others can rely on the intentions we have formed. Not always and not totally, of course: sometimes we say 'I may', and sometimes 'I definitely will', and there are important differences here. But I now prefer to put my point in these terms, and I think this suggests less plasticity, less capacity to mould our dispositions through choice, than the way I put it in the book.

Prisoner's dilemma by Christopher Bertram

In *The Wealth of Nations* Adam Smith postulated an 'invisible hand' that would lead individuals to further the common interest through the pursuit of their own self-interest. One problem for social theorists, economists and moral philosophers has been that this happy congruence between individual and collective interest often fails to occur. Anyone who has been stuck at a busy junction when traffic lights fail will know that the pursuit of self-interest by each, doesn't bring about a better situation than when the pursuit of self-interest is regulated and controlled. One type of situation which illustrates this is the so-called prisoner's dilemma.

Imagine two prisoners called Cain and Abel. They have just been arrested by the police who suspect them of a bank robbery but can only prove the charge of shoplifting. The investigating officer, having placed the two criminals in separate cells, approaches Cain with a deal. 'If you give evidence against Abel for the bank job, then I'll grant you immunity on all charges, unless he also gives evidence against you (and I'm offering him a similar deal) in which case I'll proceed against you both on all charges.' What is Cain to do? Clearly the best outcome for Cain is one where he gets off scot-free by denouncing Abel. He knows the best outcome for Abel is one where Abel escaped prosecution by denouncing *him*. It would be a good idea to find some way of securing Abel's co-operation and keeping quiet, but this he has no way of doing. If he refuses to grass on Abel then there is every prospect that Abel will take him for a sucker. The result: both confess and bring about a situation that is worse for themselves than if both had kept quiet. This can be represented in a diagram where the number on the left of each pair represents years of prison for Abel and that on the right years in prison for Cain:

		Cain	
		Not confess	Confess
Abel	Not confess	2, 2	11, 0
	Confess	0, 11	10, 10

We can make the problem more general by using not years of a sentence but simply ranking of possible outcomes for each 'player'.

	Cain Not confess (co-operate)	Confess (defect)
Not confess (co-operate)	OK, OK	worst, best
Confess (defect)	best, worst	bad, bad

Abel appears to the left, between the two Abel rows.

There is a slight tension between the terminology employed in the story from which the prisoner's dilemma derives its name and the terms normally used in game theory: the prisoner who does *not* confess is said to be *co-operating* (with his fellow prisoner) and the one that confesses is said to be *defecting*. In a single game between two players the equilibrium is mutual defection, bringing about a suboptimal outcome since there is an alternative where both players do better. If defection is always the best thing to do if two players play the game once, does it follow that the best strategy to adopt if the same two players play the game many times is 'always defect'? The answer is no. Two players can use patterns of defection and co-operation to secure conditional co-operation (I will if you will). In an *iterated prisoner's dilemma* the best thing to do is to co-operate with me, then I'll co-operate with you, but if you seek to exploit me by defecting then I'll retaliate in the next game. This simple *tit-for-tat* strategy does better for those that employ it in iterated games than any other. In many situations of repeated encounters between people, playing the 'tit-for-tat' strategy means that rational self-interested people will act *as if* they are motivated by moral concerns even though they really only care about themselves. Thus, to steal an example from Kant, a shopkeeper may refrain from cheating his customers because a reputation for honesty will secure their business in future rather than out of a sense of moral duty.

A puzzle: tit-for-tat may work best in repeated games, but does it determine what it is rational to do? Every sequence of games comes to an end and surely the right thing to do in the last game is to defect since there is no next game in which to suffer the consequences. If this is the right thing to do in the final game, then shouldn't I steal a march on my opponent by defecting in the penultimate one? And how about the one before that . . .?

Cogito: It is customary at this point to ask our interviewees what they do when they are not doing philosophy. Do you climb mountains, or play golf, or what?

Gauthier: I'm afraid that most of my leisure activities are fairly sedentary. But I do like to travel, to go to different places and enjoy the sights. I like old buildings, churches, art galleries, the theatre – and I'm especially fond of railways and trams.

Cogito: A lot of philosophers clearly enjoy travelling around – that seems to be fairly common. And many seem to share your enthusiasm for railways. Is a love of trains an appreciation of a rational way of getting around? Or is it just an aesthetic preference?

Gauthier: I don't know. The idea of vehicles moving on rails obviously has a certain fascination, but it's not something I try to explain. The other day I ran into the philosopher David Lewis at Oxford, but not because either of us was engaged in any philosophical activity whatsoever. I ran into him on the platform at Oxford station. He and I had just arrived, independently, on the Steam Special from Didcot. I was returning to Oxford, and he was going back on the return Steam Special to Didcot. That was, I think, the sum total of his stay in Oxford. So it shows how important trains can be to philosophers.

14

BERNARD WILLIAMS

Bernard Williams is Professor of Philosophy at the University of Oxford, and one of Britain's most distinguished moral philosophers. His works include *Morality: An Introduction to Ethics* (1972), *Problems of the Self* (1973), *A Critique of Utilitarianism* (1973), *Descartes: The Project of Pure Enquiry* (1978), *Moral Luck* (1981), *Utilitarianism and Beyond*, with A.K. Sen (1982), and *Ethics and the Limits of Philosophy* (1985). His latest work is entitled *Shame and Necessity*, published by the University of California Press, 1993.

Professor Williams (interview 1994) has recently published a third volume of philosophical papers, *Making Sense of Humanity* (1995), containing his papers from the years 1982–93. There has also appeared recently a collection of articles on Williams' work, *World, Mind, and Ethics: Essays on the Ethical Philosophy of Bernard Williams*, edited by J.E.J. Altham and Ross Harrison (1995).

Cogito: Perhaps you could start by telling us something about your own philosophical background. How did you come to study philosophy, and what have been the main influences that have helped to shape your thought?

Williams: I started learning philosophy formally at Oxford, where I went, in the first place, as a student of classics. Indeed, when it was agreed at school that I would go to Oxford to study Latin and Greek, no one told me, I think, that the course included philosophy. Very fortunately, I discovered when I came to do philosophy that it covered quite a lot of questions that my friends and I had been discussing anyway. It turned out that we'd been doing philosophy without knowing it.

Cogito: Were there any particular philosophers who influenced your early studies?

Williams: When I was at Oxford, the so-called 'Oxford' or 'linguistic' philosophy was very much to the fore, and I suppose that the chief influence on me, in some ways, was Gilbert Ryle. Although I didn't entirely agree with his way of doing philosophy, he did have considerable influence on certain aspects of my general outlook. I was less influenced by J.L. Austin, partly because I never believed that the problem with British philosophy was that it was liable to metaphysical excess and needed to be cut back, which seemed to be his view. He always seemed to me like a Treasury official who thought that the British economy needed deflating, when there were already three million unemployed. I also had an interest in, and a feeling for, certain more literary aspects of philosophy, which weren't really catered for at that time.

Cogito: In a recent talk you gave at Bristol, you said that there were only half a dozen works of moral philosophy that are really worth reading. Perhaps you could give our readers your personal shortlist?

Williams: Perhaps you will allow me half a dozen philosophers rather than half a dozen works. I think my list would then be as follows. Certain works of Plato (counting that as one choice), Aristotle's *Nicomachean Ethics*, Kant's *Groundwork of the Metaphysics of Morals*, Mill's *On Liberty* (and perhaps also his *Utilitarianism*), Nietzsche's *Genealogy of Morals* and *Beyond Good and Evil*, and the first part of Hobbes' *Leviathan*. I think that would do.

Cogito: Looking back over your philosophical work, one gets a clear sense of 'Williams territory': personal identity, the self, the subjective/objective distinction, the nature of practical reason and the foundations of ethics. It's much harder, though, to discern a 'Williams thesis', a single guiding thought or principle. Is there any one leading idea that brings together all the various aspects of your work, a 'figure in the carpet', to use Henry James' metaphor?

Williams: You are quite right in saying that my philosophy isn't full of positions and theses. But there's more unity to it than just in its areas of concern. I think that there's a certain continuing element of style or approach which might be called 'scepticism without reductionism'. I tend to be very suspicious of high-flown metaphysical answers to philosophical questions, while on the other hand rejecting scientific reductionism. It's not an accident that my work isn't full of positions and theses. I think one of the things that I acquired from my formation, and haven't lost, is my suspicion of philosophical theory. I'm much less suspicious of theory in some other areas of philosophy than I am in ethics, and some areas certainly demand theory. But I'm still not somebody who naturally expresses himself by coming up with a lot of theoretical positions.

There are subjects on which I do hold definite positions. One of them concerns 'internal' and 'external' reasons for action, on which subject I have defended – and still defend – a position against criticisms. And on the subject of personal identity, too, I've defended a position – perhaps we'll come to that later.

I suspect that there is one area, or perhaps obsession, which does tie together a number of the things I've been interested in. It's related to a phrase of Nietzsche's about *becoming what you are*. One thing that has continued, in various forms, to interest me is the question of what constraints, what sorts of authority, there are over ways in which one might develop, ways in which one's life might develop. Are those constraints somehow given internally, given by an ethical order, or given by something you already are? Although I find the phrase 'self-realization' distasteful, and a lot of the philosophy associated with it (e.g. of a Hegelian kind) misleading, I suppose that certain ideas that philosophers try to capture by notions of self-realization are at the basis of some of my deepest concerns.

Cogito: One subject on which you have done a lot of work is that of personal identity. In your early paper, 'Personal Identity and Individuation', you rejected the Lockean theory that it is continuity of consciousness that constitutes personal identity and argued instead that bodily continuity is at least a necessary condition of identity. Is this still your considered view?

Williams: My current view on this subject could be summarized like this. I think that, in the manner of the time (1955) when I wrote that first paper, I thought that the question had a more straightforwardly determinate answer than I now think. That was partly because of the time, and partly because of my age – at that age, one prefers nice clear solutions. I now incline to think that the concept of personal identity is less determinate, and therefore of course one can find things to say in favour of other views. But I still hold to the basic opinion which I put in 'Personal Identity and Individuation', and also in another paper called, 'Are Persons Bodies?' The essence of it is this: if the identity of a person is to be the identity of a *particular* thing, then it should be bodily identity. That's the only way of linking personal identity firmly to the notion that it's the identity of a particular thing. If you don't take that route, you are faced with only two alternatives. You are either left with the person being an allegedly particular thing of an immaterial character, such as a Cartesian soul, which I take to be quite unacceptable for various well-known metaphysical reasons. Or alternatively, and I think this is what a number of the examples in the literature have led to, you have the notion of a person as a *type*, which can have multiple tokens. Now this notion of a person as a type is one which, as actual life has led us, we don't have much use for. But it's one that we have a metaphysical base for, and you could imagine information–theoretical or other similar developments which might actually give us, at some future time, an everyday use for it.

Cogito: The philosophical arguments over personal identity tend to turn on a variety of bizarre thought-experiments involving the fusion or fission of persons. *Star Trek*-style transporters, brain bisection, and so on. Non-philosophers often find such thought experiments crazy and irrelevant. Do you have any sympathy with such objections?

Williams: Yes, I do to some extent, although I think it's a complex question. My colleague in Oxford Kathy Wilkes has written a book in which she rejects all such thought-experiments as quite irrelevant, unable to offer us any help with the subject. Let me put one thing on the side first. I think that you can tell a different story when you are dealing with metaphysical questions such as personal identity than if you are dealing with moral notions. I do think that fantastic examples in ethics are helpful only in a few rare cases. Judith Jarvis Thompson's famous article on abortion, which turns on a surreally horrible example, is extremely valuable for that very reason. I think that the awfulness of the example actually serves in an ethical way to concentrate the mind; but this is a very unusual case.

In metaphysics, I think the issue is this. It's very easy for fantastic examples to outrun our conceptual resources, and in that case they are irrelevant. When this objection is put to Derek Parfit, however, he has an answer which is clearly a very good first move. 'The objection would be pertinent', he replies, 'if, confronted by such bizarre examples, people didn't know what to say. But when people are confronted by a strange and artificial example and *do* still know what to say, that is surely significant.' That seems to me to be a fair point, as far as it goes. But now we must think, perhaps rather more searchingly, about what brings it about that people know (or think they know) what to say. That is, we have to question how far people think that they have something to say because the examples have been presented to them in a certain order, in a certain context, or in a way that brings out one analogy rather than another.

Cogito: So there could be ways of deploying arguments to produce plausible 'intuitions' for either of two conflicting conclusions – at least as regards personal identity?

Williams: I think that's right. But I don't think it's necessarily a waste of time to have done that. I obviously don't think that, because in my paper, 'The Self and the Future' I do employ some fantastic thought experiments to arrive at two conflicting conclusions – or rather, tentative conclusions. Thinking about how you arrived at these conflicting conclusions may, in my opinion, give you more insight into the basic situation. But thinking about how you got there involves thinking about what the examples do to you. In 'The Self and the Future' I do try to address, at least to some extent, questions of this kind.

I thus think that fantastic examples can be helpful, but not if they are regarded uncritically, just as 'intuition pumps'. If they are handled more carefully, they can help us to understand some of our own illusions, help us to become aware of models we have that are probably inadequate. All this means that there is a limited valid use of fantastic examples in this area, although I do think that they have to be used rather more self-consciously and self-questioningly than I used them, when I first deployed them, and than they sometimes are in the literature. Somebody once said to me that I was partly responsible for the literature which consists of gigantic numbers of fantastic examples about personal identity. If so, I think it's one of those things that one has to regret.

Cogito: Do the questions that philosophers discuss under the heading of 'personal identity' bear any relation to what ordinary people are talking about when they refer to such things as 'identity crises' or the 'identification' of an individual with a group or society?

Williams: Yes, they do, but too few philosophical discussions acknowledge the fact. With regard to your second example, I do think the identification of an individual with a group is very important, but in that case one has to think in terms of the relation of a particular person to various properties he or she has. An important feature of an identity in this sense is that it is a general thing, that is, it is something you can share. Not only is it something you can share; it is something the whole point of which is to be shared. But it also bears on the matter that I mentioned earlier, about self-realization. People talk about identification with a group when that relationship with the group is particularly significant for them. I don't think people would identify themselves with the local tennis club, for example; it tends to be more with nations, religions, and so on. In the case of sexuality, the identification of gay people with gay groups may be what is basically most important to them. There is an extremely interesting philosophical question about the sense of importance that makes an allegiance into an identification. What makes someone say, for example, 'I have recently come to discover that I am really (basically, essentially) a gay person'? What is this discovery? This question takes us back to our earlier discussion of the notion of self-realization.

On the other matter you mentioned, that of identity crises and that sort of thing, one of the things that is often overlooked in the philosophical literature on personal identity, and which I think has quite a close connection with the metaphysical issues about minds and bodies, is the fact that people can have a fear for a future in which they will be very different – even, perhaps, *because* they will be very different. Let's take the example of somebody afraid of ending up with Alzheimer's disease. That person may want to make provision now to ensure that he or she won't have to go on living in a profoundly vegetative condition. Still worse, perhaps, is the prospect not of being vegetative and kept alive on a machine, but of losing all one's faculties and ending up, to use an old-fashioned and rather objectionable expression, 'gaga'. People can be deeply concerned not – as they would naturally put it – to end up in that state.

Now some theories of personal identity seem to leave no room for this perfectly natural thought. Advocates of such theories either wish us to believe that the heavily handicapped future being is not a *person* at all (this seems to me an outrageous thing to say, but some philosophers say it); or they say that this being is a person but its relation to me is more like that of a descendant – it is not, at any rate, identity. Now I think that such views are simply belied by the nature of our concern for that person. One of the ways in which they are belied is the one I mentioned: I can be very concerned not to spend the last ten years of *my* life – as I would put it – in that condition; and one thing I can do, reasonably and defensibly, to prevent this is to bring it about that I die before that period, either by killing myself while there is still time to do so, or by bringing it about by means of some acceptable structure of euthanasia. (I'm not denying that there are institutional problems about euthanasia, but that is not the present point.) I have an absolute right to do this, because if I have a right over anything, I have a right over my own life. Now in order for this to be a correct perception of the situation, it has to be *my* life that would otherwise end up ruined by Alzheimer's. It seems to me that this is something which is integral to the notions of identity crises and the sorts of associated personal problems you mentioned, on the one hand, and to the metaphysical questions of personal identity on the other.

Cogito: So, on your view, many of us have this concern for a future state in which we might be radically different from how we now are; this concern seems perfectly rational; so any theory of personal identity which is obliged to dismiss it as resting on confusion or misunderstanding must be wrong for that very reason?

Williams: Such theories offend against our deepest understanding of the nature of personal identity. It's not only that I *say* that the future person will be *me* – it's not just a *façon de parler*. Of crucial importance is the fact that I have a right over this person's very existence. If you take the view that my later 'selves' are like my children, then suicide would be like contraception. This certainly belies the fundamental notion that *what I cause not to exist by killing myself is me.*

In my latest book, *Shame and Necessity*, I talk about the Homeric conception of the world. Here one has some concern for what happens to one's body after one's death. You don't want your body to be eaten by dogs or birds, for example, but prefer to be decently buried. Some people draw the line before that; my late mother, for example, used to say that she didn't care what happened to her body after her death. I don't quite believe that: I think that attitude is only appropriate for dualists, who regard their bodies just as the boxes that they happened to live in. One could still have a sentimental attachment for such a box, of course, just as one can for the house one used to live in or the clothes one used to wear. But I don't think that my body is like that. When you go to a funeral, you can say both that what is in the box is auntie's body, but also that 'we buried *Auntie* today'. It seems to me that the fact that we say both these things is very significant.

Cogito: Questions about the nature and boundaries of the self crop up at a number of different places in moral philosophy. One important topic here is that of moral luck. Kant of course denied the very possibility of luck playing any role in morality. The only things I can be held morally responsible for, he argued, are those within my power. But with regard to my bodily actions I am not completely in control: it is always possible that I intend to do X but, due to circumstances beyond my control, Y is what ensues. So, he concluded, it is only the self *qua* locus of will that is the moral agent, not the self *qua* embodied and socially located human being. You, of course, dissent from his conclusions. But how do you account for the persuasive force of his argument?

Williams: That's an extremely interesting question. Of course, most people dissent from that conclusion, even Kant himself as a matter of fact, when he had to accommodate his moral philosophy to a more realistic view of the world. But the question of the diagnosis of that thought is a deep one. I think that it's partly a moral matter, and partly a non-moral matter. The non-moral part is connected with the phenomenology of action itself. There is a problem in the theory of action, introduced in this form by William James, though in a way it goes back to Descartes. Suppose I were blindfolded and paralysed in some way, and then told to raise my arm. I might think that I had raised my arm, when in fact I hadn't. Yet when it's pointed out to me that my arm hasn't gone up, I have the absolute conviction that I've done every thing that I do when I raise my arm. This suggests that actually raising my arm – in Wittgenstein's famous phrase, what I'm left with when I subtract from raising my arm the fact that my arm goes up – must be (a) something purely mental, and (b) something that I do every time I raise my arm. Now there's a long story to be told about that in the theory of action, but I take it that the answer to your question is in part connected with the phenomenology of bodily movement and the notion of trying.

For Kant's concerns, however, there are a very rich set of answers that lie in the relation of the theory of action to moral judgement. One way of putting it is that it is an attempt at once to contract and enormously to expand the notion of control, the power of the will. If you just take the will in an everyday sense, the world is only very imperfectly under its control. There's an enormous temptation to try to find something over which the will has *total* control. But of course you only find that by contracting its domain, because so long as it still gives hostages to fortune, so long as some things are 'up to nature', then we're still in the mixed and imperfect position. So the mysterious 'something' over which we would have complete control would have to be very small indeed.

I think, though, that there's a further question we should ask here. Why do we want something over which we have complete control? This is because we want to have a notion of the *real authorship* of our actions. We want it not to be the case that our actions are just things that simply happen to us. We know, at a reflective level, that our actions emerge out of a whole set of factors – some of which we know about, some of which we don't know about; some of which are under our control, some of which are not under our control. We have within us a whole set of desires, projects, principles, fantasies, and so on, which issue in our actions. We are, as Nietzsche said in one of his many images on this subject, a kind of polyp. Out of this mass of stuff emerge our actions. But we want to defend the idea of the authorship of actions, and authorship requires a point at which, as it were, *I* intervene in all this stuff, stuff which is part of me but also partly not-me because it's only very imperfectly known and controlled. There has to be, or so the myth goes, a point which is *me* as the ultimate author or gate-keeper, mediating between the hidden and only partly understood stuff which is desire, on the one hand, and the external world, on the other. And this has to be the will.

I think there is yet a further reason why we want there to be such a thing as the will. We want it partly for reasons of our own self-conception, but also because of a relation we have to other people (and to some extent also to ourselves), namely, the relationship – and this takes us precisely back to Kant – of *blame*. We know that people sometimes do horrible and nasty things to us; we often can't either punish them or prevent them; but we have a tremendously powerful feeling that there is a point at which, as it were, this agent could have acted otherwise. That was the point of application of the will. We need this thought in order to represent to ourselves how it was that this agent might not just have been changed by external force but might have changed himself. If we think only in terms of change by external forces, we are simply concerned with our failure to control him (as if he were a part of the external world), but that's not the thought involved in the feeling of blame. It cannot merely accept that (as Nietzsche put it) a reprehended action means a reprehended world.

I think – and this is the most speculative part of what I am saying – that our notion of the will is actually linked to a certain fantasy, the fantasy of entirely retrospective control. The fantastic thought is that our rage, our resentment, could actually *make him not have done it*, not by the application of force but simply by inserting itself into his mind at the crucial point. This is the kind of fantasy, I think, which goes with certain conceptions of blame.

What I've done in this story is the following: I've moved from considerations of phenomenology, through some fairly uncontroversial thoughts about how such a picture might build up, to considerations about blame and moral control that are a little more disputable, to introducing a fantasy that some may recognize and some may not. The last part of the account, of course, is Nietzsche's story, as told in *The Genealogy of Morals*. That's why he says at various places that in the introduction of the will we tend to double the cause and the effect. We tend to think that there is an action, and then again an agent of that action, which as it were requires the introduction of the notion of agency *twice*. This, I think, is a very profound idea.

Cogito: So this is one of the reasons why Nietzsche is on your short list – as a sort of diagnostician of the failings of the metaphysical model, as it were, behind Kantian moralism?

Williams: Yes, that's right. Not *only* of Kantian moralism, but above all of Kantian moralism. I don't see Nietzsche as the sort of philosopher whose views you just adopt: there are all sorts of problems with his positive views about the future, about politics, and so on. I see him in the same way that Foucault saw him, as a sort of resource. Foucault said that there isn't any *one* Nietzsche: everybody gets out of him what they find most helpful. I'm also convinced, from my own experience, that you get most out of him when you've got part of the way there on some path of your own. I think it's arriving at some thoughts of my own which turned out to be not dissimilar to things that Nietzsche had developed in greater depth that has greatly increased my interest in him. I do think that his genealogies are very remarkable constructions, and deserve our attention and respect. But of course they go beyond the metaphysical psychology of Kantian moralism. They also extend much more generally to the sources of our moral conceptions and their associated metaphysical models. I find that I now take these sorts of historical questions more seriously than I did earlier in my career.

Cogito: Another related area of moral philosophy concerns the relation of the self to its roles. Are the roles played by an individual externally related to the self, or are they constitutive of it? In his work, *After Virtue*, Alasdair MacIntyre argues that the nature of these relations has changed over the centuries. In Homer's *Iliad*, he suggests, Achilles can't divorce himself from his various roles. For him, there is no 'is–ought problem': from 'Hector has killed Patroclus' and 'Patroclus was my best friend' it simply follows deductively that 'I must kill Hector'. The 'is–ought' division, on MacIntyre's view, is a sort of twentieth-century pathology, *not* a timeless conceptual truth. How do you regard this claim?

Williams: I think that, like a lot of things that MacIntyre says, it is an immensely stimulating mixture of the true and the false. I also think that it forces us to address some important issues. But I don't entirely agree with him. As a matter of fact, Achilles was a wonderfully unfortunate example to take. Achilles is the one hero in the *Iliad* who actually questions his own destiny: he has asked himself the question of whether he should live the life of a glorious hero who dies young, or should give it up. Just on the historical point, even if there were a strong identification with the heroic role in the ancient world, it's quite clear that it was already under question, in ways that MacIntyre would recognize. Indeed, there is a very interesting contrast between Sophocles' *Ajax*, on the one hand, and Euripides' *The Madness of Herakles* on the other, which raises exactly this issue. Herakles, as it were, retires – he does something that no hero is supposed to do. So I don't think that the pure history in MacIntyre's account is quite right.

Now I don't believe – and here MacIntyre and I are on the same side – in an abstract, logical, is/ought distinction as such, as taught by, for example, my old teacher Richard Hare. Apart from purely technical objections, I don't find it a very illuminating tool. I do think that there are certain distinctions between the pre-modern world and the modern world that have something to do with the is/ought distinction. That is, I think it's true that in pre-modern society certain roles or statuses were both more firmly defined and more readily accepted as given to individuals than is typically the case in a modern society. That's because the notion of *a job* has changed in modern society, because the notion of social mobility is more developed, and because hierarchical notions of caste and class have become less important – all for reasons familiar from sociologists of modernity such as Max Weber. All these factors naturally tend to make the distinction between what I do *qua* such and such, e.g. as the holder of a certain role or office, and what I do at the end of the line on my own responsibility, a clearer distinction than it was in pre-modern societies. I can ask, with greater freedom and a wider range of choices, what I am going to be. The child's question, 'What am I going to be when I grow up?' is, in certain ways, a rather modern question. Of course it could still be asked, within a certain range, in pre-modern societies; but if you go back to a really traditional society the range would be much narrower. This is just a matter of sociological fact.

I think that MacIntyre exaggerates the extent to which these manifest social changes are either necessary or sufficient conditions of changes in our conceptual structure. People in pre-modern societies could ask questions about whether they ought to do what is expected of them or required by their role; just as many people in modern society still take a great deal of their ethical world as given.

There is, however, another item which has changed our view of the relation between 'is' and 'ought', or fact and value. That is the rise of modern science. I think that the rise of science has actually changed ethical conceptions in certain ways; MacIntyre thinks that, if it has done so, it has done so only by misleading us. For instance, he thinks it's a mistake to suppose that Aristotle's ethics rested on Aristotle's biology. I don't agree with him over this point: I think that certain important features of Aristotle's ethics did rest on his biology and on his wider cosmology. I think that it was possible, and indeed perfectly reasonable, for Aristotle to believe that there was a pattern of real natures in the world that had a human significance. It's not that we don't believe in real essences or natures these days – some philosophers of science do, others don't. But even those philosophers who believe in real natures think of them as belonging to such things as subatomic particles, fields of force, or whatever. What they do not believe is that the world is written, fundamentally and ultimately, in a script that will tell us a lot about how to be. Now it seems to me that Aristotle did believe this. In the course of the development of modern science we have thus come to reject an important assumption of pre-modern thought. It's no good trying to whistle it up again by invoking the name of Aristotle.

You might well say that this is the thing that unites Nietzsche and Kant. Kant tried, above all, to come up with a theory of morality that would deal with the fact of autonomy – that is, the fact that we aren't told what to do by the way the world is. He realized that fact at the greatest possible depth. Nietzsche is responding, at a rather similar depth, to the fact that he finds Kant's acknowledgment of this fundamental truth does not go far enough.

Cogito: Now you've disagreed with MacIntyre about identity and roles, but then you have raised another example of your own where conceptual change has resulted from a major historical development – in this case, the rise of science. But if either case is correct, might we not find ourselves forced to do a lot of rethinking about the nature of analytic philosophy? Your old teacher Richard Hare, for example, presumably *didn't* think of himself as discovering conceptual truths valid only for twentieth-century modernity?

Williams: No, he certainly didn't. Instead, he used to spend quite a lot of time trying to find traces of the is/ought distinction – perhaps of a somewhat benighted or anticipatory nature – in Plato's dialogues! I don't think that Oxford philosophy, or perhaps any of the analytic philosophy of those days, was very historically conscious. There was something called 'the history of philosophy', but that mostly consisted of exposing the errors of various writers, read in a somewhat anachronistic manner. Analytic philosophy seems to have a sort of resistance to the historical, although there has been, oddly enough, some very distinguished analytic history of philosophy. It's a curious genre, analytic history of philosophy, but some of it has been very good.

What I think has often happened is that when analytic philosophy has been thinking about philosophical topics rather than the history of philosophy, its use of history has been very linear. In particular, it tends to confine its use of history to the history of *philosophy*. But one thing that we surely know is that our conceptions about a lot of things are deeply influenced by the history of things other than philosophy – science, religion, and literature. This is manifestly true, but one of the difficulties about acknowledging this manifest truth is that it gives you too much to do. If you can't write about anything with any depth or seriousness without knowing a lot about its history, you're never going to write anything at all, because there's an awful lot of history to know. Also, it makes you too much the servant of the conceptions of the past. A lot of good things are written by people who don't know much history and just write something new. I'm very much in favour of that: I don't want us to sink into history. But having said that, I think that my sense of the degree to which the fundamental way of understanding the phenomena is historical has grown, on the whole. It's no accident that my most recent book is in good part a work of history – though it's also got quite a lot of philosophy in it.

Cogito: Questions about the self also play a prominent role in your critique of utilitarianism. In your contribution to *Utilitarianism: For and Against* you suggest that utilitarianism cannot do justice to our notion of the *integrity* of the moral agent. But why, the utilitarian will reply, should we care so much about integrity, especially if it frequently leads us to admittedly undesirable outcomes?

Williams: This has been the subject of a great deal of misunderstanding, which is in some part my fault. The main problem, I suspect, lies in certain preconceptions about what arguments in moral philosophy should look like. My objection to utilitarianism is taken to be in the form of a counter-intuition to a principle. But that wasn't my point. It isn't that you are supposed to read the examples, think, 'Oh yes, they were quite right to act on the principle of integrity', and thus conclude that utilitarianism must be wrong because it doesn't allow for that. If that had been the point, I would have had to tell you more about the cases than I did. (Actually I do suggest that there may be some reason for thinking that Jim might have to do the nasty thing in question, whereas George certainly doesn't.)

My point was that utilitarianism gives us a depleted way of thinking about such cases. 'Here', I was saying, 'are two examples of a fairly familiar form. I've given you enough for you to understand what the issues are. First of all, what do *you* think these people should do? Secondly, how do you think that they should think about what to do? And what sorts of things could we say about them if they acted (or thought) in one way or the other?' Now there's a concept that many people find natural to apply to such situations, namely the concept of integrity. Most of us think that there is space for such a concept in our moral thinking. There are a very large number of things that this *doesn't* entail, and that I never intended it to entail. First, it doesn't entail that the agents themselves are thinking about their own integrity. I more or less said in the *Utilitarianism* essay, and I certainly said it in a later paper, that I *didn't* suppose that they needed to do so. Thinking about one's own integrity is almost always a terrible idea. Second, it doesn't entail that integrity is always a good thing. Indeed, there are obvious cases in which the possession of this quality may make things worse. That doesn't prove, however, that it isn't a virtue. Courage often makes things worse, but it's still a virtue. If a man is engaged in a particularly foolish or destructive project, it may be better, both for himself and for others, if he is a coward. Likewise, if there are people with hideous principles, such as Nazis, it may be better if they lack integrity. The Jews in Nazi Germany had a better chance of survival if the local *Gauleiter* could be bribed.

What's completely mad is the idea of some of the objectors, to the effect that I'd supposed that integrity itself represented a principle operated by the agent, a principle which on their view he would be better off without. This is the idea that a fanatical Nazi who not only has fanatical Nazi principles but has the principle of integrity as well, would be better if he dropped the latter. What do they think he becomes if he does so? A less fanatical Nazi? It just doesn't make sense.

The point is this. Integrity occupies a space in which a lot of people (not necessarily the agents themselves) think about cases of this kind. I then ask, what would it be like if you didn't have that thought at all? The answer is that it would be like what utilitarianism says it is like. If you ask why that should be so, you will see that a moral philosophy which made everyone into direct utilitarians would necessarily be a world in which there was no space for the notion of integrity. That's because of the way in which utilitarians conceptualize the relation between an agent, his actions, and his circumstances.

Now of course you are absolutely right – and I say this in the book – that the utilitarian has a possible answer. He can say, 'Fine, I don't believe in integrity. I don't think there is space for such a thing. I think that a conception of action which requires, or allows, such a notion is mistaken. I think that we are all simply channels between circumstances and outcomes, functions for mapping circumstances onto outcomes.' Fine. That's what I think they believe; it's what a few of them are honest enough to admit that they believe. It couldn't actually last very long, because there's no way of living in a world in which everyone believed that. I'm just inviting everyone to think about what the relation is between, on the one hand, certain things we say and think about people, and certain things we find valuable about people, and on the other hand the philosophical theory of utilitarianism.

Cogito: In *Ethics and the Limits of Philosophy* you criticize the attempts of Aristotle to found morality on human nature, and of Kant to found it on the nature of reason itself. But if all the big theories have indeed failed, and if there is no prospect of a successor, what is left of moral philosophy?

Williams: I think an awful lot is left of it. People are always asking, 'What would you put in its place?' If they mean, 'What item(s) of the same sort would I put in its place?', the answer is *none*. There is a great deal of difference between, on the one hand, theoretical structures that enable us to think about the relation of ethics to the world and, on the other hand, moral or ethical theories that are supposed to tell us how to decide what to do. The removal of the latter, which is the main focus of my book, seems to me to remove very little at the moral level. Take, for example, the ethics of Aristotle. Not everyone who is a good agent, on Aristotle's view, needs to be armed with Aristotelian *theory*. In fact, one of the things he says in his book is that you won't be able to understand it unless you are already a good agent.

I simply do not believe that what keeps most people going through their ethical lives is something in the form of a theory; and I don't think that what is needed to sustain moral life is philosophers' producing more theories. I do accept that there are images and conceptions which help people to organize their experience, and may thus be useful at the *political* level. I have in mind images of what societies are – whether they are organic, or based on a contract, or whatever. Such images may help us to think about our relation to the State, what the powers of the State should be, and so on. Some sort of conceptual apparatus for thinking about these issues is especially important in modern society, where such things as open discussion and transparency are both particularly important and particularly vulnerable. And of course these political conceptions will have consequences and implications for ethics. On my view, it is a mistake to start with the theories of ethics and then ask what we are to do if they are all discredited. Rather, we should say, 'Look, we find ourselves living under certain kinds of pressures to make the world sensible to ourselves. How much and what kind of theory do we need?' Then we'll see how 'theoretical' the structures will need to be to serve their purpose.

Cogito: In ethics, as in other areas of philosophy, principles are tested against our intuitive judgements regarding particular cases. Here, too, philosophers often conjure up bizarre test cases. I remember asking my pacifist mother what she would do if a child were about to stumble over the red button that would trigger World War Three, and the only way she could prevent the catastrophe was to shoot the child. She not only refused to answer, but didn't see why the case should be seen as a threat to her principles. At the time I saw this as merely evasive; after reading *Ethics and the Limits of Philosophy* I began to reconsider. You, I presume, would take her side in this argument?

Williams: I rather think I would. We need to recognize the fact that, most of the time, moral thought and practice have to operate against a set of expectations about what sorts of things change the world. If the world were full of stray buttons which would cause everything to blow up, or people who exploded if you touched them, then a very different set of expectations would come into play. Indeed, we have examples not totally unlike that, e.g. people's beliefs about leprosy, or about diseases so hideous and so contagious that the people who suffered from them had to be treated as pariahs or scapegoats. But we have to start our moral thinking with some sort of set-up, and counterfactual examples which totally violate that set-up are usually not very helpful.

At the same time, we certainly can't take the *providential* view, which is taken by Professor Anscombe, for instance, when she says that discussing certain kinds of example (e.g. hideous threats by tyrants) is (a) bad for you, because it inures you to thinking in extremes, and (b) beside the point, because if you are a good person you will never find yourself faced with that kind of situation. I have some sympathy with her first point, but none with her second. In fact, I don't think that even all Christians accept her version of providentialism: many believe that the world has been sufficiently deserted by God that events don't conspire to protect an innocent agent against extremities of that kind. We also have to accept, in my view, that human affairs are largely shaped by luck, contingency, and even absurdity. People sometimes *do* find themselves in situations that seem to them to be absurdly, even surreally horrible.

There is therefore a tension here. Ethical thought is bound to address itself to the usual – that's almost a matter of necessity. But we live in a world in which the usual is constantly subverted by contingency, absurdity, and horror. How can we reconcile those two things? It may help to distinguish here, not between the fantastic and the real, but between extraordinary and ordinary cases. Having made this distinction, I think there are two things we can say about the use of extraordinary examples. The first is that the extraordinary should be represented in realistic terms. If we draw our extraordinary examples from science fiction, or from wildly counterfactual stories, the effect can be very misleading. It insulates you from their horror, for one thing. Also, it confuses the difference between the fantastic and the extraordinary because, by being contrary to the laws of nature, such examples make us think that the extraordinary belongs to another world. And it's very important that it doesn't.

So we should take realistic examples of the extraordinary. Some of the torture and threat cases are relevant here, e.g. those that turn on the sorts of threat that actual terrorists do use. Take, for example, being in a room with twenty innocent people, where the terrorists take one out of the room every hour and shoot them. Questions about what you should do in cases like that are, I think, perfectly proper in moral philosophy.

The second consideration which is very important here is whether the extraordinary case is one from which anything can be learned. One of the troubles about the method of principle and counter-example in moral philosophy is that it always assumes that the case is one from which you can learn something of a general kind, that is, that you can modify your principle. Now some cases are of this kind: what you may learn is that a certain kind of extraordinary case is continually coming up, so you'd better be prepared for it. But consider, on the other hand, the sort of extraordinary case that comes up in tragic drama. Such cases may teach us something about *moral psychology*, but nothing about general questions of moral principle. Some moral philosophers seem to think that the whole of the moral world can be tamed by principle, and if your current principles aren't serving too well, you should get yourself some more complicated ones. But not every form of extreme situation should be reacted to in that way.

Cogito: There has been a trend in recent moral philosophy to make a sharp distinction between rules on the one hand, and ideals on the other. The basic thought seems to be that we might reasonably hope for *consensus* in the former area, that a group of rational individuals might come to agree on a small set of mutually advantageous social rules, while continuing to hold widely divergent ideal goals. What do you think about this approach to moral philosophy?

Williams: I think that it has great limitations. What it tries to do is to structure a great deal of moral and of course political philosophy by reference to the kind of principles which inform American constitutional practice and the conception of a pluralist state as it's written into the constitution of the USA. The most complex attempt to do that is John Rawls' recent book, *Political Liberalism*, which applies the structure of his *Theory of Justice* to a more overtly political subject matter. I think, personally, that the method has more limitations than Rawls admits. The idea that the set of rules, the determination of *right*, can be kept out of the theory of the *good*, seems to me over-optimistic. This is partly because I agree with Charles Taylor, who claims that the conceptions of the right which govern the structure of the rules are more informed by or grounded in certain over-riding goods than Rawls typically allows. I also think that the goods or ideals held by the various pluralistic parties are going to have more effect than Rawls allows on the way in which they promote the shared structure of right.

A clear example of this is an extreme consequence that Rawls has drawn in his latest book. If you are voting in a national election in a pluralist state, he says, your conception of the good shouldn't inform the way you vote. That does seem to me to be a quite extraordinary view. In the USA, for example, you couldn't vote for a candidate because of his or her views on abortion, or because of his or her religion. So I'm afraid I am more sceptical about this than Rawls' supporters.

I actually think the case goes better if you have a less purified view of the right. Rawls is extremely emphatic that the shared structure of the right is not to be regarded as merely a *modus vivendi*. It's got to be a principled idea of right. Now I think, oddly enough, that we can combine more various views of the good if we do regard the rules of the right as a mere *modus vivendi*. I think a Hobbesian solution is more robust here, because it gives people a more vivid sense of what's at stake. They know that they are not going to get the best order, which is homogeneity in beliefs about the good; they know that the cost of constant strife will be hideous. That gives them a vivid sense of why they have to stay together and make a few shared notions of the right work. This, I think, gives a stronger account of the matter than Rawls' more idealized version of it.

Cogito: You describe morality, in *Ethics and the Limits of Philosophy*, as a 'peculiar institution'. Presumably you intended the word 'peculiar' to bear both of its normal English-language meanings. But why have you come to think of morality as something odd or strange?

Williams: I think you have missed out the other reading of that phrase. 'The peculiar institution' was the expression that was used, in the slavery debate in the USA, for Southern slavery, and that echo wasn't absent

158

from my mind when I adopted this phrase. That is to say, I was hinting that the form of the ethical, supposed by Kant and others to be the very stuff of freedom, might in fact be a form of traditional slavery.

Cogito: Well, that partly answers my next question as well. You suggest that we might be better off *without* the 'peculiar institution', i.e. without the domination of our practical reasoning by what you call 'moralism'. Is this a purely professional philosophical judgement, or is there some personal *animus* involved as well?

Williams: Like any such judgement, it's obviously in part a result, in some sense, of my own experience, no doubt of my upbringing. But I may not be the best person to judge.

One thing that has always struck me, since I was at school, is the sort of conflict that sometimes arises between art and the conditions which produce art, on the one side, and the demands of morality on the other. When I was at school I was thinking in terms of romantic artists, 'art for art's sake', and so on. I admired Oscar Wilde, for instance, and D.H. Lawrence interested me, although in hindsight I see him now as an intense moralist and a highly puritanical thinker.

I suppose I was also dimly aware of something that Nietzsche reminds us of, which is that the material conditions for the production of things of value, including morality itself, often rest on the violation of morality. I've always been impressed by the thought that if you took morality absolutely as seriously as it demands, almost nothing that we value would exist. It seems to me that this conflict requires us to rethink entirely the balance between rules and constraints, on the one hand, and various sorts of creativity on the other.

Cogito: In 1979 the *Williams Report* was published, the report of a committee you chaired on pornography. In view of your rather modest conception of the competence of moral philosophy, what role do you think philosophers can and should play in the formation of public policy on such matters?

Williams: I don't have modest views about the competence of moral philosophy. Or rather, I have modest views about one thing in particular: its supposed authority as based on theory. It seems to me that a lot of the pretensions of moral philosophy to contribute to public policy are based on a false view of its authority as based on theory. The idea seems to be that someone will turn up on a Royal Commission, or a hospital board, and claim to have an authoritative voice because they have taken a degree in moral philosophy, or have a PhD in applied ethics, or whatever, I really do think that, taken at face value, this is just nonsense.

You can get an academic qualification without having any practical judgement whatever; and how can we expect that someone who hasn't got any judgement in other matters will be competent to make good decisions in, say, medical ethics?

However, I don't underestimate the powers of moral philosophy – particularly if it's historically informed – to serve a number of valuable roles in relation to public policy. For one thing, it's helpful in sorting out one argument from another. I am strongly opposed to the claim that analytic expertise is a monopoly of philosophers – that, I think, is an insult to other people who think clearly about anything – but there is a certain level of abstraction that philosophers, in virtue of their analytic training, may help with.

For example, I was once involved in an argument about the rights and wrongs of inheritance. Is inheritance based on the right of the children to receive, or the right of the parents to give? It makes a big difference. Again, is the right to inherit a *house* a special case, or is it just one smaller part of a general question about inheritance? If you think there is something particularly wrong about inheriting a house, perhaps because of a distortion in the housing market, should that consideration be confined to inheritance, or is it a point about housing as property? These are perfectly sensible questions, and some analytic training may help us to grasp them more quickly.

Second, some expertise in moral philosophy may help you to get some hold on aspirations and ideals that are rather ill-defined, and to focus them onto a particular case. They may help you to see that a certain dispute is a species of a more general kind of argument, or resembles an argument that is going on in another area. If you are lucky and approach the matter in the right way, you may be able to unite ethical ideas from apparently very different domains. So I don't think that moral philosophy is all that limited in relation to public policy; I think its limitation is only in respect of a false model of its authority as based upon theory.

A further point about the pornography case is that you have to remember that the report was a public policy document of a very special kind, namely, a *legislative* proposal within a given state. As such, it is a public document, and one that must couch itself in terms of the discourse of that politics and that legislature. For instance, suppose that my colleagues on that commission and I had felt that the constitution of the USA was much better in this respect than that of England, because it founds pornography legislation on the First Amendment, on a right of free speech of a very unqualified kind. It would have been no good our saying, 'Everyone has an absolute right to free speech, as expressed in the First Amendment to the US Constitution', because that is not part of the political tradition in which we were operating. You have to start from the law, and the understanding of the law, that are already in place.

This produces a particular kind of political discourse. It's not necessarily *conservative*, but it has to be *continuous*, i.e. it must address itself to the ideas that are expressed in existing institutions and practices. Moral philosophy may help here because it may help you to see what is essential and what is not. But of course it isn't sufficient, because you still have to have the political judgement to determine what is practicable.

Cogito: Campaigners for a ban on pornography have traditionally cast their argument in *causal* terms – porn is sometimes defined as material that will 'deprave and corrupt'. Now according to conventional views about causality, causal claims involve us in *counterfactual conditionals*, i.e. claims about what would have happened if . . . But claims about what would have been the case raise notorious problems for philosophers interested in their truth-conditions. Do you think such propositions *have* definite truth-conditions? And if so, could we hope to know them? Or is this an area in which ideological bias will always prevail on either side?

Williams: I don't think that the metaphysical issues about the truth of counterfactuals are relevant here, because there are clearly *acceptable* counterfactuals about public matters. For example, we may all agree that if certain events hadn't happened at Chernobyl, there would not have been an explosion; or that if a lot of people hadn't started smoking, the incidence of lung cancer would be much lower. So I'm not worried about that.

There is, however, another feature of counterfactuals which is clearly relevant to public policy debates. In philosophers' jargon, counterfactuals are not monotonic – that is, you can't get from 'if p then q' to 'if p and r, then q'. This is of course the whole basis of David Lewis' theory of counterfactuals, which relies on the similarity of possible worlds. In asking what would have been the case if p had been the case, you try to imagine the *nearest* possible world to the actual one, i.e. you leave as much as possible of the rest unchanged while changing the contrary-to-fact condition. So counterfactuals come out in the form, 'if p had been the case, and as much as possible of the background had been kept constant, q would have been the case'.

The trouble is that in matters of public policy, such as pornography debates, people say things like, 'If there had been less pornography available, there would have been less rape.' But in any realistic scenario in which there is less pornography, a lot of other things would be different as well. A society in which less pornography is available is also a society less exposed to material pressures, less open to the rest of the world, less given to discussion of sexual matters, and so on. So what you end up with is some wonderful result such as, 'If the modern world were less like the modern world than it actually is, a lot of things about it would be different.'

That's the trouble. People trot out comparative statistics about, say, how there is less pornography and a lower rate of sexual crime in Singapore. Well, it's no doubt true that there is less pornography and less sexual crime in Singapore – but a lot of other things are different as well. There's a rather robustly enforced public order, for instance.

In general, my view is this. In the report, we did the best we could in dealing with pornography in the light of these sorts of causal considerations. We had to do so, because that's the way in which it has been treated both in British law and in public controversy. I'm sure we were right to say that all the alleged causal connections are pretty dubious. What received less emphasis in the report was that this level of discussion is rather unrewarding. I now think that the treatment of the issue of pornography as if it were a public health problem, like the link between cigarette smoking and lung cancer, or between poor drains and cholera, is a mistake. You sometimes have to address causal arguments in their own terms, because the law is formulated that way, but it's better to think about pornography as a cultural phenomenon, and to enquire into its expressive content and its relations to such things as structures of social power.

Cogito: The difficulty of sustaining the causal argument has led many anti-pornographers to adopt a different line. Pornography should be banned, argue a number of feminists, not because of its causal consequences but because it is itself degrading to women, i.e. because of its expressive content rather than its causal powers. What do you think of this line of argument?

Williams: There has been a lot of literature since the report was published, particularly by feminists such as Catharine MacKinnon and Andrea Dworkin, which attempts to get away from the public health model. The trouble is that the moment you try to put considerations of cultural significance, for example the relation of pornography to questions of gender and social power, into a *law*, you haven't got a hope of legitimating it until you turn it back into a public health issue. So the concept of defamation or damage to women, which is deployed in MacKinnon's draft statute, is in fact just another causal concept. It's true that it's been moved from the area of public health to the area of tort, but it carries with it exactly the same problems as other causal accounts.

Cogito: Your most recent book is entitled *Shame and Necessity*. Can you give our readers, in a few words, some idea of its contents?

Williams: It's a study, in good part a historical study, of ethical ideas found in the earliest ancient Greek literature, particularly Homer and the tragedians. I'm concerned mainly with literature that was written before Socrates and Plato, although there is some discussion of Aristotle. Its negative aim is to combat a certain view of our relation to those ethical ideas, a view that I label 'progressivism'. On this view, the ancient Greeks had certain primitive, elementary, pre-modern (even pre-moral) ethical ideas on such matters as moral responsibility, guilt, and so on. That progressivist view is associated with celebrating what all of us will regard as improvements: the abolition of chattel slavery, an improved respect for the equality of women, and so on.

My thesis in brief is, firstly, that the ethical ideas of ancient Greece have been misunderstood; secondly, that we have much more in common with the ancient Greeks than we believe. A lot of the ideas that actually 'keep us going' are fundamentally the same, I argue, as those of that world; and in so far as ours are different in some respects, they may even be worse. We have fooled ourselves into believing that we have a more purified notion of moral responsibility than we have. This belief is thus a form of illusion.

To the extent that our situation represents progress or an improvement over theirs, understanding that progress requires the ancient ideas rather than our modern ones. Put another way, the degree of self-understanding of post-Enlightenment ethics is rather poor. I don't want to take the archaising, reactionary view and say, 'The Enlightenment has been a terrible disaster – back to the Greeks!' If you were to go all the way back to the ancient Greeks, you'd get a very black picture indeed. Of course there has been some progress: our ethical situation is not theirs, because the modern world isn't the ancient world. But there is more in common, ethically, than people think, and we actually mislead ourselves when we suppose otherwise.

Cogito: We always close these interviews by asking our interviewees about their extra-philosophical interests and activities. So, Professor Williams, what do you do when you are not doing philosophy?

Williams: I have a lot of interests outside philosophy; perhaps I'd better confine my answer to two of them. I have had a long involvement with the world of opera, and was on the board of the English National Opera for nearly twenty years, which gave me great pleasure and satisfaction. I still write about opera. In fact, I recently agreed to do something which no sane and well-informed person would have done, which was to write an article in the new *Grove Dictionary of Opera* under the entry, 'opera'. Nobody who was actually an expert on the subject wanted to write so general an article.

I'm also involved in some issues of public policy, notably the Labour Party's new Commission for Social Justice, although I am not myself presently a member of the Labour Party. The Commission is supposed to deal with difficult issues concerning social security, pensions, and so on, and I hope to make a contribution to its deliberations.

15

ADAM MORTON

Adam Morton has been, since 1979, Professor of Philosophy
at the University of Bristol. His books include *A Guide
Through the Theory of Knowledge* (1977), *Frames of Mind*
(1980), and *Disasters and Dilemmas* (1991). He is currently
completing a new philosophy textbook.

Adam Morton (interview 1995) is still Professor of Philosophy at Bristol,
and has recently become President of the Aristotelian Society. His
Philosophy in Practice: An Introduction to the Main Questions appeared
in 1996, and was followed by a new edition of his *A Guide Through the
Theory of Knowledge* (1997). He is currently completing his book on the
theme 'folk-psychology is ethics', and then plans to launch into 'a wild
eccentric project about mind-expanding languages'.

Cogito: How did you come to study philosophy, and what first motivated
you to take up the subject?

Morton: I'd been reading philosophy since my early teens. I remember
when I was in high school in Canada, there was a fellow-student who was
considerably older than me. (In Canada, unlike in this country, it's not
unusual for older people to return to school.) We used to talk about all
manner of subjects, and from time to time he would throw books –
including some philosophy books – at me. I remember some works of
Russell, and Dean Inge's book on Plotinus, which may well have been
the very first philosophy book I read. That set me off on a philosophy
reading binge. I read all sorts of weird stuff, including Schopenhauer and
Nietzsche. I remember going back, a few years later, to reading Russell,
and being outraged by his low-minded, anti-metaphysical stance. I was
also doing quite a lot of mathematics at high school, and I remember
reading a book on symbolic logic that happened to be around, and experiencing a sort of burst of recognition.

Cogito: When you came to study philosophy more systematically, what were the greatest influences on your own philosophical thinking?

Morton: Where I studied, at McGill in Montreal, the philosophy department was very scholarly and historically oriented. This was probably good for me, as I'm not a very scholarly sort of person. We started with Thales in the first year, and inched into the twentieth century in the final year. I remember being enthusiastic about some of the individual lecturers, but the overall approach didn't greatly excite me. It was a great discovery when, between the end of the last year of teaching and my final exams, I discovered Nelson Goodman's *Fact, Fiction, and Forecast*, which I then thought was wonderful for its crispness. That was, I think, the most vivid impression from that early period.

Cogito: As a young academic, you spent a few years at the very high-powered department at Princeton. What was the atmosphere like there at the time?

Morton: It was a high-powered department, but it wasn't just the established figures who made it so. Gilbert Harman was there, and Paul Benacceraf, C.G. Hempel, Stuart Hampshire, and Gregory Vlastos. But there were also people who are now very eminent, such as Thomas Nagel and David Lewis, but who were then much less well known. So the atmosphere was of younger people who were very active, and always trying out new ideas. They were still in the shadow, at that time, of dominant figures like Quine and Goodman, and weren't aware that they were going to become famous themselves. So it was very exciting for me to be among these bright people before they got slightly puffed up by the sense of their own importance.

Cogito: I understand that between Princeton and Bristol there were a couple of years back in Canada?

Morton: Yes, in Ottawa – and it felt like going home, returning to Canada after almost ten years in the States. I still don't know why I didn't stay. I was perfectly comfortable in Canada, and had a good life being organized for me there. Though it wasn't the greatest of departments, I was quite at home there, and Ottawa is an interesting bilingual university in a truly bilingual city – perhaps the only one left in Canada now that Montreal is no longer so. Then the Bristol job came along. I applied, was interviewed, was offered the job, and accepted, thinking it would be nice to have maybe five years in this country. And here I am fifteen years later. That's the way life goes.

Cogito: So the Bristol job was just something that turned up? Was it just like that, or was there something about Bristol that appealed to you?

Morton: When I was maybe six years old, I spent an afternoon in Redland, a suburb of Bristol; and for some reason the event stayed with me as one of my very earliest childhood memories. Then as an undergraduate, I'd read Stefan Körner's book *Kant*, and his *Conceptual Thinking* too, which had stuck in my mind. So Bristol did have an identity for me, and various English friends in Canada had told me it was a nice town. I can't put my finger on it, but when I came for interview it just struck me that it was a place I'd like to live in for a few years.

Cogito: Let's now turn to your work in the philosophy of mind. Your book *Frames of Mind* is primarily concerned with the nature of everyday psychological explanation. Many modern philosophers have claimed that our ability to explain and (sometimes) predict the actions of our fellow human beings shows that we are in possession of a body of theory, usually called 'folk-psychology'. You argue that folk-psychology is not so much a theory as a *scheme*. What does the distinction amount to?

Morton: That question has become important to developmental psychologists, studying what it is that children learn when they acquire competence in folk-psychology. Some of these psychologists seem to base their position on the slogan, 'Adam is wrong: it *is* a theory after all.' That's a useful role to have played. When they say, 'it is a theory', what they mean is that the child learns it from his or her immersion in a culture; that it's justified by its explanatory success; and that it *develops* – you try out one thing, and then if it doesn't work very well, you change it and try out something else. Actually, I don't want to deny any of these things. What I do want to deny is that what you know when you have the concept of a mind is a result of absolutely free theorization, that you've just got all this data, of human behaviour, and you're trying to find the best explanation of it. What I meant to emphasize is the possibility – I would say the probability – that the way we think about mind is shaped by innate constraints, so that when a human is faced by other humans he or she cannot but see them as having emotions, being moved by desires, and so on. In short, we can't help seeing one another as minds. It's a bit like a child coming to acquire its first natural language. Which natural language he or she acquires depends, obviously, on the surrounding culture, but if Chomsky is right there are strong innate constraints at work. The human's capacity to acquire language constrains what sorts of language it can learn. Similarly, I think, we have an innate capacity to acquire social life, and this innate capacity constrains the kinds of concepts which we can use in handling our relations with other people. In the last few years, philosophers and psychologists have begun to talk to one another again, and I think a consensus has begun to emerge. You can accept the points that are emphasized by the people who insist that folk-psychology is a theory – namely that it develops and that it has explanatory value – and at the same time grant that there are strong innate constraints, which is what I want to emphasize.

Another point that I now want to stress is that the concept of mind is not something we have just out of intellectual curiosity: it also helps us to get on with one another in a variety of ways. Sometimes we just want to please other people, or to avoid hurting them. But to do that success-fully, you have to have some grasp of what is going on inside them. So I want to trace the innate tendency to have a concept of mind to the innate social nature of human beings. We have evolved as social beings living in small groups, and have therefore evolved ways of thinking which are useful, perhaps even necessary, to such inherently social beings.

Cogito: Folk-psychology seems to have powerful explanatory resources but almost no true universal generalizations. If one tries to say, for example, 'everyone who is angry will lash out . . .', one produces propo-sitions that are manifestly false. But according to traditional accounts of scientific explanation, explicit generalizations (laws) play a crucial and indispensible role. How then do folk-psychological explanations explain?

Morton: I think they are like a lot of other common-sense explanations. Take the boring example of the window which breaks when the tennis ball hits it. Someone asks, 'Why did the window break?', and the reply comes back, 'It broke because the tennis ball struck it.' But do all windows break when struck by tennis balls? Obviously not: sometimes the ball will just bounce off. 'So why', we now ask, 'did the window break in *this* case?' The answer, we are told, is 'Because the ball was travelling fast enough and the window was fragile enough.' How do you know that the ball was travelling fast enough and the window was fragile enough? Because the window broke. These circles just are there. But we usually suppose that the obvious gaps in such common-sense explanations could be filled, at least in principle, by a *causal* claim. Philosophers of science usually think that, perhaps deep in the background, such causal claims depend on gener-alizations. But they may not be generalizations that can even be stated in common-sense terms. The situation may be similar in psychology. There may be no way, within the resources of common-sense, to spell out the psychological analogues of 'fast enough' and 'fragile enough'. It might turn out to be necessary to go all the way down to the level of neurons to provide an adequate causal story. You can't tell in advance.

Cogito: Among the people who think that folk-psychology is a theory we must of course number the eliminativists, who think not only that it is a theory but that it is a *false* theory, one that will have to be discarded as science tells us more about the brain and the real causes of behaviour. If your insistence on the innateness of the constraints is right, what will follow? Either that we can't give up folk-psychology at all; or that we can't give it up and still go on thinking about minds?

Morton: Very well put. I had a letter from Paul Churchland shortly after the appearance of *Frames of Mind*, saying that it had struck him as a revelation that the concept of mind might be innate – innate but false! And that is, indeed, a possibility. But I do think there's a mistake in that way of putting it, as if folk-psychology were a single theory with a fixed content. Churchland, in particular, tends to say that we have had exactly the same folk-psychology since Homer; that it hasn't changed over the centuries; and that there are lots of things it can't explain. It seems to me clear that this just isn't true, and that folk-psychologies vary from culture to culture, albeit with certain constant features reflecting the innate constraints, in the same sort of way that human languages do. So that when there are things we can't explain with a given version of folk-psychology, one option is to seek a better version. This seems to me to be one of the jobs that moral philosophers share with novelists. Now it may be that no single version of folk-psychology can explain all the phenomena of human behaviour; but that doesn't imply that there are phenomena that can't be handled by *any* version of folk-psychology. We may just be obliged to use different versions for different purposes.

Cogito: So one possible response to the eliminativist is to insist on this flexibility of folk-psychologies. You might grant that we haven't made much progress explaining some range of phenomena (mental illness, perhaps, or weakness of will) in folk-psychological terms. But how can the eliminativist show that *no* variant of folk-psychology could explain such things? That seems to face the eliminativists with quite a nasty challenge: how could they prove a negative claim of that kind?

Morton: It's obvious that some part of the eliminativists' claims are true: there are some things you can't do with folk-psychology. Not every tool is suitable for every job – you can't turn a bolt with a hammer. Folk-psychology is a tool for making human social life run smoothly, and such a tool is unlikely to be much use for such a completely different purpose as, say, predicting what drugs will help people recover from strokes.

Cogito: Psychological explanations are generally thought to require two components: a *belief* or mental representation to the effect that the world *is* such and such a way; and a *desire* or wish to make it some way. In your Chapters 4 and 5, you focus on these two core concepts. The theorists' concept of belief, you suggest, involves a sort of myth: that there is a definite list of propositions that a given person 'really' believes. But belief, you suggest, lies at the centre of a sort of four-dimensional 'space' surrounded by variety of fuzzy belief-like states: wishful thinking, fantasy, wild hunches, etc. We certainly *act* on such states, but do they therefore count as beliefs? But if we abandon or weaken the traditional account of belief, we surely lose the *rationalizing* component of folk-psychology too?

Morton: Yes, I think we do risk losing that. But I wonder whether folk-psychology as actually employed by 'the folk' really did have a large component of rationalization. I sort of suspect that, like a lot of philosophical ideas, it's a legacy of the Enlightenment project, a rationalized substitute for something that was originally normative. Many generations ago, folk-psychology may have been more explicitly normative: our great-grandmothers may have explained people's actions by reference to what they *ought* to have thought and done, to what was 'normal' or 'natural', or whatever. So a folk-psychological explanation, old-style, of why someone acted as they did might simply be along the lines that a decent person *would* act that way, or at least *could* act that way. Later generations of philosophers didn't want their explanatory concepts in folk-psychology to be 'infected' with folk-morality, so they 'cleaned up' the concepts by replacing them with a sanitized notion of rationality. Maybe this is an improvement, and we did get a better version of folk-psychology as a result.

Cogito: But could there be a version of folk-psychology that was purely *causal* in structure, which relied neither on folk-morality nor on rationality? In such a theory, there would be generalizations, but they would be construed by their users just as brute facts about human beings.

Morton: I can understand that question in two different ways. One would be this: 'Could a bunch of folk think that way and manage their lives?' I don't know the answer, but one might make the experiment. Perhaps the community described in B.F. Skinner's *Walden Two*, whose folk-psychology is replaced by behaviourism, comes close to it. Another way of understanding the question would be: 'Can we think in this way while using our innate bias to think psychologically?' An analogy with language may help to bring out the distinction more clearly. Suppose, faced with a given system of symbols, you ask, 'Could this be a language?' You might be asking, 'Could a group of people learn to speak this?', or you could be asking, 'Could we get our innate Chomskian apparatus to handle this for us?' Going back to folk-psychology, the two questions are clearly distinct – though not unrelated – and I don't know the answer to either.

Cogito: In your Chapter 4, you take issue with the traditional conception of desire as being desire *for* some definite object. Citing Freud, you emphasize instead the *plasticity* of desire: a desire that is currently *for* X may (without losing its identity) become a desire for Y. The *same* mental energy or *libido*, in Freud's terms, may be redirected to a different object. As in the case of belief, you seem to be accepting a sort of trade-off *vis-à-vis* more orthodox views: your position seems closer to psychological reality, but at a high cost in neatness of theory.

Morton: Don't forget that what I was trying to do was quasi-empirical. I was trying to say what our actual folk-psychology was like, not arguing that this was better than some proposed alternative. In a way, I was trying to break away from what I saw as the excessive rationalization of other characterizations of folk-psychology.

Cogito: But would 'the folk' accept the following as a good pattern of explanation? 'Why did A pursue B?' 'Because he wanted C.'

Morton: I think the answer is 'yes'. Of course, it wouldn't count as a *complete* explanation – you would need to say more about the circumstances and perhaps about the mechanism of transference. But even when people behave as paragons of rationality, there is still a further question there too, namely why this person, on that occasion, was so rational.

Cogito: Suppose we submitted the question to a sort of *vox populi* test. We go out and tell people a little story, in which Fred desires Arabella and ends up making love to Belinda. If anyone asks why Fred made love to Belinda, we say that it was because he desired Arabella. We then ask whether they find this a satisfactory explanation of Fred's behaviour.

Morton: Isn't this more or less parallel to asking, 'Why did George kick the dog?', and being told, 'Because his boss had been bullying him and his wife had been abusing him'? Surely we can all understand that? There's no *general* problem in understanding that passions *can* be transferred in this way; there are just detailed questions about what sorts of transference can be expected in what circumstances. I do think, though, that in the special case of desires, the tendency of theorists to lump together hopes, wants, aspirations, longings, etc. under the single catch-all heading of 'desire' serves only to obscure a number of important distinctions. Perhaps a want is for something definite, and a longing has only a very indefinite object.

Cogito: A few years ago, you were one of a number of professional philosophers to take a keen interest in chaos theory. Now chaos theory is, first and foremost, a branch of mathematics, with some interesting implications in the natural sciences, e.g. to meteorology. What special interest does it have for philosophers?

Morton: I got interested in it because I had a project, which I couldn't carry through because it turned out to be too hard for me (maybe someone else will do better). I was trying to characterize the sort of physical system that could have experiences – that is, could be minds. For example, are the stars conscious? How would we know? The orthodox answers did not satisfy me. Like many modern philosophers of mind, I had nagging doubts about functionalism, and I wanted to develop some apparatus for finding the right level of generality to describe what kinds of system could be minds. I don't think I made much progress with that. But now Peter Smith is writing another 'Adam is wrong' book, inspired by my attempts. So it wasn't all wasted effort.

There was also a coincidental interest, which arose from some other work I was doing on mathematical modelling. When you are working with complicated dynamical systems, you realize very quickly that exact predictions are usually out of the question. In order to get a handle on the system, you have to have some limited purpose in mind. You ask, 'What kind of predictions am I looking for?', or 'What aspects of the system am I seeking to understand?', or 'What kind of theory will be useful for providing the kind of understanding I need?' So you are interested in *partial* explanations and *partial* predictions, and you come up with theories which are probably not true, but are useful for certain limited purposes. It seems to me that there are analogies here between philosophy of mind and philosophy of physics. The full *true* theory of some complicated system (like the brain, or the Earth's atmosphere), even if we had it, would be completely unusable. So you have to make models, that is, partial theories which are not literally true but serve special purposes. I think different versions of folk-psychology are a bit like different models, supplying the place of what we manifestly don't have – a complete theory of the mind. Each of these different models may have its proper range of uses, e.g. to different cultures.

Cogito: You were hinting, a moment ago, that you might have seen some deep metaphysical significance in chaos theory. It almost sounded as if you had in mind the striking metaphysical claim that *only* a chaotic system could be a mind. That would be a very interesting, not to say provocative claim since it would exclude digital computers – not on the boring ground that they are machines but on the more interesting ground that they have perfectly discrete states.

Morton: It would be nice if one could say something like that. It wouldn't be that simple, of course: it would have to be the right *kind* of chaotic system that constituted a mind. The right sort of balance between order and disorder might turn out to be essential. This might indeed rule out certain kinds of digital computers – while not excluding purely mechanical systems. This would divide the camps on these issues in a rather neat way. I do think that, sooner or later, someone will understand the physical conditions for having a mind, and that there may well be some very striking and surprising conclusions here. But I've gone into the subject far enough to be pretty sure that that person isn't going to be me.

Cogito: Your next book, *Disasters and Dilemmas*, is about the nature of practical reason. Reading it recently, I became increasingly struck by its Aristotelian aspect. In the *Nicomachean Ethics*, Aristotle speaks of *phronesis* or practical wisdom and its role in the pursuit of the good life. We recognize, he says, that some people are better at practical decision-making than others; but we can't spell out any definite rules that such people employ. Your book seems to be an attempt to do just that.

Morton: When I wrote that book, I was reading lots of work by orthodox decision-theorists. And I was impressed with the fact that the rules for decision-making that they were setting out didn't seem to apply very well to a whole range of perfectly everyday situations. My main worry was that my attempt to say something enlightening about how a sensible person might make decisions in such situations might not seem systematic enough.

In the preface, I put my picture of decision-making like this. At the top level, there's *phronesis*, which I think of as the mysterious faculty which gives you your options to choose from. Ordinary decision-theory has nothing to say about this: it only tells you how to evaluate the options presented to you. At the bottom level, there's orthodox decision-theory, with its probabilities, utilities, and weighted sums. In between these levels, however, there is a middle level, concerning such things as how a long list of options gets boiled down to a short list, how choices are structured, and so on. It's this middle level of the decision-making process, between the mysterious and the mechanical, that the book is about. It's not like doing ordinary arithmetic – that would correspond to the bottom level. Nor is it like finding a new proof, which requires insight – that's the top level. It's more like solving differential equations, perhaps in the presence of some complicating boundary conditions. The most interesting and important part of this middle level decision-making is, I think, trying to decide which of a list of options to take seriously. Being finite creatures, we can't take all the items on a long preliminary list of options as serious candidates for action. We have to find ways of whittling a long list down to a short list for further deliberation. Much of the book is concerned with the not very systematic ways in which we do this.

Cogito: Traditional accounts of decision-making have tended to be broadly utilitarian in structure, and have thus involved a theoretical commitment to the possibility of 'weighing' one type of good against another. Politicians, for example, are routinely required to balance, say, deaths against liberties, or jobs against environmental damage. What led you to take issue against this tradition?

Morton: I just don't think we actually do it. I don't think we have constant trade-offs between such incomparable goods. Suppose we're planning a new road, and that Plan A will be safer, but will involve destroying an area of outstanding natural beauty, whereas Plan B will probably cost a few extra deaths but will leave the forest unscathed. Some economists think that a rational decision in such a case requires a fixed trade-off, but I don't think that's so. Anyone who claims to have a systematic way of making such trade-offs is, I think, fooling themselves. Anyway, since no such procedures and trade-offs are currently agreed, we are left in practice fumbling around without them. I'd like to help us to fumble around a bit more intelligently.

Cogito: In moral and political debate one sometimes hears people say, 'no amount of extra wealth could compensate for the death of a child'. This suggests that they might be attaching an effectively infinite weight to life as against 'mere' money. But such people rarely – perhaps never – follow through the implications of that thought, e.g. perhaps the complete abolition of the motor car. Perhaps what they are really saying is, in your terms, that lives and money are 'incomparable' goods, and that there is something morally suspect in *trying* to balance one against the other?

Morton: People's actual practice is never consistent with saying there's no trade-off between the risk of death, on the one hand, and money on the other. People are always risking their children's lives for money, and it would be wrong not to. Saying that two goods are incomparable isn't saying that you *never* balance them, but that there isn't a *fixed* trade-off. This can be conceptually very tricky indeed. You are sometimes obliged to balance one thing against another, but at the same time it's a misunderstanding to suppose that there is a single, determinate, objectively right trade-off value.

Let me make what might seem a surprising connection. There are issues concerning population which are relevant here. Here's a moral intuition that many people share: that it's never morally obligatory to have a child. If you're faced with the possibility of having a child, the choice is often morally open. If you do have a child, you may be morally obliged to give it the best life you can, but that's only a conditional obligation. In many situations, it is permissible to have a child; but it's never obligatory.

173

I would like to be able to explain why it is that we think of people as being terribly valuable, but *don't* think of ourselves as being obliged to create more of them. Perhaps this will only seem paradoxical to those of us whose moral intuitions are basically consequentialist. A utilitarian, for example, can find it puzzling that people are valuable, but that more people aren't obviously more valuable. This isn't just a boring point about overcrowding: it would still be true in an underpopulated world that a couple wasn't morally obliged to have children.

In a recent *Aristotelian Society* symposium with John Broome, I tried out the following line of reasoning. The explanation for the apparently puzzling facts is that the values of lives are incomparable: a world with all the people who now exist *plus* the child you might have is therefore incomparable in value to a world in which that possible child does not exist. That can be expressed by saying, 'Lives are infinitely valuable, and two infinities aren't greater than one infinity.' I think that this pseudo-mathematical language is something one finds oneself pushed into when one is grappling with problems concerning incomparable goods.

Cogito: The way you put it in the book is this. Suppose I accept a payment of $1,000 for an additional risk of 1/10,000 to my child's life. It doesn't follow that I have tacitly placed a value of $10,000,000 on that child's life. I could vigorously – and consistently – reject such an offer, even if I accepted $1,000 at odds of 10,000 to one.

Morton: It's as if we had different trade-offs at different levels of probability. Some economists have tried to develop systematic ways of showing that this can be done without inconsistency. It seems that such probability-dependent weightings of goods *can* be consistent, although the mathematics gets quite difficult. So in a way I'm just defending the rationality of something we all do anyway, that is, having such probability-dependent trade-offs.

Cogito: The book contains a variety of strategies for *avoiding* being forced to choose between incomparable desires. One can, for example, satisfy one directly and the other indirectly; or one can 'revalue', i.e. specify more precisely just what it is that one values in such a way as to avoid the conflict. (One may think that it's money one wants from one's job, and find out that self-esteem is actually much more important.) But can one always find such a stratagem? And if not, are we not faced with a terrible dilemma between a crazy rationalism on one hand and an equally crazy existentialism on the other?

Morton: I accept that you can't always avoid being forced to make such choices. But there might still be a half-way house between the extremes that you label 'crazy rationalism' and 'crazy existentialism'. Suppose you're deciding on the route for a new road, or the location of a new airport. You have to balance the risk of death against environmental damage. You have no very clear intuitions about trade-offs, but you are obliged to decide. One technique discussed in the book is to look at greatest and least possible trade-offs. So you say, 'the most extra risk I would accept to preserve the forest is this'; and then, the other way round, 'the most environmental damage I would accept for a 1 per cent improvement in safety would be this'. This gives you a first-cut among your options, eliminating those that fall outside those limits. So you first reject all those options that look likely to be disastrous, and then deliberate about those that look promising, ending up with a final decision based on a trade-off somewhere between the two extreme values. This isn't the same as accepting a trade-off in the middle right from the start, because if you do that you might end up accepting something which has a disastrous consequence. So you first exclude options that lead to disaster, and then look for a middle way among the surviving options. This may enable you to make a decision that looks rationally defensible, even if it isn't uniquely determined by a prior set of weighted values.

Cogito: One of the most striking parts of *Disasters and Dilemmas* is the chapter entitled 'Misery and Death'. Here you suggest that our existing medical institutions are faced with making choices between two sets of incomparable goods. There are 'A goods' on the one hand (roughly, keeping more people alive longer) and 'B goods' on the other (improving the overall quality of life of the living). You suggest that health services should devote more of their limited resources to B goods, at the inevitable costs of a few more deaths. Why do you think this would be a better world?

Morton: I wanted to suggest that it might be a better world, and that we should at least take the suggestion seriously. The main reason for making the suggestion is that our present attitudes to medicine seem so heavily biased the other way: we seem to rank avoiding death so highly that we fail to address the question of whether it might not be better to have less misery at the cost of more death. The reason we get pushed that way is that we are taught to regard lives as something incomparably, perhaps infinitely, precious. I wanted to suggest that we should take an opposed moral point of view more seriously.

Why might a world with less misery and more death be a better world? To describe a world as 'better' presupposes a set of values. I think it would be better because more people would lead better lives. They might be shorter lives, but they would still be better lives. Most of us agree that it is more important to have a good life than a long life. I certainly think

175

this for myself, and most other people say the same. Yet when we are making decisions for other people (e.g. for aged parents), most of us seem only to pay lip service to this judgement. There seems to be a sort of moral confusion prevalent here. When it's a matter of individuals making particular decisions for particular people, this moral confusion perhaps isn't so wrong. But when we are thinking about setting out policy-goals for *institutions*, a different trade-off of misery against death may be appropriate.

Cogito: You further suggest that a 'revaluing' strategy might enable us to 'capture' what is really so important about our concern for A goods (that people *not* be treated as dispensable), *without* obliging us to devote such massive resources merely to keeping people alive. How might this work in practice?

Morton: The suggestion was that we first ask *why* we have certain Kantian-sounding intuitions about the value of each human life. You then try to find different ways of paying respect to this underlying value, short of keeping people alive no matter what. The doctor can then, as it were, tell the patient, 'I won't try to keep you alive at all costs, but I'll do all I can to honour and respect you while you are alive, and will see that your memory is preserved after you've gone.' Other people are thus required to recognize that such a person had lived, and what was unique about him or her. I was thinking, primarily, about children born with severe physical handicaps, and how one might try to overcome the very natural revulsion at the proposal that they be simply allowed to die. I sketched a set of institutions that might be of service to us in such cases. Such people's names, identities, family histories, etc. are ceremonially recorded – they are given, as it were, a sort of honorary place on the roll of citizens, even though the decision was made not to expend enormous resources on keeping them alive. Maybe more imagination is needed to show in convincing detail the ways in which social institutions and practices show respect for people as individuals. Perhaps a novelist could do this better than I have.

Cogito: Have you found any connection between theory and practice here? Has a period of intensive study of practical decision-making stratagems changed the way you make decisions in your own life?

Morton: Possibly: I've certainly had a lot of difficult decisions to make since then. In talking through decisions with people I know, I do sometimes find myself saying, 'Let's use a strategy of such and such a kind.' But that, of course, may be just pinning labels on types of decision-making process that I was already employing. More to the point, I often find myself insisting that we separate very clearly that part of the decision-making process where we settle what the options are from the part where we choose between them. I think it makes it much easier to make decisions if you do make this separation; and I think in everyday life we often don't make it. So that's one difference I've found in my everyday life as a result of writing the book.

Another thing that has emerged, for me, out of writing the book, is that I've come to be more aware of my lurking suspicion of the idea of a fully-balanced life, of a sort of ideally harmonious fulfilment of all our capacities. I now find myself in sympathy with the view that people can properly lead very specialized lives. I think that if one person commits herself absolutely to an academic career, while another devotes himself to his family, or to politics, that's perfectly fine. They shouldn't feel bad about 'missing out' on other things, and shouldn't be made to feel incomplete by others on that account.

Cogito: You have recently been working hard at a new introductory textbook in philosophy. What made you set aside your own research work in order to write a textbook?

Morton: It was actually a series of accidents which trapped me into devoting several years of my life to producing a textbook. But one of the ways by which I got myself into the trap is by having very unorthodox ideas about how philosophy should be taught. Philosophy students pick up skills rather than acquiring knowledge. They need to be able to ask the right questions (out of the vast number that could be asked), to be able to pursue an argument while sticking to the point and avoiding distraction, and so on. I don't think you pick up those skills by passively reading books and attending lectures; such skills are only acquired by *doing* philosophy – that is, by discussing, arguing, and criticizing. Over the years my own teaching, in a fairly disorganized sort of way, had come to reflect this emphasis. At the same time, I'd been experimenting with breaking a large lecture-class down into small groups and giving them exercises to work at. Again, the emphasis was on activity as opposed to passivity, and on skills as opposed to knowledge. Given that I had all these scattered materials from several years of teaching, it wasn't too crazy an idea to try to put them together to make a textbook. The result is that I now have a marvellous, innovative, first-year textbook which covers most of the standard topics in such a way as to allow a large class to be broken down into small groups and to enable the students in those groups to develop their philosophical skills. It's due to be published by Blackwells this autumn.

Cogito: Finally, what do you do when you are not doing philosophy?

Morton: Raising children takes up a great deal of my time – though there's only one child needing a lot of attention at the moment. When I'm not doing that, I enjoy making music. I've played the oboe, very badly, for many years, and have recently started taking piano lessons. Music is important to me for a reason of principle: it's the one thing I do really badly but haven't given up on. I also try to be outdoors – walking, cycling, sailing, or whatever – as much as I can.

16

DEREK PARFIT

Derek Parfit is a Fellow of All Souls College, Oxford, and author of the controversial and widely acclaimed book *Reasons and Persons.*

Derek Parfit (interview 1995) is the subject of a volume of papers edited by Jonathan Dancy, *Reading Parfit* (1997), in the series, *Philosophers and their Critics.*

Cogito: We usually start these interviews by asking our interviewees something about what turned their interests towards philosophy. Was there some particular person, or problem, or work, that made you a philosopher?

Parfit: Yes, there was. As an undergraduate, I did only modern history. Then I read David Wiggins's book, *Identity and Spatiotemporal Continuity*, and in particular his discussion of the actual cases in which the hemispheres of people's brains have been disconnected, in attempts to treat epilepsy. As a result, these people seem to have two quite separate streams of thoughts and experience, in having each of which they are unaware of the other. Wiggins then imagined a case in which the two halves of our brain would be successfully transplanted into a pair of empty skulls, and there would later be two people each of whom has half our brain and is fully psychologically continuous with us. Since these would be two different people, it can't be true that each of them *is* us. So how should we regard our relation to these people? I found that a fascinating question. It was this imagined case that drew me into philosophy.

Cogito: It is, of course, for your views on personal identity that you are best known in the philosophical world. But personal identity is only one area – and by no means the simplest, where metaphysical conceptions of reality have been thought to be practically important. Do you have a general view about the nature of the relation between metaphysics, on the one hand, and practical reason, on the other?

Parfit: Yes. What interests me most are those metaphysical questions whose answers seem to be relevant – or to make a difference – to what we have reason to care about and to do, and to our moral beliefs. Personal identity is one such subject; two others are free will and time's passage. Free will is the most straightforward. Many people have argued that, if determinism is true, no one can deserve to be punished, and what Strawson calls our 'reactive attitudes' – such as resentment, indignation, or gratitude – would be unjustified. I believe that, in this and some other cases, metaphysics should affect our attitudes and acts.

Cogito: So you're not impressed with the view, usually ascribed to Hume, that we can care about anything – that caring is not constrained by the facts? On this view, even if time isn't really passing, or no one has free will, that need make no difference at all to what we should care about.

Parfit: No, I reject that view. It has become the dominant view in much of philosophy and economics. On this view, while we can have reasons for *acting*, and our acts can be irrational, we can't have reasons for *caring*, except of a derivative kind, and our desires can't be in themselves irrational. If that were true, metaphysics couldn't have the significance that I think it has. But I see no reason to accept this view. On this view, what we have reason to do is what would get us what we want. But most good reasons for acting are not given, I believe, by our desires. They are given by our reasons for having these desires. I have the old-fashioned view that there can be straightforward truths about what we have reason to want. To defend that view, it's better to start not with ethics, but with simpler and less controversial reasons. Mackie claimed that 'objectively prescriptive values' were too queer to be part of the fabric of the universe. But our ordinary reasons for caring and acting don't seem too queer. If we believe that there can't be such reasons, we ought to conclude that there can't be reasons for believing either, and then we might as well give up both philosophy and science.

Cogito: But presumably the queerness is not in the reasons for acting; the queerness is in the idea that the reasons for acting are connected with the metaphysical nature of the world, by some direct means that doesn't involve any dependence on what we happen to care about.

Parfit: There isn't a sharp distinction between metaphysical and ordinary facts. Both kinds of fact are involved in one of the questions that interests me most: that of the rationality of our attitudes to time. One such attitude is what I've called the *bias towards the near*: caring more about the near future than about the distant future. This attitude is most pronounced when we're considering events that are good or bad to experience, or live through. Pain provides the clearest case. Since we care more about the near future, we sometimes choose to postpone some ordeal, knowing that this postponement will only make the ordeal worse. In such cases, I would claim, the fact that our ordeal will be worse is a reason for *not* postponing it, and the fact that it will be further in the future is *no* reason for postponing it. That it will be further in the future won't make it, at the time, any less painful, or any less ours.

Our bias towards the near can, I think, be usefully compared with a purely imaginary attitude to time. I described someone who has what I called *Future Tuesday Indifference*. This person cares equally about his whole future, except that he doesn't care at all about what will happen to him on future Tuesdays. So, if he had to choose whether to have a mild pain on either Monday or Wednesday of next week, or great agony on Tuesday, he would choose the agony on Tuesday. Here again, I would say, the fact that the agony will be much worse is a reason for *not* preferring it, and the fact that it will be on Tuesday is no reason for preferring it. This attitude would be quite irrational. Some people think this attitude too crazy to be worth discussing. But it's like our bias towards the near, except that it's more obviously arbitrary. I also imagined an intermediate case: caring more about the next year.

In these examples, the fact that some pain will be more painful isn't a metaphysical fact, nor are the facts that some pain will be on a Tuesday, or further in the future. But some of our attitudes to time do rest on facts that involve metaphysics. One is what I called our *bias towards the future*. This applies to events that are good or bad to experience, or live through. We care more about these events when they are in the future rather than the past. And this distinction raises deep philosophical questions. On one view about time, the property of being present, or occurring now, is an objective feature of reality, and time's passage is the movement of that feature into the future. This is the view that can seem to justify our bias towards the future. On another view, which I'm inclined to accept, 'now' is no more objective than 'I' or 'here', time's passage is a myth, and there is less metaphysical difference between the past and the future. That supports the attitude of caring equally about good or bad experiences, whether they are in the future or the past.

Cogito: But isn't our bias towards the future so deep-seated that no metaphysical reasoning could ever dispel it?

Parfit: There are two ways in which metaphysics can affect our attitudes. First, it may only change our beliefs about whether our attitudes are justified, or what we have reasons to care about. Second, it may also change our attitudes, or desires. On the first, more pessimistic view, we are just lumbered with certain attitudes. We may come to see that these attitudes are irrational, but that will do nothing to get rid of them. But even this might make a practical difference. Suppose, for example, that thinking about free will won't enable us to get rid of reactive attitudes like anger. There's still a difference between anger which we regard as irrational, and *resentment*, since the latter includes the belief that the person we want to make suffer *deserves* to suffer. If we come to believe this attitude to be unjustified, that may make a difference to what we do.

It's less easy to say how the metaphysics of personal identity should affect our view about what we have reason to care about and do. The implications here take longer to describe. But there is one well-known example. One central claim of early Buddhism was that most of our suffering arises from a false belief in the self. The remedy was the 'no self view', according to which there aren't really any selves or persons. But it was also claimed that the no self view was very hard to believe. One main aim of Buddhist monks, when they meditate, is to try fully to internalize the truth of this view, so that it can affect their attitudes and emotions.

Cogito: Can I ask you about another of Mackie's points? When Mackie doubted that there could be objectively prescriptive values, part of what he doubted was that there could be facts about values, or about reasons, which it would be impossible to recognize without being moved to act.

Parfit: It might be puzzling if beliefs about reasons could necessarily motivate us. That's one of Hume's main arguments: moral beliefs necessarily motivate, but mere beliefs can't do that, so moral beliefs must really be a kind of desire. But I would reject that argument's first premise. Beliefs about reasons do not, I think, necessarily motivate.

Cogito: But presumably you think that such beliefs *could* motivate us, and that they would then provide the explanation of why we act. Isn't that what Mackie finds puzzling? If reasons are facts about the world, how could such facts bring it about that we act in some particular way?

Parfit: It wouldn't be the fact itself, but only our belief in this fact. Those who hold my kind of view – or what are called 'Externalists' – might claim at this point that most of us have a standing desire to do what we believe that we have reason to do. That could be how, if we believe we have a reason, that belief together with that desire leads us to act. This reply accepts the Humean account, according to which we cannot act without some desire. That account can be challenged, but Externalists don't need to challenge it. According to Ross for example, if I remember right, most people have some desire to do their duty, but we could know that something was our duty even if we completely lacked that desire.

I've not tried to reach a view about the Humean account, because it seems irrelevant to the questions with which I'm concerned. If I was persuaded that we couldn't believe that we had some reason unless we had some corresponding desire, I would have to consider this issue. But I'm persuaded by an example of Christine Korsgaard's: that of someone who is so depressed that she just doesn't care about anything. Such a person could still believe that she had a reason to act in some way, because she will later regret it if she doesn't. If she lacks all motivation, we don't have to conclude that she can't have that belief.

Cogito: When you mentioned the Buddhists, I wondered if you might say something like this. Perhaps the difficulty of coming to act on a reason that is given you by the metaphysical facts is the same as the difficulty of coming to believe in the metaphysical facts in the first place. So what the Buddhists are doing is acquiring the belief, and, through that, the motivation.

Parfit: In some cases, such a claim may be true; but I don't think it's always true. If we take free will, which may be the clearest case, many people have not found it difficult to believe in determinism. Many, indeed, have found it difficult to believe that determinism could be false. If they conclude that the truth of determinism undermines desert, the effect on their attitudes can be more straightforward. They can still have the strong conviction that what some criminal has done is a terrible thing. And, as I've said, they may still feel anger. But they won't endorse ill-will towards the criminal. They won't think either that it would be good if the criminal suffered, or that it matters less if the criminal suffers than if some innocent person suffers.

Cogito: So the metaphysics might have an effect on our 'second-order attitudes', i.e. our attitudes towards our own first-order attitudes, and this second-order difference might in turn have an influence on our behaviour? We might come to regard our anger, perhaps, as merely a pathological reaction, and seek therapy for ourselves rather than demanding punishment for the criminal?

Parfit: Yes; and I think it's also likely that this would make our anger less intense and less lasting. We all have these natural reactions, but if we don't endorse them that helps to overcome them. I'm helped in this area by the fact that I get angry with material objects all the time. I sometimes want to kick my car, for example. Since I have this anger at material objects, which is manifestly irrational, it's easier to me to think, when I get angry with people, that this is also irrational.

Cogito: I was surprised to hear you say that many people find it easy to believe in determinism. Didn't Kant claim that, at the moment when we are actually making a decision, we necessarily act 'under the idea of freedom'? Isn't than an essential aspect of facing up to a decision?

Parfit: Some people have thought that that we can't, at the time of making a decision, believe in determinism. Others, of whom I'm one, see no tension here. When I consider what it's like to make a decision, I don't think I am presupposing the falsity of determinism.

I would now distinguish two ways in which metaphysics can make a difference. In the clearest cases, there is one intelligible metaphysical view whose truth would justify some attitude or moral belief of ours, and another metaphysical view whose truth would show that our attitude is unjustified. In such cases, whether the attitude is justified depends on which metaphysical view is true.

Some cases are more complicated. Thus, in the case of free will and time's passage, there is one metaphysical view whose truth would undermine some of our attitudes. If determinism is true, there can be no desert; and, if time's passage is an illusion, we cannot justify our bias towards the future. In both cases, there are other metaphysical views whose truth might *seem* to justify our attitudes. But I'm inclined to believe that this is not so. I agree with those who think that, even if determinism is false, there could be no basis for desert. And I doubt whether, even if time's passage were not an illusion, we could justify our bias towards the future. In such cases, it may seem that metaphysics *doesn't* make a difference, since the justifiability of our attitudes doesn't depend on which metaphysical view is true.

Mark Johnston defends a view that is sharply opposed to mine. On his view, which he calls 'Minimalism', metaphysics is always irrelevant to our practical concerns. It would support that view if we decided that, whichever metaphysical view is true, our attitudes or moral beliefs *are* justified. But, in the cases I've just mentioned, my conclusion is that our attitudes *aren't* justified. And that means that, in a different way, metaphysics still makes a difference. The justifiability of these attitudes may not depend on *which* metaphysical view is true. But we need to think about metaphysics to see that, on any of the possible views, these attitudes are not justified.

Cogito: Can we return to the cases in which, on one metaphysical view, our attitudes are justified, but, on another view, they are not? In such cases, some people might say, our views about metaphysics are likely to depend on our views about ethics, rather than vice versa.

Parfit: Some people have said this; but I think that in some cases this clearly gets things the wrong way round. Suppose someone argued, 'We can deserve punishment for what we do; but we couldn't deserve punishment if determinism were true; therefore determinism is not true.' As it stands, this argument seems to me useless, since it's hard to see how we could be sure that we did deserve punishment for our crimes if we thought that this could not be true unless determinism were false, and we weren't sure that determinism was false. We might add an extra premise to the argument. We might believe that God treats us as deserving punishment for our crimes, and that God wouldn't treat us unjustly. Then we would have a useful argument against determinism. But it would now be another metaphysical premise, about the existence and nature of God, which would give us reason to accept the metaphysical conclusion. At the moment I'm inclined to doubt whether it's ever the case that we can believe both that some moral belief presupposes some metaphysical belief, and that the metaphysical belief must be true because the moral belief is true.

Cogito: That suggests that you think that, as a general rule, the grounds of metaphysical arguments provide a better or firmer basis than the sorts of attitude that lead people to hold the moral convictions that they do.

Parfit: That isn't quite it. My view is rather that, when our moral beliefs appeal to certain facts, they *rest* on those facts. Since that's so, we can't decide whether those facts obtain by appealing to those beliefs. That isn't exactly wishful thinking, but it involves the same kind of mistake.

Cogito: Yes, but what we've got to compare are the grounds for our beliefs in metaphysical facts on the one side against the grounds for acceptance of ethical convictions on the other. For what you're saying, you need to be convinced that the grounds for metaphysical views are of a sort that gives them greater strength than the grounds for our ethical attitudes can give to those attitudes.

Parfit: Not quite, because I agree that there may be areas where, as Johnston claims, metaphysics is irrelevant. In such cases, perhaps, we can be confident of our moral beliefs, and justifiably confident that these beliefs cannot be threatened by metaphysics. All I was saying was that we couldn't usefully argue both that our moral belief requires some metaphysical view to be true, and that, since our moral belief is true, the metaphysical view must be true.

Cogito: Perhaps we ought to shift, at this point, and discuss in a little more detail your views about personal identity. How did you come to take such a special interest in this particular subject?

Parfit: It's not hard to explain that interest. It's easy to be specially concerned about our own continued existence over time. But perhaps I could say this. Consider Wiggins's imagined case, in which my brain will be divided, and each half will be successfully transplanted into the empty skull of some other body. And suppose we agree, as most people would, that there are two resulting people. If that is so, these two people can't each be one and the same person, *me*. And, since there's no reason to believe that I would be one of these people, we ought to conclude that I would be neither of these people, and that I would therefore cease to exist. This case seemed to me to show that what we have reason to care about, in caring about our future, isn't that we ourselves should continue to exist. If we were about to divide, in this way, we should conclude that our relation to each of the resulting people, though it wouldn't be personal identity, would contain everything that matters in our ordinary survival. If that is so, it seemed to me, our reason to be specially concerned about our future can't be, as we assume, that this will be *our* future. Personal identity is not what matters. But that's very hard to believe.

Cogito: It might help some of our readers if you could relate your view to the famous discussion of personal identity in Locke's *Essay*. Locke argued for psychological continuity as the real *criterion* of personal identity, or as what makes us one and the same person over time. I suppose you would say that his theory can't adequately handle cases of division?

Parfit: Locke does mention a case of division, though it involves, curiously, the continuity of consciousness in a severed toe. I like to think that Locke could have been won over to the view that what matters is not identity but psychological continuity. Because he thought that both of these mattered, he was led to claim that if we are conscious of some past act, it must have been us who did that act, and if we cannot remember it, we can't have done it. That can't be right.

Cogito: It's central to your view that what we should care about is not personal identity. So it's puzzling that you none the less spend a great deal of time discussing identity and rather less time on those things that, on your view, we should care about.

Parfit: The main reason for that is that it's so hard to believe that identity – or our own continued existence – *isn't* what matters. Another related point is the following. It seems to me well worth considering the bizarre problem cases that Locke introduced, and that still dominate the literature. By considering these cases, we discover that we are deeply inclined to hold certain beliefs about ourselves, and our identity. If we imagine that we are about to undergo one of these bizarre operations, we may not know what we should expect to happen: whether, for example, we should expect ever to wake up again. But, if we ask, 'Will the person who wakes up be me?', it can seem that this question must have an answer, which must be either yes or no. We take our continued existence to be a kind of fact that must be determinate, and all-or-nothing. If someone will later be in pain, we assume, that person must either *be*, or *not* be, us.

That assumption could only be true, I believe, on something like a Cartesian view. On such a view, we either have or are persisting, indivisible immaterial entities – souls, or pure egos – whose identities must be determinate. I'm not claiming that most of us accept that kind of view. Most of us, nowadays, reject such views. But we continue to think about our identity in a way that could only be justified if some such view were true. In order to come to see that identity isn't what matters, we need to be shown that we continue to think in that way – that we believe that our own continued existence does have this very special character. That belief, I think, underlies our view that identity must be what matters.

Cogito: It's now ten years since the appearance of *Reasons and Persons*. How have your views about personal identity changed in the intervening decade?

Parfit: The main change is the following. In my book I was inconsistent in my attitude to the criteria of personal identity. In the first printing, I argued in favour of a purely psychological criterion. I now think that it's a mistake to spend much time discussing the choice between the different criteria. What's more important is to see that, when these criteria conflict, questions about our identity are what I call *empty*. Even without answering these questions, we could know the full truth about what was going to happen. And I now think that, even in ordinary cases, where questions about our identity *have* answers, these questions are, in a way, empty. If we know all the facts bout physical and psychological continuity, we know what's going to happen. Questions about our identity are merely questions about how we can redescribe what's going to happen. They are, in a sense, merely conceptual questions.

Cogito: If these questions are 'merely' conceptual, does it follow that the answers can't provide reasons for having some particular attitude or other?

Parfit: That doesn't strictly follow, but I think it's true. Let me give another example, to illustrate the difference between questions about reality and conceptual questions. Suppose I learn that my brother's plane has crashed. I ask, 'Is he still alive?' This might be a question about reality, since I may have no idea whether my brother is quite all right, or has been blown to pieces. Suppose next that I learn that my brother is in hospital, and that because of damage to his brain he is irreversibly unconscious. His heart is still beating, and his other organs are still functioning, but that is only because he is attached to some machine. Once again, I ask, 'Is my brother still alive?' But that is now a question of a quite different kind. I know what state my brother is in. My question is no longer about two different possibilities, either of which might be true. It is only about how we can re-classify my brother's state, or about our concept of being alive.

Suppose that, given our use of that concept, there is no doubt that someone whose heart is still beating, and whose other organs are still functioning, is still alive. The fact that this person's heart is beating doesn't *cause* it to be true that this person is still alive. The relation between these facts is closer than that. In such a case, that's *what it is* for this person to be still alive. Many people assume that, if such a person is still alive, it must be wrong to stop his heart from beating, since we would then be killing him. On my view, if we decide that, in itself, it is morally unimportant that this person's heart is still beating, we should conclude that it's unimportant that he is still alive. That's because, in the sense I've sketched, that is a conceptual fact. Concepts like 'alive' and 'kill' have, we assume, great rational and moral significance. But, on my view, it doesn't matter *that* such a concept applies. What matters is *why* it applies. In this imagined case, even if my brother is still alive, he is irreversibly unconscious. If his being still alive just consists in the fact that his heart is still beating, it is not morally significant that he is still alive. Nor is it significant that, if we stopped his heart from beating, we would be killing him. If that's what he would have wanted, that is what we should do.

Cogito: The philosophical literature on personal identity often sounds, to the outside, like a wild excursus into science fiction. You have played your part in this trend. Recently, however, there has been a reaction in the literature against the use of bizarre thought-experiments. Kathy Wilkes, for example, in her book *Real Persons*, tries to do without thought-experiments and use only real examples. And Bernard Williams, though he has used bizarre thought-experiments in the past to argue for a criterion of personal identity based on bodily continuity, now warns that you can tell what is essentially the same story in different ways to generate different (and conflicting) intuitions.

Parfit: People appeal to bizarre examples for different reasons. Some people hope to vindicate one particular view about the true criterion of personal identity. I agree that can't be achieved. I also agree that, as Williams says, we can produce different intuitive responses by giving different descriptions of the same case. But I appeal to such cases for a different reason. That is to get us to see, as Williams was the first to argue in his wonderful article 'The Self and the Future', that we are inclined to believe that our identity must be determinate. Suppose we imagine ourselves about to undergo some bizarre operation, and we ask, 'Will the resulting person be me? Or am I about to die? Is this the end?' As I've said, it's natural to assume that this question must have an answer. I appeal to such cases to show how compelling that assumption is.

On my view, our question would be empty. If we knew what was going to happen to our brain and body, and what kind of experiences would later occur, we would know everything there is to know. We would know everything, even though we didn't know whether we were about to die, or would wake up again. Instead of asking, 'Would the resulting person be me?', it would be clearer to ask, 'Would it be correct to call that person me?' That reminds us that there are not here, at the level of what happens, two different possibilities. There are merely two ways of redescribing what will happen. If we come to understand that fact, we ought to conclude, I believe, that our identity is not what matters. To use a slogan that I now find tempting, what matters is reality, not how it is described.

Cogito: Someone might try to resist your views at this point by admitting that, in some of the bizarre cases, there is no determinate answer to the question 'Will it be me?', but insisting that in almost all ordinary cases this question has a clear answer. Such a person might ask, 'Why should I take the subversive Parfitian message on board by generalizing from the bizarre cases?'

Parfit: That depends on what the message is. My claim is that what matters isn't personal identity, but certain other facts which normally go along with personal identity. I advance two different kinds of argument for this claim. The first appeals to imagined cases in which personal identity and these other facts come apart. When we think about such cases, we can be led to see, I believe, that it is the other facts which matter. Someone might say, 'I agree that, in those bizarre cases, identity isn't what matters. But it *is* what matters in all ordinary cases.' That response is, I think, unreasonable. I'm appealing to a kind of inference that we often make. If X and Y always go together, and we think that X-and-Y together have a certain significance, we may wonder whether both matter, or only one of them matters. The obvious move is to imagine cases in which X and Y come apart. If we decide that, in these cases, it would be Y that mattered, we have good reason to conclude that, even in ordinary cases, it is Y that matters. This is like the use of artificial experiments in science. We create a purified situation in which two factors come apart, and then extrapolate our answer to the ordinary cases in which these factors hold together.

The other argument I've mentioned is quite different. That appeals to the general claim that, when we know the facts about physical and psychological continuity, there is a sense in which we know what would happen. Given a knowledge of those other facts, claims about personal identity do not give further information about reality, but merely tell us how, given our concepts, what happens can be redescribed. I then appeal to the claim that what matters is reality, not how reality can be described. This argument does not appeal to bizarre examples. It appeals to the implications of what I call a Reductionist view. On my view, though facts about personal identity are not the same as facts about physical and psychological continuity, they just consist in those other facts. When we see how that is true, we should conclude, I believe, that it can only be the other facts which matter.

Cogito: You are a revisionary metaphysician, in the sense that you think that we all hold certain deeply held, but incorrect, views about reality. Many such philosophers adopt a twofold strategy. First, they explain why our deeply held views in some area are incorrect; then they go on to provide an 'error theory': an account of how people come to hold such incorrect beliefs. Do you have an error theory to account for what are – on your view – our mistaken beliefs about personal identity and its importance?

Parfit: I have some thoughts on this subject, but they're not original. A partial explanation is that we are misled by our conceptual scheme. For example, as Williams argues in his 'Imagination and the Self', if I try to imagine being Napoleon at the battle of Waterloo, it is easy to confuse that with imagining *myself* being Napoleon. If I confuse these two, I may conclude that what I really am can't be a particular human being, Derek Parfit. It makes no sense to imagine Derek Parfit's being Napoleon. So, if I think I can imagine *my* being Napoleon, I may assume that what I really am is not a human being, but what Williams calls a 'featureless Cartesian ego': one that might have swapped places with Napoleon's ego. Kant makes similar remarks. Our belief in such egos partly derives, he suggests, from our misunderstanding of the way in which the concept 'I' features in our thinking. This could provide part of an 'error theory'. But I think we also need other explanations, of other kinds.

Cogito: You claim that it would in principle be possible to describe all the facts about people in what you call an 'impersonal' way. You also seem at times to be recommending the adoption of a wholly impersonal conceptual scheme: one that that did not even use the concept of a person as an abiding subject of experiences. You suggest that we could adopt that scheme without any real loss. Is that your considered view?

Parfit: It's clear that, if we fully adopted such a scheme, that might make a great difference to our lives. Some people think that it would undermine most of what matters, or has value. Others think that we would gain.

Some Buddhist monks spend much of their time trying to think in impersonal terms. There's a fine book by Paul Breer, *The Spontaneous Self*, which recommends this approach. When we're really angry, he suggests, rather than thinking, 'I am angry', we should think, 'Anger has arisen here'. Even that, I think, might make a difference.

My present view is somewhat different. I have tried to imagine beings who are in other ways like us, except that their conceptual scheme contains no concept of a person, or subject of experiences. They have the concept of persisting bodies, and the concept of sequences of thoughts, experiences, and acts, each of which is directly related to some persisting body. But they don't ascribe thoughts to thinkers, acts to agents, or experiences to subjects. I am inclined to believe that this conceptual scheme, though very different from ours, would not be worse. It would provide, in its way, for as good an understanding of reality. I do not accept the Buddhist no self view, since I believe that persons exist. *We* are persons. But I believe that persons are not entities of a kind that must be recognized in any adequate conceptual scheme.

Some have made a similar claim about the concepts of persisting physical objects. We think of such objects as having spatial but not temporal parts. What exists, at any time, is the whole object. Quine and others argue that there could be an adequate scheme which did not use such concepts. On such a scheme, we would think only in terms of four-dimensional entities, which have temporal as well as spatial parts. The most familiar concepts of this kind are those of continuing processes. What occurs, at any time, is not the whole process but only one of its parts. Thus, when we see some person, we see the whole person, but if we see that person for only five minutes, we see only a very small part of that person's life. I am inclined to agree that, if we thought only in terms of four-dimensional entities, our scheme would be no worse. But that is different from my claim. Compared with the notion of persisting objects, which are all there at any time, the notion of persisting *subjects* is a much more isolated part of our conceptual scheme.

Cogito: What exactly are we supposed to learn from discovering the possibility of such alternative conceptual schemes?

Parfit: When we see that there's an alternative to our scheme, which would be no worse, that can free us from certain kinds of mistake. If we have only one scheme, and don't see that there could be alternatives, we may take too seriously some elements in our scheme. We are, as it were, imprisoned in it.

Cogito: So you think of this device of looking for alternative conceptual schemes as a sort of method for doing metaphysics. But you don't apply

191

it directly: you don't for example conclude, from the existence of a coherent and adequate impersonal scheme, that there are no persons?

Parfit: No. Of those who defend the four-dimensional scheme, some claim that *all* objects have temporal parts: that there are no persisting objects which are all there at any time. That seems to me a mistake. I think we should recognize that there can be alternative conceptual schemes which are both adequate, and which both make true claims about reality. That's why I'm not tempted to deny that there are persons.

The Buddhist no self view could be interpreted like this. As I've said, we are inclined to have certain strong beliefs about personal identity, such as the belief that our identity must be determinate. We might regard such beliefs as entering into our concept of a person. That would explain the claim that there are no persons. That would be a way of claiming that there are no entities with the special properties that we take persons to have: subjects of experience whose identity must be determinate. But I prefer to say that *we* are not entities like that.

Cogito: One of the uses to which the traditional conceptual scheme has been put is to provide a rational grounding for prudence. If we believe that we have a special relation to ourselves in the future which we don't have to other people, that has been thought to make prudence a pre-eminently rational form of practical concern. What implications do your views of identity hold for this subject?

Parfit: That question raises some difficult and complicated issues. Butler said of Locke's theory that, if it were true, we would have no reason to care about our future. I don't think that's right. We do have reason, I believe, to care about our future. But we may not have as *much* reason as some of us think we have. We have several kinds of concern about our future. One kind, which we might call *anticipatory* concern, we can't have about other people's future. If we know that our child will later be in pain, we may care more about that pain than we care about our own future pain; but we can't anticipate our child's pain. This kind of concern may, I think, be in some ways tied to certain false beliefs about personal identity, or what is involved in our own continued existence. If we lose those beliefs, that concern might be weakened, and shown to be groundless. But there are other reasons for special concern, which might be unaffected.

Cogito: What other sorts of reasons are you thinking of?

Parfit: One class of reasons are those described by Perry in his article 'The Importance of Being Identical'. These reasons appeal to our present desires, projects, or ambitions. As Perry points out, we are likely to be the people who are best able to fulfil some of these desires. That gives us a derivative reason to want to remain alive and well. But such concern is very different from our ordinary concern. Suppose we know that we shall be destroyed, but that scientists will later make an exact replica of us. Though that replica will not *be* us, his similarity to us would make him just as good at fulfilling many of our plans and projects. Thus he could finish the book that we were writing. Perry claims that we would have as much reason to be specially concerned about the future of our replica.

Cogito: What if there was someone completely different – not a replica – who would be as good, or better, at carrying out our projects?

Parfit: That would also give us, on Perry's account, less reason to want to survive ourselves.

Cogito: So the big change here is that our reason to be prudent, or to care specially about our own future, becomes something entirely contingent?

Parfit: That's true, on Perry's account. But, as I've said, that account explains only one kind of reason for special concern. There are others. Thus, as several writers claim, most of us care specially about certain other people – such as our family or friends – and we might care specially about ourselves in the same kind of way. Since our family and friends are not identical to us, such concern would also be in a way contingent, and would not be founded on the fact of our identity over time. This concern is unlike Perry's, since it would also not be founded on our present projects. If we care about our friends, that need not be because we and they are trying to achieve the same things. But if we cared about ourselves in the future *only* in the kind of way in which we care about certain other people, some elements in our ordinary concern would, I think, be missing. The most obvious element is anticipatory concern.

Cogito: Is our concern about our friends based on reasons at all? Isn't this more like a Humean concern, that exists independently of reasons?

Parfit: That's a disputed question. Some writers, such as Whiting, defend Aristotle's view that our friendship should be based on our friends' admirable qualities. Others insist that love is not based on reasons, and that we should go on loving people however much they change for the worse. It's hard to decide when, and how, we have reasons for caring about our friends.

Cogito: But, when we do have such reasons, some of these don't look as if they would also justify our caring about our own future.

Parfit: Williams suggested that, on Aristotle's view, the ideal friend would be a three-dimensional mirror image of ourselves. And some suggest that, on such a view, we admire and love such friends because they have the qualities that we admire and love in ourselves. But this seems not to capture much of our ordinary self-concern. We can be specially concerned about our own future even if we don't admire ourselves.

Cogito: What other changes in our thoughts and attitudes might flow from this different way of thinking about persons?

Parfit: Another attitude worth mentioning is our attitude to our death. I know that, after a few more years, I shall not exist. That fact can seem very disturbing. But, on my view, it can be redescribed. It is the fact that, after a certain time, none of the experiences that occur will be connected in certain ways to my present experiences. That does not seem so bad. In that redescription, my death seems to disappear.

Time's passage is also relevant. When we are depressed by the thought of ageing and the approach of death, we are depressed by the fact that we shall have less and less to look forward to. That seems so bad because of our bias towards the future. If we lost that bias, perhaps because we concluded that time's passage was an illusion, that would make a great difference. I imagined someone who was temporally neutral, and who cared in the same way about good or bad experiences, whether they were in the future or the past. Such a person would not be disturbed if he was about to die. Though he would have nothing to look forward to, he would have his whole life to look backward to. His position would be no worse than if he had only just started to exist, and had nothing to look backward to. Wherever he is in his life, he would have his whole life to look either backward or forward to.

Cogito: But your imagined man could still be upset that his life is less long than it could otherwise have been?

Parfit: Yes. If he had just come into existence, he might regard it as bad news that he had only 80 years to look forward. He might prefer to live for several centuries. Even so, if he was temporally neutral, he would regard it as no worse when, because he is about to die, he has *nothing* to look forward to, not even the pleasures of looking backward. He would still have 80 years to look backward to. If we had this attitude to time, that would change our attitude to ageing and death.

These remarks overlook those many attitudes of ours which involve our plans or projects. Since we can't affect the past, looking backwards cannot be just like looking forwards. But that's not what affects us most when we think we have nothing to look forward to. That is an attitude, not to the fulfilment of our plans, but to our experiences. Even after our death, our plans may be fulfilled. What disturbs us is that *we* shall not exist.

Cogito: We traditionally close these interviews by asking our interviewees about their extracurricular activities.

Parfit: I have, I think, only one distinctive activity: architectural photography, in colour. My subjects are Venice in all weathers, and Oxford and St Petersburg in mist and snow.

17

NANCY CARTWRIGHT

Nancy **Cartwright** is Professor in the Department of Philosophy, Logic and Scientific Method at the London School of Economics. She has published numerous articles in the philosophy of science, and two books, *How The Laws of Physics Lie* (1983) and *Nature's Capacities and Their Measurement* (1989). *Otto Neurath: Philosophy Between Science and Politics*, written with Jordi Cat, Lola Fleck and Thomas Uebel, will be published in December 1995.

Nancy Cartwright (interview 1995) continues to advance her vision of science at the LSE. The volume on Otto Neurath referred to in this interview has since appeared, edited by Cartwright, Jordi Cat and Thomas Uebel under the title *Otto Neurath: Philosophy Between Science and Politics* (1996).

Cogito: Can you remember how you first came to take an interest in philosophy? Was there a particular book that stimulated you, or a particular issue that troubled you?

Cartwright: Not exactly. I started out with an interest in maths and physics, and an unfortunately strong religious education, that being the only intellectual outlet in my home town. So I grew up knowing a lot about predestination and foreordination and issues like that. But those have never been at the heart of my concerns as a grown-up philosopher. When I went to the University of Pittsburgh, which, from my small town in Western Pennsylvania, was a big move, the maths department was not very exciting. The physics department was considerably more interesting, but Pittsburgh had this really expanded, wonderful philosophy department, and I simply got pulled away from maths and physics into philosophy. I ended up with my major in maths and a minor in physics but the rest of my time was spent in the philosophy department.

Cogito: And were there particular people at Pittsburgh who stimulated your philosophic thinking, particular issues that you found exciting at that time?

Cartwright: Well. I was terrifically interested in the philosophy of science and there was Adolf Grunbaum, and I studied logic with Nick Rescher ... but I had a wide range of interests. I was keen on ethics, which I studied with Jerry Schneewind; and Sellars had come there, and I was very interested in what I now don't believe in any more, metaphysics and epistemology, which I learned from Sellars and his students.

Cogito: Now, you taught for some years at Stanford University in California, where there was a very active programme in the philosophy of science. Would it be appropriate to talk of a 'Stanford School', and if so, what are its distinctive features?

Cartwright: Yes, I think so. Let me go back a minute, though. You asked if there were things that I was particularly interested in as a student that got me into philosophy, and I think I answered that question, but really, there's another, more interesting question about a somewhat later period as a graduate student. I was a post-graduate student at the end of the 1960s and the early 1970s, and at that time there were two movements that I and my fellow-students firmly believed in. One was feminism, and the way to change the way we think about things from a feminist perspective, which, as you know, can take a variety of different expressions. My belief has been that the movement in philosophy, as in other academic disciplines, has been fairly successful. When it started out, it didn't have much to build on; the work was necessarily rather vague at the beginning and open-ended. But we now have a body of very important and substantial work, a number of different kinds of questions and new perspectives, that didn't exist when I was a beginning graduate student. The other thing that we were very keen on was the application of philosophy in life. Philosophy is, it seems to me, necessarily a very abstract discipline, and of course, that could be much reinforced if you study it as I did, as an undergraduate looking up to Wilfrid Sellars. But we didn't think of it as an abstract discipline that simply solved its own intellectual problems, building on a philosophical tradition of problems that were internal to the subject itself. I thought of philosophy as an important relevant subject. I always thought it important to think about things and to think things through, and that a thoughtful approach, where you've taken as much into consideration as possible, is, if you have the time for it, the best way to go about solving problems. And so I really did believe that philosophical considerations made and ought to make a difference in the very details of concrete life. This ranges from philosophy of science to political philosophy; if metaphysics was worth doing it was worth doing because it would make a difference to the way one practised life – maybe life in the laboratory, maybe life with one's friends, maybe life in the larger political arena. But the point of doing it was that it really did bear in concrete ways on what one was doing.

Cogito: Are you saying that that movement hasn't been as successful as the feminist movement?

Cartwright: That's exactly what I think. I find that there's a small region in philosophy of science, but a very, very small region, where the concerns are directed toward understanding how philosophy is brought to bear on real scientific problems. In my own field, we tend to think entirely of scientific theory, very, very high theory, and the only place that philosophy makes an impact is in somehow clearing up the interpretation of high theory. That's not at all my picture of how philosophy works. I think if it's worth doing for me, it's worth doing in every aspect of human endeavour, and ... it does make a difference in all kinds of scientific activity, to think about things philosophically. I think that's also true of political activity. What we've tended to get in philosophy is, rather, people who do, say, theoretical ethics, and then applied ethics. But applied ethics isn't really applied theory – applied ethics tends to be thinking at a very local level philosophically – an important thing to do – but thinking sensibly at a very immediate level about ethical problems rather than knitting together. I thought of philosophy as working in a way similar to the way in which quantum theory informs the construction of lasers. You don't derive how to construct a laser from quantum theory, but it certainly informs it; and it seems to me that ethics informs ethical decisions in much the same way: similarly for philosophy of physics, and physics itself.

Cogito: And is this just your personal view, or did you actually find like-minded people at Stanford who took similar views?

Cartwright: Well, this was before Stanford. I was wanting to back up, this was the movement of the 1960s and early 1970s. It was fairly widespread, optimistic, at that time, but slowly we've drifted away from that. Unlike feminism which got a group of people who succeeded in pursuing it and building and building and building, I don't think we've built very much on this. At Stanford there was more attention to this kind of thing than I think is usual elsewhere, and that's one of the reasons why I very much enjoyed being at Stanford. But I still think if you were going to characterise a 'Stanford School', it would be in terms of more abstract philosophical positions. But they are ones that are motivated by wanting to look at how things are actually done and not construct pseudo-rational ideals of how they might be done. So the Stanford School – there was Suppes, Patrick Suppes, and then to Stanford came Ian Hacking, and me, and then Peter Galison, John Dupre, and that whole group of people. Well, I think, Pat Suppes's book, *Probabilistic Metaphysics*, is a good description of views vaguely held in common, almost by accident, or at any rate people came together, and were sympathetic with these views, which urge reading the structure of science or the structure of the scientific world from how science is actually practised. So not to have a kind of transcendental argument that Nature must be deterministic – this is just an example, the simplest example – or that science must be unified, but to look at what we've got and figure out how it's working.

Cogito: Now this takes us fairly neatly into your best-known book, *How the Laws of Physics Lie*. There you argue that scientific laws have been understood in two very different ways: as descriptions of what actually occurs in nature, and as providing explanations of observed events. Now realists characteristically try to bridge this gap by arguing that the explanatory value of the laws is some indication of their truth. You reject this argument. Why?

Cartwright: I don't think that I reject it any more because I've gotten more confident and my confidence lies in rejecting a picture of laws which I was brought up with. Which is a picture that – it's described as an empiricist picture. It's the doctrine, more or less, that, really God spoke the predicate calculus. Now, the primitive predicates: with Hume they started out being the predicates that describe sensible properties. There were these primitive predicates and you could ascribe them to objects, and then maybe you could put a universal quantifier in front, and as time passed we are almost all of us now willing to stick a modal operator out in front of that. So we are talking about necessary, universal generalisations. We nowadays admit not only the necessity operator at the front, but we also tend to admit that they may not be universal generalisations: they could be probabilistic generalisations, but still there's a sense of the distinction between necessary and accidental frequencies of association.

But, crucially, there was supposed to be this special set of privileged properties – and I was never very clear what was privileged about them. In the first instance it was supposed that they were privileged either because those were the ones to which we had secure epistemic access, or because they wore their meaning on their faces. Now, few people really defend either line any more, but they still think there somehow are some set of privileged properties, and then all that can happen is that the properties occur or they don't occur. We can note this, so then there are associations between them, and there might be something very special about nature, so that some of those associations are law-like ones, and some of them are purely accidental because you are dealing with finite samples or something like that. That picture of laws of nature seems to me on reflection of how physics works – and physics ought to be the place where we find them if anywhere – just a false picture.

What goes along with that picture usually is a covering law model of explanation. You have a universal generalisation, and what you really see, the thing which is explained, is an instance of that generalisation. Or sometimes it's a more concrete generalisation that follows from the more abstract generalisation. Kepler's Laws are universal generalisations, and they are simply what Newton's laws amount to when certain boundary conditions are specified. But what you've always got is a kind of universal generalisation, and everything which gets explained, gets explained by being seen as an instance of that.

I just don't think that's how explanation works in physics at all, never mind in any of the other sciences. If you render laws of nature as modalised universal generalisations or probabilistic generalisations, if you render them that way, then I think you can't get explanations out. But if you think of them in a different way, as I now am trying to get a handle on how else to think of them – I now think of them as ascriptions of capacities – one can see, I think, how these claims could be true and explanatory. But they have nothing like the form of universal generalisations. Science then becomes much less tidy because the received body of knowledge gives us only guidelines for how to explain things, and it gives us as well guidelines for how to construct new devices that work, like lasers. But it doesn't contain within it already, in some surreptitious hidden form, the very information we want to get out at the end. So the deductive model of explanation, and the deductive model of theory-application, goes.

I think that's all for the best because it seems to me that that's not how science works. We have got, say, quantum theory, but how to build a model of a laser requires a good deal of creative effort. If you believe in the deductive model of explanation and the universal generalisation view of laws, then all in principle that that creative work can consist in is getting the right boundary conditions, the right input conditions – which, admittedly, if that view were right, could still be very difficult – and doing the mathematics. But that doesn't seem to me to be how science works at all. We piece together different bits of theory to build models of real-life systems such as lasers and the method of doing so is in no way deductive. It's not even approximately deductive; it's just not like that at all. It's like my knowing that you're irritable and then having to figure out how to cope, in different circumstances, with that; that's the analogy. We know the capacities of different kinds of devices or features, we know a range of situations in which we know explicitly what those capacities will lead to. We think that something systematically related will occur in different kinds of circumstances, but exactly what that is isn't already built into the theory. And there's this terrific creative leap, which is why models often don't work, not because the unsuccessful models don't follow from the theory – the physicists made a mistake in their deductions – it's that they made a bad bet in their constructions.

Cogito: To state a law in such a way as to give it a chance of being true, you claim, one needs to fence it round with *ceteris paribus* ('other things being equal') clauses. Such conditions are perhaps only fulfilled in the controlled world of the laboratory. Are there no laws that are not *ceteris paribus* laws?

Cartwright: I think there are no descriptive laws in the sense of modalised universal or probabilistic generalisations – there are none of those which are not *ceteris paribus*. I don't think it follows from that there are no true nomological type statements in physics. When you ascribe a capacity to an electron, because of its charge, to repel other electrons or attract protons, I think that capacity-ascription is universal and it's true. But I think it in no way can be translated into a modalised universal generalisation. It has to be seen as a capacity statement which works in a very different way than one of these laws as traditionally conceived. So I now have this rather unusual view. I think, that all laws in the sense of regularities are generated by something I call a nomological machine, deploying and harnessing capacities, getting them situated in just the right circumstances, in just the right connections with each other, keeping the whole thing stable enough and shielding it and setting it running, and then we can get regularities emerging. Most of these nomological machines are made by us, but some have been made, as it were by God – the planetary system is a nomological machine. We've got an arrangement of parts, the parts have fixed capacities and the arrangement is such that the whole thing has a stable capacity – put the planets in certain positions, and you get out certain motions. But that's due to the capacities of bodies with inertia to stay in motion unless acted on to do otherwise and it's due also to the capacities of bodies with mass to attract other bodies. And I honestly believe that if you try and cash all that out in terms of universal generalisations about relations within some privileged set of sensible, or measurable, or 'occurrent' properties, you won't succeed. It's not how Newton's Laws work in general; you end up with a false picture of how you construct explanations and successful applications in physics. And I keep focusing on physics because it's the case where you'd expect this doctrine to work if anywhere. It's not that I think physics is the important science, but it's the important test-case for these philosophical views.

Cogito: Outside the laboratory it is notoriously difficult to isolate the effects of any given cause. In classical mechanics there is the assumption that forces act independently of one another, allowing us to represent the resultant force as a simple vector sum. But what can we do if causes interact, i.e. if the presence of one cause affects how another cause operates?

Cartwright: I don't think there's anything in general we can do. I don't believe in universal methodology, so it's not a surprise that I don't believe in it in this case. There are cases where we have interaction – the notorious cases being in chemistry – where one comes to an understanding of how they operate. There are other cases where interactions may not follow any rules. I think most cases of causation are cases of interaction and that they're not intelligible in a scientific way. That is, not much of what happens in the natural world is governed in a systematic way, that it takes an enormous amount of effort in special background conditions in special circumstances before you get regular and repeatable behaviour. The more standard view is that everything that happens is an instance of some regularity, albeit a very complicated or a very abstract one which we may never know. And since I think it's very difficult to get regularities at all, they're not just lying around and everything that happens is an instance of them, then I genuinely believe that most things that happen in the world can't be subsumed under a regularity, or ought to be subsumed under a regularity. A lot of what happens simply is a result of interaction which we can't have a handle on.

I want to make one caveat to that – one of the reasons I like to think in terms of capacities is because I think it allows us to account for the fact that we do have scientific knowledge – and it is genuine knowledge – even in cases where there aren't regularities. Acorns have a capacity to give rise to oak trees. Now, I think that's true and I think that it goes hand-in-hand with a lot of singular causal claims: like 'That oak tree in my garden came from the acorn that we planted there twenty years ago'. And there are a lot of true singular causal claims like that that go hand-in-hand with the fact that acorns have the capacity to grow into oak trees without there being any regularity about what would repeatedly happen in any of the circumstances in which an oak tree did result. You know, the standard view is – take those circumstances and if you had a good microscope and had sufficient time, in every one of those cases in which the singular causal claim is true, you could find some description of the circumstances for that very acorn such that, if only you could repeat those circumstances, there'd be a universal generalisation. Now, I think basically that's all just a metaphysical pipedream.

Cogito: Why?

Cartwright: Well, it's probably got to do with the fact that I see no reason why we should start with this ontology of some given special properties and their associations with one another. Which is a long story and it goes through trying to get rid of a bad history in metaphysics and epistemology. I think we had at one point a genuine belief in the idea that there were sensible properties. One could really make sense of the concept of a sensible property, one whose essence was given in the way that it appeared in experience. At that point we at least had something that singled out these special properties, and then we could talk about the associations among them. Having given up that view, I don't think that there's any other reasonable way to pick out some handful of special properties which have somehow no modal content, to make a distinction between occurrent and dispositional, between modal and non-modal, I just think there aren't any such distinctions. So causal happenings are as much part of the fundamental ontology of the world as anything else and then it's very hard to construct a reason why there can't be causal patterns – acorns tend to give rise to oak trees and that's borne out in a lot of singular causal happenings – without there having to be universal generalisations in the background. Besides, I don't think that this whole story makes sense, that there's some description of every circumstance, and if you just went through the whole catalogue of all the properties that obtain on the occasion you'd finally find exactly that arrangement of them that would give rise to repeatability. I think that reality is far more multi-faceted and I don't accept that whole ontology of properties being already sorted out and given, there's three hundred or three hundred thousand of them and we could just, in principle, tick them off – was it red, was it blue, was it six inches long, was it eight inches long . . .

Cogito: Of course the belief that nature falls under universal laws was sometimes presented dogmatically, but it's also presented by Kant, for instance, as a regulative claim. He says, you know, I can't prove this is so, but reason requires us to look at nature in that light. Do you have no sympathy at all for that view that, even if there's no guarantee that there are universal generalisations there, it makes sense to look for them?

Cartwright: Well, one thing is, the specific Kantian arguments that reason requires us to see the world in this way, and I don't believe in those arguments. But I'm not the best person at all, by a long shot, to talk to you about Kant, but let's just say that I don't start from taking those kinds of arguments seriously. Now, there is a more local argument: my empiricist friends tend to say this is a regulative ideal. But the question is, why should it be a regulative ideal? One answer is that it would be nice if we could have it. I'm not even sure it would be nice if we could have it – I mean we're getting along fairly well, and we don't have it at all in the sciences.

The second thing that worries me is that I don't think that one should hunt the Holy Grail when it doesn't exist. It's a bad idea to have as a regulative principle to do your science in a certain way, if that's the wrong way to deal with nature. Now, it's not that I know that nature is disunified, but I wouldn't think it was very sensible to build an entire scientific methodology on an assumption that it must be unified. And if it's not unified, in certain specific ways, then certain specific methodological assumptions that we make in doing science are mistaken, and they're going to be costly and lead to mistakes, and I don't want us to make method-ological mistakes based on a kind of Holy Grail metaphysics.

Cogito: Let's move on to your second book, *Nature's Capacities*. Reading that work recently, I was struck by the resemblance in a number of places between your views and those of Mill. Is this just because he was discussing some real and fundamental problems that were bound to come back anyway, or had your ideas actually been influenced by reading him?

Cartwright: I don't know. He's certainly discussing some real fundamental problems that were bound to come round again. I noticed that rather strangely, I started reading Mill again – I started reading the sections of Mill to which these views are relevant and then I found, travelling around, friends in California, Pittsburgh or Berlin were reading the same things, without contact with each other. Another person I found people reading now again, is Max Weber. When I was a graduate student, it was very out of fashion to read Max Weber, partly because he was accused of a kind of mysticism, and now people, very serious – I don't mean the others weren't serious, but very analytic people who like language to be used in a very careful way – are terrifically interested in Max Weber.

So I don't know if these ideas are bound to come round again or that you have an idea which was a very good one but ran out. It served a purpose, it provided a way of doing certain jobs that needed to be done, needed doing, but it doesn't do all the jobs, and it's not the biggest picture, and we don't need those jobs to be done any more, they're already done. I feel this about Popper's falsificationism, which to many people seems rather trivial – why keep going on about it? – but at the time when it came up there were battles to be fought and it was a neat way, though we now think terribly over-simplified, of fighting those battles. But it didn't tell anything like the whole story and if you look at it from a totally different point of view, it didn't even tell the right story. Anyway, I think that what's happened is that we've played out a lot of the consequences of the covering law account, the focus on laws, the focus on a require-ment that science be wholly articulated.

Really, that's what's going on, I think: it's a battle between people who still want to cling to the idea that science, scientific knowledge, must be completely articulated, so that there's no space for any individual whim, or pseudo-science; that if it's all there, clearly stated, then objectivity is secured, objectivity of a certain kind, a kind of mechanical objectivity. And the reason that you want that mechanical objectivity, I take it, is to guard against individual whim or, as a lot of our Eastern European friends thought, to guard against making up whole stories about what's true. Well, I think that what's going on is the realisation that of course science can't be and isn't completely articulated, but insisting on the articulation, and those aspects of it that were articulated, served a certain purpose, and it did highlight differences between the kind of science that the people who argued for it liked, and the kind of thinking that they didn't like. So it's not a surprise to me that people are reading Mill again these days, and thinking about things a little differently, since we've learned the lessons of the covering-law account, and we've outrun the need for insisting that science be completely articulated, and that all the results simply follow by deduction from what's already been written down.

Cogito: Now a number of philosophers of science have tried to explain the causal relation in terms of probabilities. C causes E, they say, if and only if the presence of C raises the probability of E. There are a number of well-known objections to this claim, cases where C is intuitively the cause of E but where its presence may actually lower the probability of E. What should we learn from such cases?

Cartwright: Well, I think they point to the general conclusion, which I believe anyway, and which a number of other remarks point to, that there is no interesting scientific method. There's no interesting articulation of a scientific method, which will give you the right result if only you follow it. There are guidelines, which I think are genuinely useful, and insightful, but they're very vague. And the attempt to lay down a probabilistic measure of causation, which you can take to any problem, and, again because you want objectivity in some sense, just turn the handle and get out a result; it just seems to me to be foolish. I think that what happened was that we started out being suspicious of certain content claims in science – with the Vienna Circle period, and Popper – and didn't want to assume we knew those for sure, but hoped to secure the objectivity, rationality, the truth, the possibility of knowledge in science, by moving up to thinking that there was a content-free methodology. If only one followed this content-free methodology, one could be assured of knowledge or objectivity. And we don't any longer have good reason to believe in this content-free methodology. So that's what we're seeing here – the attempt to say it's very difficult to know what the real probabilities are, but if only you knew the real probability of E on C you'd know whether C caused E or not. Or maybe you needed to know something more complicated, maybe you needed to know a partial, conditional probability, or maybe you needed to know a whole set of probabilities of the kind Spirtes,

Glymour and Sheiness proposed. Maybe if you just had the full probability measure, which is something you aim for, though it's very difficult to get, if you just had that, it would tell you what the causal relations are without having to put in any background knowledge that's content-dependent. You don't have to know anything about social welfare, you don't have to know anything about education, you don't have to know anything about drugs – you can just go to any discipline and take this methodology and grind it out, and you end up with a causal conclusion. Well, I think it's pretty clear that doesn't work in case after case. You can use probabilities as a tool, just as you can use an oscilloscope as a tool, but you can't use probabilities as a tool if you don't put in some content, some specific content, in the first place.

Cogito: So the probabilities will only be an intelligible, a helpful guide to causes, to someone who already knows a fair amount about the subject matter involved?

Cartwright: Yes. Including, I argue, that you have to know a lot of facts about how causes are already operating in that discipline, in order to use probabilities to get at new causes. But I think that's fairly typical – I mean, of course the standard problem in philosophy of science nowadays is: if we grant, as a starting point, that there's no content that we want to help ourselves to, and now we move on to the new conclusion that there's no methodology which is certain and has any meat to it, any real ramifications, other than 'think carefully' or something like that, which doesn't really tell you what to do, how do we ensure that we have objective knowledge? That's the problem that all philosophers of science are worried about nowadays. My intuition about what has happened is to go back to the beginning and argue that we never had any reason to think we couldn't help ourselves to content in the first place. But that's a whole big story about epistemology. It is, at any rate, where I think philosophy of science is right now – this big question about objectivity.

Cogito: Right, so the Positivists had a particular picture about how objectivity in science is secured, and the collapse of that picture of how science is done makes the very notion of objectivity problematic.

Cartwright: That's what people think. And my attacks, for instance, on being able to use probability as a sure-fire way to infer causes, have come to be seen as an attack on objectivity, though I'm not at all sure that's right. As I've said, though, that's another story, in epistemology.

Cogito: Now, one of the things I found most interesting in *Nature's Capacities* was the contrast you draw between idealisation and abstraction.

To idealise, you say, is to extrapolate from the real to some ideal state or condition; to abstract is to separate out in thought one real feature in nature from others with which it is always associated. So, on this view, abstract properties are really there, they just tend not to be found in isolation. What turns on this distinction?

Cartwright: Let me begin by saying that that's not the only interesting way in which we use the notion of abstraction in science. So this is a particular distinction, a particular sense of 'abstract' in which I talk about Aristotelean abstraction, when you think of properties as really there and then go on to make a distinction between abstraction and idealisation. There are lots of other senses of abstraction. For instance, I worry a lot about Duhem's concerns that a lot of the properties of physics are abstract in the sense he uses the term – symbolic representations. They're not abstract in Aristotle's sense that you've abstracted them from real situations; they somehow are purely representational, but do a really good job.

So it's the sense of Aristotelean abstraction versus idealisation that's at stake in the discussion you were talking about. What hangs on it is that I think that you learn about certain situations or certain properties, what capacities they have, and you also learn about the capacities they have by putting them in very specific circumstances – like, if you put a ball on an inclined plane, and make it as frictionless as possible, and you try to learn from that about the capacity of something with an inertial mass, say, to keep moving unless acted upon by a force to make it stop. Now, in that very special circumstance ... well, let me back up.

We very often talk about capacities in terms of some characterising behaviour, like, inertial masses have the capacity to keep moving unless something acts to stop them. That's a characterising behaviour – it's not all inertial masses do, but we point to the capacity by talking about some particular characterising behaviour that we think is somehow particularly salient. Now, that characterising behaviour is often associated with constructing some special circumstances in which that characterising behaviour is exhibited, or almost or approximately exhibited, like the frictionless plane. But the question is, why are those circumstances particularly interesting circumstances? What's so special about them – they're after all just some circumstances: you could have this degree of friction, that degree of friction, you might not think about friction at all but something else, you might paint the inclined plane red ... What's so special about the circumstances we call 'ideal' is that we have these two concepts working at once – we have the concept of a capacity and its characterising behaviour, and then we have the concept of interference and distortion and the idea here is that you deploy your concepts of interference and distortion to come up with instances of the characterising behaviour, and the whole point about the characterising behaviour is that it's behaviour that you learn how to change systematically in order to account for what happens in more complicated circumstances. So it's a rather complicated ontology of all these things playing together, because I don't think there's any natural notion of what circumstances are ideal for a certain property. It's that those circumstances are ideal in which it exhibits a certain behaviour, a special behaviour, and what's special about that behaviour is that it's behaviour which we have some system for calculating from it some different behaviour that will actually happen in a more complex situation.

Cogito: Perhaps we could illustrate that by applying that thought to economics. Economics, you agree with Mill, deals in abstractions. So there will be lots of cases where predictions based on economic theory turn out to be wildly wrong, but where the economists will say, well, that doesn't discredit the theory, because what's gone wrong is the result of some disturbing factor. But do we need to know, when we try to formulate a theory, what will count as a refutation, and what will count as a disturbance?

Cartwright: Now, that's a nice case, because economic behaviour, the behaviour of the Economic Man, the Economic Person, is – crudely, if we go back to the time of Mill or Menger – is behaviour of someone acting only out of an economic motive. Very often nowadays, economists say 'acting rationally', but that really means acting only out of greed. But, anyway, it's behaviour out of some specific motive, that's one simple way to characterise economic behaviour; there are various other ways, but you can stick with that. Now the nice reason for focusing on that particular way of characterising economic behaviour is to realise that there may be no behaviour which is ever purely economic behaviour. Not even approximately so. It's worse than the case of the frictionless plane. There's no pure frictionless plane, but we get closer and closer and closer, and we can chart the accelerations as we get closer and closer to a frictionless plane. But in economics there may be nothing like this pure economic behaviour which is even approximately exhibited in any real situation. Nevertheless, most economists claim that theories of pure economic behaviour are explanatory, which is where we started this question.

The question was, do we need to know what counts as an interference in order to have a theory? I think so, yes. I think that why physics is successful is that it has a very good handle on what kinds of things count as interferences. Regularities are hard to come by, and one needs to take systems with known capacities and arrange them in very special ways, put them in very special circumstances, before any regularity comes to be true – or even a counterfactual could be true if there were enough repetitions of the circumstances. Now, if you think along those lines, then what you need to know in order to have a science which is successful in application, is you have to have a pretty good handle on how to build those special circumstances in which your capacity will give rise to a regularity. And you do have to *know* that, even if you don't have a rule that articulates it. You've got cases which are good cases where you know what will happen, you have some handle on the systematic variation, the output behaviour: you know the output capacities of several different components, you begin to know how to harness them together. It's like building a new bicycle. You do build new machines, and the knowledge deployed is of the behaviour of simple machinery – or you build new electronic circuits. We build lots of new things, using our old knowledge, but we don't go too far afield. And that seems to me, of course, what's missing in economics, because we are very seldom in a position where we're arranging background circumstances. So in order to have successful science, you do need to have an understanding of the capacity, how the capacity operates, what are the range of circumstances across which it will give rise to a regularity. That isn't all contained already in the science, but a lot of information of that kind is there, and you can have good bets about how to build new machines. But we aren't in such a good position with respect to socio-economic issues.

Cogito: Might your views on these subjects have any implications for the use of economic theory in political decision-making?

Cartwright: Yes, but I think I ought to think a lot more about it; that's my project over the next several years.

Cogito: This is taking us back, of course, to where we started, that philosophy should have some practical import.

Cartwright: I think the reason why I want to pursue these metaphysical views – that capacities are basic, not laws – is not as a piece of metaphysics, that I want somehow to get the ontology of the world right, but rather that I think that certain ways of picturing the world lead to certain scientific methodologies, and that some are better than others. I'm particularly interested in thinking this through, because I think it has implications for how one goes about doing economics as well as fundamental physics. The last thing that we want is what's always been accused of happening, that economics is following a model of physics. Well, we've always worried that their problems are different so it might not be a very good model – but now we worry a lot about the fact that what we call the model of physics isn't the way that physics itself works. So I think it does have implications about policy; both in physics, in building a laser, and in developing an economic policy.

Cogito: You're not yet clear what those implications are?

Cartwright: Well, I've got vague ideas, but the point of thinking of it differently is to look at concrete cases and see whether and where it matters. One place it does matter is in collecting cross-national, cross-cultural statistical data, and then writing down econometrics equations, and trying to estimate those equations, and thinking one learns something from those equations about, say, the relation between direct government expenditure and standard of living in developing countries. To suggest that there's some kind of a universal generalisation which is true independent of the structure, the institutional structure of a society that might give rise to such a generalisation seems ludicrous.

Cogito: Or, to take a very topical case, debates about minimum wage legislation. Does it create jobs, destroy jobs? Is there going to be a systematic answer to questions of that sort? And I suppose that on your views the answer might well just be no.

Cartwright: It might not be, it might be like the acorn and the oak, that there's a tendency which is a pretty good one to bet on, if you can cushion the circumstances in the right way. One important point is a cautionary note on the relation of some of these ideas to policy. There is a movement in economics to discount macro-economic models and using them as bases for policy, saying some of the same things I say – universal generalisations are hard to come by, that they're unstable, they must be generated by something else. But this movement says they have to be generated by a certain kind of micro-consideration of individual preferences and decisions; then models of those are built, and the models are used to argue that certain kinds of macro-regularities could never be stable. None of what I say commits one to that. None of the arguments that I see as being valid against universal generalisation insists that the arrangements that give rise to them have to be microscopic, as opposed to macroscopic. The arrangement of the planetary systems is as it were at the same level of description as the output regularity. So there's nothing about claiming that you need some kind of harnessing of capacities in institutional arrangements to give rise to a regularity which says that the arrangements – say in economics, if you have macroscopic economic regularities – that the arrangements have to be fixed at an individual level rather than an institutional level. The kind of philosophical arguments I've been giving are very neutral about that.

Cogito: Now, quite a prominent feature of your recent work has been scepticism about the thesis of the 'Unity of Science', so dear to many positivists. From your point of view, I presume, this thesis is a sort of unseen legacy of rationalist or Kantian metaphysics, something that a good empiricist ought to be suspicious of?

Cartwright: Yes.

Cogito: So even someone like Carnap, who prided himself on his empiricism, was smuggling some non-empiricist elements into his own philosophy?

Cartwright: Oh, I think definitely so. Yes. And one of the reasons I'm very fascinated by Otto Neurath, who was one of the other founders of the Vienna Circle, is that Neurath had a quite different view of the Unity of Science from the one we usually attribute to Carnap. I think also it's over-simplified to attribute that to Carnap. But at any rate, Neurath had a quite different view, that really read more from the way that science is practised – he didn't want to do metaphysics at all. His view was that he observed that in many cases we were able to unify the sciences at the point of action. It was when you had to make a decision to build a better hospital, we found out that we were not so bad at doing it. We had to piece together medical knowledge, and psychological knowledge, and knowledge about building materials – that you really had to piece together knowledge from a wide range of scientific endeavours in order to do anything concrete. But he was very optimistic that that could be done. That was his view of the unity of science. It wasn't that science would come to be unified in a grand picture at some time, but rather that we had learned that it could be unified to serve our purposes.

Cogito: Are you writing papers on Neurath? A book? Are we going to see the results of this work?

Cartwright: Yes, there's a book just finished which three other people and I have written, called *Otto Neurath: Philosophy Between Science and Politics*, which should be coming out at the end of the year from Cambridge Press. The authors are Jordi Cat, Lola Fleck and Thomas Uebel.

Cogito: And yourself.

Cartwright: And myself. It advocates – Neurath advocates – this kind of doing philosophy by looking at the world. He doesn't think of philosophy as an internal discipline driven by its own problems, starting from premises and using long chains of deductions. And hence, I think, a lot of analytic philosophers have thought he's not such a good philosopher. Well, Thomas Uebel makes a major effort in the middle of this book to show that his philosophical arguments are quite sophisticated. But what I admire about him is that his philosophy was constantly adjusted by his encounters with scientific and political life.

Cogito: Right at the polar extreme to your views about science would be those of someone like Stephen Hawking, who thinks that physicists are on the brink of finding the one master-formula, the grand law, from which everything else follows. And then, when they've found that, everything else is just filling in details, applying the big law to particular cases. How do you regard such a view of science?

Cartwright: Excessively optimistic. I think the optimism about the particular kind of unification that Hawking thinks – or has thought – that we can achieve in physics itself turns out to be not so probable now. But even if we had it, the bearing that would have on the rest of scientific endeavour seems to me to be very small. In part I want to use a term I disapprove of, but which I've used a lot here, that's the term 'in principle'. I think that even in principle, you couldn't deduce much from knowing the laws of physics.

Cogito: Do you have positive grounds for believing that your rival picture of the disunity of science is true, or do you insist on it merely to draw a contrast with the metaphysical picture of the people who believe in the unity of science?

Cartwright: I think there are positive grounds for believing the picture to be true. I don't really approve of doing metaphysics, but I think I find myself much in the position of Hume, in his *Dialogues Concerning Natural Religion*, that I think, in so far as we have to make bets about metaphysics, because our methodology hinges on it, they ought to be very small bets. But also I think that the positive evidence suggests that nature is disunified, that there are pockets of things that are quite distinct from one another, that behave in fairly regular ways that we can get a handle on. I think that the best bet about how Nature is ought to be read from the structure of our science. I don't see our science being unified in any way in this kind of pyramid structure, and the idea that eventually it must be, or in principle it is – I don't really understand this notion of 'eventually', or 'in principle it must be'.

Cogito: So if you are forced to do metaphysics, you will do metaphysics, as it were, from the bottom up, not from the top down. You'll look at science as existing bits of knowledge, and say; What must the world be like for us to have this patchy, fragmented knowledge of it?

Cartwright: Well, I think your original distinctions of rationalist versus empiricist were more to the point than top–down/bottom–up. I think that knowledge of the way the world must be should be very closely tied to knowledge of the way the world is, and that great inductive leaps are chancy, and we should be very cautious about them, hedge our bets a lot. I personally am very suspicious of arguments that start: things must be thus and so, because ... And I am also very suspicious – and I try not to, though myself caught up very much in my philosophical upbringing – we should not talk so much about the way 'the world is'. Certain psychological characteristics may work very differently from the way inertial mass works, and there's no reason at all to think there's some way 'the world' works. And when I argue for capacities in science, it seems to me a reasonable way to construct our endeavours in economics and physics and a few other places. But it's not as if we can learn, from looking at physics, the way the world works.

Cogito: A few years ago, you came from Stanford to the LSE. Have you experienced any sort of culture-shock? Are there any big differences between British and American philosophy that have struck you?

Cartwright: British philosophy seems to be more separated from philosophy of science than I expected, and that really does have a lot of repercussions. I find that the intercourse between the two groups is very small and I think this is to the detriment of both subjects, and moreover I don't think there's very much respect on either side of the divide. You get people who behave in polite ways, but deep down don't respect one another. I really do find that quite harmful to developments on both sides. I suppose in America people are more constrained in what they can say, and so there's a lot more nods to the acceptability of the other side's work than there are here. And I've always had this perhaps foolish American view that if you don't say it for long enough, you stop thinking it.

The other thing I've found that's got nothing particular to do with philosophy, I mean the intellectual side of philosophy, is that I'm shocked by the situation for women in Britain. I don't tend to think of America as being a great haven for any kind of liberal political views, but I find the system here – I suppose one learns to work within it and I haven't learned to do that, I'm still trying to work in my old way within it – but I don't understand how it's possible to be a woman academic and have a family, or if you're a male academic who wants to devote a great deal of time to the family; I don't see how it's possible. There's just the structure of the working week, people's attitudes, the scheduling of conferences (which in fact has something to do with the structure of the working week, conferences tend to be structured, to be scheduled on Saturdays, because it's so difficult to miss a day of teaching), the whole structure of the academic life and teaching seems to make it impossible, I can't understand how a successful academic can manage to raise children. You teach till late at night – it doesn't matter, what good does it do if you have a six-week holiday between second and third terms – if you're not home to see your children at nights during term. I look around the room and there just aren't any women around me here. And I'm not surprised when I think what the structure of my life is like.

Cogito: You experience something like what is experienced by the people who argue for more women in the House of Commons – that the way the institution works more or less prevents it from happening.

Cartwright: Yes.

Cogito: Not necessarily a deliberate policy, but just inertia, or thoughtlessness, or what?

Cartwright: Yes, inertia I think, that the system worked well when dons were monks. And it doesn't work very well for family life. And it has managed to creep along during the period in which academic people were in the old-fashioned sense middle-class, university teachers, who had servants, but anyway, none of them were women. And it works OK if it's just a man who doesn't expect to see much of his children, but it's just not a system that's geared to allowing women, women who want to have a certain kind of life-style, at all.

Cogito: Well, finally, a question that we ask all our interviewees, what do you do when you're not doing philosophy?

Cartwright: I try to stay with the children.

18

JOHN COTTINGHAM

John Cottingham is Professor of Philosophy at the University of Reading. His books include *Rationalism* (1984), *Descartes* (1986), *The Rationalists* (1988), and *A Descartes Dictionary* (1993). He also led a team producing a new translation of *The Philosophical Writings of Descartes* for Cambridge University Press (3 vols, 1984–91).

John Cottingham (interview 1996) is still Professor of Philosophy at the University of Reading. Since this interview, he has edited a large volume of classic philosophical writings, *Western Philosophy: An Anthology* (1996). His growing interest in different types of ethical theory is reflected in his new book, *Philosophy and the Good Life: Reason and the Passions in Greek, Cartesian, and Psychoanalytic Ethics* (1998).

Cogito: Perhaps we could start by asking you how you came to become a professional philosopher. Did you study the subject at university?

Cottingham: At school I studied classics – Latin, Greek, and Ancient History. Then, when I went to Oxford, I took the course called 'Mods and Greats', which involved doing two years of Greek and Latin literature, and then two years of Philosophy and Ancient History. So rather than having a strong initial urge to study philosophy at university, I was channelled into it by the system.

Cogito: So what was it that first drew you to the study of philosophy? Was there a particular issue or question that you used to puzzle over as a young man?

Cottingham: Before I went to university I was interested in the sorts of questions teenagers often get obsessed by – the grand questions about the meaning of life. I read quite a lot of existentialist philosophy, especially

Nietzsche. When I studied philosophy at Oxford I found it rather dry and dull: in those days it was very much linguistic philosophy at its narrowest. I only got fired up about the subject relatively late, once I had embarked on graduate studies. What has always attracted me most about philosophy is the broadness of its scope, the way in which it links issues in the sciences and the humanities. Philosophers have traditionally tried to provide a grand overview of how things fit together, or how they clash, for example in the relationship between science and ethics, or between science and religion. It's this synoptic conception of philosophy which made it more attractive to me than more narrowly specialized subjects.

Cogito: Were you already interested in Descartes during your student years?

Cottingham: No; I did no early modern philosophy as an undergraduate. In the Greats course we did intensive work on Plato and Aristotle: we had to read the whole of Plato's *Republic* and Aristotle's *Nicomachean Ethics* in the original Greek, and be examined in enormous detail on gobbets taken from the original texts. After that we jumped forward to the twentieth century, to Strawson and Ayer, with nothing in between at all.

Cogito: So how did you come to develop an interest in Descartes?

Cottingham: Perhaps because I hadn't had to slog through early modern philosophy for exam purposes I was able to approach it without any preconceptions, and I found it extremely interesting to see how so much of the recent philosophy I had been studying had its origins in the seventeenth century. Apart from that, when I started to work on Descartes I simply found him – as many others have done – to be a very compelling and engaging writer.

Cogito: You are best known, in the philosophical world, for your work on Descartes. This year, of course, we will be celebrating the 400th anniversary of his birth. How does his critical reputation stand today?

Cottingham: Pretty low, I think. Most of twentieth-century philosophy has been strongly anti-Cartesian. Descartes' perspective on enquiry – the perspective of the isolated, solitary meditator – has been largely discredited, mainly due to Wittgenstein and his followers, who have attacked the idea of private thought and private language as philosophically incoherent. Secondly, Descartes' foundationalism, his attempt to reconstruct the whole of knowledge from a few self-evident and self-standing premises, goes against the temper of much twentieth-century theory of knowledge. And thirdly, his theory of the mind, his claim that we are incorporeal, spiritual entities wholly distinct from our bodies, is regarded by the great majority of philosophers today as hopelessly wrong. So Descartes' reputation today is as a kind of monster of philosophical error.

Cogito: Descartes is sometimes described as 'the father of modern philosophy'? What precisely is meant by this? Do you find the label a helpful one?

Cottingham: As I was saying a moment ago, if you look at Descartes' actual doctrines, most modern philosophers have abandoned them. But if you look at his methods and his philosophical outlook, then I think there is some justification for the title. Descartes is one of those who inaugurated the modern outlook which rejects authority in philosophy. One of his major projects was to overturn the authority of the entrenched Aristotelian system, and to some extent that of the Bible too, and instead to appeal to the 'natural light', the rational faculty of each individual person, as a more reliable guide to the truth than past wisdom and authority. That attitude has remained with us. No one now would attempt to support a philosophical claim just by appealing to what some great authority had laid down. There are other more specific aspects of his legacy, but we'll probably come to those later.

Cogito: Historians of philosophy tend to emphasize the importance of context and background for understanding a philosopher's works. Yet first year students often *start* with Descartes, without any background at all. Does this make sense?

Cottingham: There are some problems, but I think we can teach Descartes this way. Descartes himself was a hater of technical jargon in philosophy, and claimed that his philosophy was accessible to anyone with good sense – 'the most equally distributed thing in the world', he says in the first sentence of the *Discourse on the Method*. So he claimed at least that we could come to philosophy without any baggage, and make perfectly good progress. In his dialogue, *The Search After Truth*, the character Polyander, who is really Everyman, is very much better and makes faster progress than Epistemon, who is a learned academic, steeped in technical philosophical jargon. Technical training clouds the natural light, says Descartes. I think to some extent he is right about this: we can approach his philosophy without formal training. It is also true, however, that Descartes in spite of himself often smuggles in preconceptions which he inherited from his scholastic Aristotelian teachers, and fully to understand some of his arguments there's no doubt that one does need this historical background. So it's not ideal, but Descartes' work is more suited than that of many other philosophers as a text for the beginner.

Cogito: Students of philosophy often read only the *Discourse on the Method* and the *Meditations*. How accurate a picture of Descartes' philosophy can one gain from these two works alone?

Cottingham: If you had asked people in the late seventeenth century what was important about Descartes' philosophy, they would probably have thought first of the *Principles of Philosophy*, which dates from 1644, a few years after the *Discourse* and the *Meditations*. The *Principles* is really a scientific book: most of it deals with what we would call questions of natural science such as the laws of motion, the origin and nature of the solar system, and so forth. Descartes was best known in his time as a proponent of mechanism, the view that all natural phenomena could be described using simple mechanical principles which were supposed to be derivable, ultimately, from mathematical laws. So it is a bit misleading to chop off the science and just consider Descartes as if he were only interested in the 'theory of knowledge', as we now call it, or in metaphysics. There's a recent biography of Descartes by Stephen Gaukroger which takes the line (already advocated by other scholars) that the metaphysics was really of interest to Descartes only in order to validate the science, that is, to provide foundations for his physics.

Cogito: That interpretation is not, of course, without textual support. Doesn't Descartes say somewhere that you should do the metaphysics *once* only, and then set it aside and concentrate on the science?

Cottingham: He certainly told a young Dutchman, Franz Burman, who went to interview him in 1648, not to spend too much time on metaphysics. And he gave similar advice to Princess Elizabeth of Bohemia. In the latter case he actually suggested that metaphysics could be confusing, because it could make us concentrate too much on the *distinction* between mind and body, while for the purposes of ethics and of living well we need to concentrate on their *union*. This union of mind and body, according to Descartes, we learn about not through metaphysics but by ordinary experience.

Cogito: You recently led a team producing a new three-volume English translation of Descartes. Did it change your understanding of him in any significant respect?

Cottingham: That's an interesting question. I don't think it changed my reading of Descartes in any major respects, but it did help to bring him alive. If one were re-doing a seventeenth-century philosopher into modern English – imagine, for example, doing Hobbes, or Locke – one might be struck by the differences, by the gap that separates them from us. With

Descartes one is struck, very often, by the modernity of his style, which is usually simple, elegant, and very direct. That's not true of all his writings, but is true of large parts of the *Discourse* and the *Meditations*. Doing a big translation project forces one to look at all sorts of works, not just the well-known texts, so I think it has broadened my understanding of Descartes. The third and most recent volume of the translation, which deals with Descartes' correspondence, does provide some fascinating insights which you don't get from the more familiar texts, particularly in the areas of ethics, psychology, and the relationship between mind and body.

Cogito: Perhaps we could move on now and ask a few more detailed questions about Descartes' philosophy. Let's start with the method of doubt. Descartes invites us to doubt everything, seeking something *so* certain that it resists all doubt. But does it make sense to try to doubt *all* my beliefs?

Cottingham: I'm not sure, actually, that Descartes does say that we should doubt everything. He certainly says that we should abandon all our preconceived beliefs, all the things we haven't thought about or reflected on, that we don't perceive sufficiently clearly and distinctly, in his terms. But there are certain assumptions which aren't doubted in the *Meditations*; for example the proofs of God's existence require premises which are never called into question.

Cogito: So the fact that Descartes doesn't doubt the causal principle he helps himself to in *Meditation Three* is not necessarily a lapse, on your view?

Cottingham: No: my view on this is that the doubt is principally directed towards existential propositions. The famous method of doubt in the first *Meditation* asks us to doubt whether we can be sure there is a table in front of us – we might, after all, be dreaming. The doubt is then broadened to include all existing objects: there may be no earth, no sky, no external objects at all. But I don't think Descartes means to cast doubt on the fundamental logical principles whereby we reason. If he did, then he could never get out of trouble: the doubt would be undefeatable. I think he doubts all matters of existence, and then his method shows him that there is one existential proposition he cannot doubt, namely his own existence. So on my view the scope of the doubt is not as wide as is often suggested.

Cogito: And that makes the method of doubt a more intelligible subject?

Cottingham: I think so. I think the assumption behind your question is correct: that if one was to doubt absolutely everything without exception, no enquiry would be possible at all.

Cogito: Now the Cartesian thesis that everyone has heard of is of course the formula *cogito ergo sum*, usually translated 'I think, therefore, I am'. The *cogito* has been interpreted, over the years, in many different ways. How do you read it?

Cottingham: I think that people have made a terrible meal of this. It's meant to be something extremely simple and straightforward. It's best translated as 'I am thinking, therefore I exist'. The point about it is that if you try to doubt everything, there's one thing you can't doubt, namely that you are thinking. Even if you doubt that you are thinking, it must follow that you are thinking, because doubting is itself a thought-process. So at the time when you are thinking, it's impossible to doubt that you are thinking, and it follows that you must exist, so long as you are thinking. 'I am, I exist, that is certain', says Descartes. 'For how long? As often as it is put forward by me or conceived in the mind.' That's what the *cogito* is, I think – a very simple point. It's importance is not that it yields a lot of fantastic truths but that it shows that universal existential doubt is self-defeating. So there's a faint glimmer of hope that progress can be made towards knowledge, even in the face of scepticism. Even if there's a very powerful and malicious demon doing his best to deceive you, there's one thing he can't deceive you about, and that is that you are thinking. The defeat of the demon and the defeat of doubt, that's what the *cogito* is about. Beyond that, I think its philosophical importance can be over-done – at least as far as Descartes' own aims are concerned.

Cogito: So if we're asked to categorize it as intuition, or inference, or performance, you tend to come down on the side of intuition?

Cottingham: I think those who have interpreted it as performative had an important insight: that the *Meditations* are not a set of blackboard doctrines. As the very title implies, the *Meditations* are an activity – they are something you have got to *do*. You can only get at the truth of the *cogito* by actually doing it. It's not that I necessarily think or necessarily exist – I might stop thinking, or even stop existing, at any moment. The point is simply that by engaging in the thought process – by doubting, by thinking, by cogitating – I can see that there's at least one thing that can't be doubted. So it is a practical exercise, and Descartes himself said that he wouldn't listen to critics except those who were prepared to meditate along with him. You might do one *Meditation* a day for six days – that would be one way. The important thing is that they are not so much a book to be read as a set of exercises to be engaged in.

Cogito: To move from immediate awareness of his own conscious states to knowledge of the external world, Descartes first has to prove the existence of God. Some modern scholars regard the two proofs in the *Meditations* as manifestly invalid, and suggest that Descartes was insincere in proposing them. Is there any reason to believe this? Was he simply trying to pacify the Church?

Cottingham: The claim that Descartes' proofs are 'manifestly invalid' I would probably agree with. Certainly the ontological argument of *Meditation Five* is clearly invalid. All it tells us is that to qualify for the title 'supremely perfect being' you have to exist, but it doesn't tell us whether anything in fact qualifies for that title. That is an old criticism, which I endorse. As for the so-called 'Trademark Argument' of *Meditation Three*, it seems to me to rely on highly dubious assumptions about causality, assumptions which belong to the medieval world-view which Descartes himself, in his clearer moments, was fighting against.

On the question of Descartes' sincerity, my opinion is that he was a perfectly sincere Christian believer. There's no evidence that he ever departed from the Catholic faith in which he was brought up. With hindsight, we can see that Descartes' philosophy was the first step in the move away from a religious view of the world. He certainly moved away from a view of religious authority as a touchstone of truth, as I was saying earlier. He also moved away from the conception of God as somehow deeply concerned in the running of the natural world. God doesn't *intervene* in Descartes' physics; and Descartes says that the scientist can't know anything about His purposes – they remain inscrutable for us. Descartes' God determines the mathematical laws by which the universe operates, but in a way which isn't transparent to the human intellect: we can't understand the rationale for them. And once those laws are established, the rest of physics is in a sense autonomous: we can unravel the mechanisms of the natural world without any reference to God. So with hindsight I think Descartes' philosophy does point away from theism towards the deism of the eighteenth century, which regarded God as no more than an inscrutable Prime Mover, and beyond that to atheism. But I don't think that entitles us to say that Descartes was not a sincere Christian. At any rate, there's no evidence whatever to suggest that he wasn't sincere.

Cogito: The proponents of the claim that Descartes was insincere can of course quote plenty of evidence that he wanted clerical approval for his philosophy, and wanted his physics to be taught in the schools. He thus had tactical reasons as well as purely philosophical ones for offering proofs of God and the soul. But this, of course, could only ever establish that he was acting from mixed motives; it doesn't establish the stronger claim that he was actually insincere.

Cottingham: I absolutely agree. Descartes was certainly a cautious man. He withdrew his earlier treatise on physics, *Le Monde*, in 1633, when he heard of Galileo's condemnation for advocating the heliocentric hypothesis which Descartes himself supported. When he was writing the *Principles*, he did want it to become a university textbook, and took care to avoid unnecessary confrontation with established orthodoxy. But the references to God in his philosophy are certainly not 'tacked on'; that would be a complete distortion. God is at the centre of his metaphysics, and the divinely-decreed laws of motion play a central role in his physics. God certainly isn't an afterthought or an optional extra in Descartes' system.

Cogito: When we teach the history of philosophy, we tend to divide the great philosophers of the seventeenth and eighteenth centuries into empiricists and rationalists, and pin the rationalist label on Descartes. But what does the term mean?

Cottingham: This is a terribly vexed question. I think rationalism is a cluster-concept, involving several different elements. One is the idea of *a priori* knowledge, that is, knowledge independent of experience. Unlike Locke, Descartes certainly does believe in innate ideas. He believes the mind is furnished from birth with certain concepts, and with certain truths, which are the building-blocks for subsequent reasoning and for the acquisition of certain knowledge. So Descartes is an innatist. Another element in rationalism is necessitarianism, the idea that truths – particularly the truths of science – can be somehow unravelled with strict logical necessity. We naturally think here of Hume's famous attack on the idea of necessary connection in connection with causality. It's very difficult to say with certainty where Descartes stood on this issue. He certainly compares physics to geometry: there's a famous passage where he says that the long chains of reasoning of the geometers, where elaborate conclusions are strictly deduced from very simple premises, made him think that the whole of knowledge could be exhibited in such a fashion. So he's attracted by the geometrical model, which makes him a kind of rationalist. But there are two qualifications that need to be made here. The first is that the ultimate laws are for Descartes not transparent to reason, not self-evidently true. They are just decreed by God, whose will is quite inscrutable to us. So there's a certain sense in which he is closer to Hume than is usually supposed. The Humean idea of brute facts that just are the way they are is usually thought of as a characteristically empiricist position. Descartes' way of putting it is that there are laws which are simply decreed by the inscrutable will of God. There does seem to be a degree of convergence here between what we think of as empiricism and what we think of as rationalism.

The other qualification has to do with the role of experience. Rationalists are often lumbered with a kind of caricature which presents them as thinking that the whole of science can be done from the armchair, without any experiments. Descartes is certainly not a rationalist of that stamp: he makes it very clear that deciding which hypotheses to adopt, consistent with certain general principles which are known *a priori*, can only be done on the basis of conducting experiments.

Cogito: So the rational principles put some constraints on a range of hypotheses, any one of which might turn out to be true, and then experiments help us determine which is in fact true. How are they to do this? By a sort of eliminative induction, perhaps, where all but one of the competing hypotheses are ruled out?

Cottingham: If we get on to the question of the methods of induction, it has to be said that Descartes wasn't very good at that stuff. He was in fact pretty cavalier about experiments and about scientific methodology in general. A lot of his particular scientific theories are vague conjectures, based on models drawn from the world around him. He points to a whirlpool, or a bouncing tennis ball, and says 'gravity works like this', or 'the reflection of light is like that'. As science, it's often pretty amateurish.

Cogito: But he does attempt, doesn't he, to reconcile the hypothetical method with the search for certainty? Towards the end of the *Principles* he says that each of his mechanical hypotheses, taken individually, might seem arbitrary, but that when we see how they all fit together and help to make sense of the universe as a whole, we will be convinced of their truth.

Cottingham: It's extremely interesting trying to work out exactly what is going on at the end of the *Principles*. He makes a distinction between *absolute* certainty, which is rigid deductive certainty, and *moral* certainty, which is certainty enough for practical purposes, and he claims that his physical theories are morally certain. But he then goes on to make a rather stronger claim, with the aid of the following analogy. Suppose, he says, we are trying to crack a code. We come up with a key which gives us a word, then another, and so on. If, using the same key, we go on to produce page after page of intelligible English or French, there will come a point when it is practically inconceivable that we haven't got it right. Descartes claimed, rather arrogantly perhaps, that it was likewise practically inconceivable that his physical theories were not right. He was of course to be proved wrong not many years after his death.

Cogito: Another aspect of Descartes' philosophy which has tended to attract hostile criticism is his metaphysical *dualism*, that is, his insistence on a sharp divide between mind and body. You have suggested that the nature and grounds of Descartes' dualism are often misunderstood. Can you explain where your reading departs from more traditional interpretations?

Cottingham: I think the interpretation which is most common now sees Descartes as dividing all properties into two exclusive and exhaustive categories, mental and physical. So one typically hears modern philosophers, if asked to give an example of a mental state, refer to something like a toothache. If you think about it, you'll soon see that this is a rather strange thing to say. The underlying assumption is that it must belong in one box or another, so, since it involves some element of consciousness, it must belong in the mental box rather than the physical box. Descartes' own position, I think, is rather more complicated. He does think there are purely incorporeal, spiritual aspects of us, namely intellect and volition, thinking and willing. He also thinks there are purely mechanical aspects of human beings, like digestion and (involuntary) muscular contraction. But what about toothaches, hunger, thirst, and so on? What about the passions? In my view, all these things belong to a third category in Descartes' thought. There's a sense in which *trialism* might be a more appropriate label than *dualism*. Sensations and passions cannot be ascribed to mind *simpliciter*, nor again to body *simpliciter*; they must be ascribed to what Descartes calls the 'substantial union' of mind and body. Now this mind–body union is composed of two elements – a spiritual entity, the thinking self, and a mechanical entity, the body – so in a sense the term *dualism* still remains appropriate. But if we want to understand what a human being is, as opposed to a kind of bloodless angel which just happened to be using a body (and this is a distinction Descartes often discusses), then we need to focus on bodily sensations and passions as key sources of evidence for the fact that we are not just minds inhabiting our bodies but are, as Descartes puts it, intimately united with them.

Cogito: So when he rebukes his disciple Regius for saying that a human being is an *ens per accidens*, a merely accidental unity of two distinct things, it's not just for tactical reasons – that it's a foolish thing to say, and bound to give offence? He also, on your view, has genuine philosophical reasons for rejecting that expression.

Cottingham: Yes, I think he has. If I said to you that a human being was a completely non-physical substance which just happened, for seventy years or so, to be plugged into a body, that would suggest that such a being was, in the jargon, merely an 'accidental unity', without any genuine *oneness*. Now I think Descartes did sincerely believe that we have such a genuine oneness, that a human being is a thing in its own right. The evidence for this is that there are properties ascribable to the human being – pain, hunger, the passions – which cannot straightforwardly be ascribed either to the spiritual soul or to the mechanical body.

Cogito: Closely related with the issue of dualism is the question of the status of animals. Descartes draws a sharp distinction between humans and 'brutes', using the capacity for *language* as the basis of his distinction. We could expect him, then, to be hostile to the modern 'animal rights' movement. Two important questions arise here. One concerns the relation of metaphysical issues to moral ones in general; the other concerns this particular issue. What are your views?

Cottingham: The first is a very interesting question. Nowadays we tend to separate ethics off as a specialized discipline of its own. That way of thinking is quite alien to Descartes. In his famous metaphor, he likens philosophy to a tree: the roots are metaphysics, the trunk is physics, and the branches are particular sciences like medicine, mechanics and, perhaps most important, morals. So ethics were not a sort of optional extra. Nor were they separated from the main body of philosophy: they were an integral part of an organic structure. The metaphor cashes out in other ways, too: it is from the branches that you get the fruits. What Descartes had in mind was partly instrumental things like how to prolong life and remain healthy. But he's also thinking of how greater understanding will enable us to lead better lives. One aspect of this is the regulation of the passions, a subject which had preoccupied moral philosophers all the way back to the Greeks. Descartes thought that his science would show us how the passions were generated by casting light on the physiological mechanisms that underpin them. This understanding would enable us to control them where necessary, and to use them to our advantage where possible.

As for the more specific issue of the status and treatment of animals, this raises complex questions. Descartes' official doctrine is that animals lack souls completely and are just complex machines. If they are not even sentient, we need have no scruples about exploiting them. But did Descartes really hold this extreme view? According to his biographer Baillet, he kept a dog, 'Monsieur Grat'; it is very difficult to believe that he could have regarded the animal as non-sentient. And if you look at the *arguments* about animals, in Part 4 of the *Discourse*, they all have to do with thought and language rather than sensation and feeling. Descartes insists, surely correctly, that animals have nothing that could count as genuine language. You may be able to train a dog to bark to get a biscuit, but that's not language, it's just a stimulus-response mechanism. There's nothing that's as rich and innovative as the linguistic responses of human beings.

Cogito: But can Descartes, consistently with his dualism, ascribe sensation to animals? You have said earlier that, for humans, Descartes' theory is a sort of *trialism*. But such a trialism still requires there to be a spiritual soul in the body as a precondition of the human passions and sensations. Now if there is no spiritual soul at all in animals, does it make any sense to ascribe sensations to them?

Cottingham: This is a tricky one. It depends on what you mean by the absence of soul. There is no intellection, no understanding or volition, nothing that could be expressed *propositionally*. That, presumably, we would nowadays agree to be true. There's nothing in a dog or a cat which corresponds to propositional awareness of the states of its body or events in its environment. Could there nevertheless be something that we could legitimately call *pain* in the absence of a rational soul?

Let me first say that I don't think this is something Descartes ever fully sorted out, so there is a certain fuzziness – or at least unexploredness – in trying to specify what he would have said on these issues. But his general line is, I would say, reductionist rather than eliminativist. That is to say, if you look at what he has to say about physiology in the early *Treatise on Man*, what he says is that very complicated operations like digestion and muscular contraction, and even what we think of as psychological functions like memory and imagination, can all be performed without any soul. Now that's reductionism, but it's not eliminativism. He's not saying that we don't really remember or imagine things, just that memory and imagination can be accounted for in mechanical terms. So I don't see why a Cartesian shouldn't take precisely that line with respect to animals.

Cogito: So psychology is going to divide into a physiological discipline concerned with how the nervous system and brain work, and which is *common* to us and the animals, and an 'extra' element concerned with those psychological functions that only a rational and spiritual soul could perform?

Cottingham: I think that's right. We can think of psychological predicates as covering a whole range of things – both the activities Descartes ascribes to the rational soul and those faculties (sensation, imagination, memory) which he explains reductively in mechanical terms. We may find that difficult as an interpretation of Descartes because when we hear the word 'psychology' we think in terms of modern categories, and immediately apply it to 'mind' as opposed to 'matter', assuming that Descartes' distinction must have been the same.

Cogito: Perhaps we could pursue this point a little further before moving on? If we now have this reductionist programme explaining the 'lower' mental faculties (sensation, imagination, memory) in mechanistic terms, is that going to have any implications for ethics? If we find that we can give a reductionist account of *all* the psychological powers of animals, and only *some* of those of humans, will that have important implications for how we ought to regard and treat the so-called 'brutes'?

Cottingham: I don't think we can give a proper answer to that question in terms of what Descartes himself actually said; I just don't think his views on these matters are sufficiently worked out. If you are asking for my own reaction to the question, 'Is there an important ethical difference between a non-rational, non-linguistic being that is in pain, and a being which has a similar physiological state but also formulates it propositionally, "I am being tortured"', then I think the answer is yes. The rational awareness of what is going on will make a great deal of difference to its significance and indeed to the amount of evil that is being inflicted. I do myself believe that it's worse deliberately to inflict pain on a human being that on an animal, and this is doubtless due – at least in part – to the presence of propositional awareness in the one case and not in the other. But this is, I confess, an off-the-cuff answer, not something I've thought through in any detail.

Cogito: Shifting from the seventeenth century to the twentieth, are there still lessons for the modern philosopher in the study of Descartes?

Cottingham: I think there are. Descartes' determination to keep the whole of human knowledge within the purview of philosophy is something I find both attractive and instructive. In my view, if philosophy just becomes a series of very highly specialized disciplines, accessible only to experts, it loses much of its *raison d'être*. Descartes was combating a certain sort of scholasticism, in which enormous intellectual energy was devoted to making minute distinction which, from our modern point of view, are almost entirely worthless, although a lot of people made their living out of making them. The scholastics had lost sight of the wider importance of what they were doing. I'm thinking of scholastic debates about intentional forms, sensible and intelligible species, and so on. All these terms were defined, redefined, and argued over with great mental agility, but the debates had somehow lost contact with serious problems about human nature or our understanding of the natural world. It does seem to me that some aspects of philosophy nowadays are in precisely that condition, and

Cartesianism can help to call us back to the question of the relevance of technical philosophy for our world-view as a whole.

Cogito: That's a very general lesson we might learn from the study of Descartes. Are there any more specific lessons?

Cottingham: There are a lot of problems Descartes worked on which one could point to as being philosophically fruitful. Perhaps the most important of these problems, still not properly resolved today, concerns the relationship between the subjective perspective and the objective description of the world. Descartes thought that a correct description of the world could be given in mathematical terms, that is, in terms of the sizes, shapes, motions, and arrangements of particles. (We might change the list, or add in mass, charge, and other fundamental physical properties, but such changes wouldn't affect the philosophical issue.) This complete account of the physical universe still leaves out the perspective of the meditator, the *subject* of experience. Part of the reason why Descartes introduces the rational soul is that, having given (to his own satisfaction at least) a reductive account of digestion, locomotion, sensation, memory, and so on, he just couldn't see how language and thought could be explained in the same sort of way. Now we're still pretty much in the same predicament, I think. The relationship between the language of science and that of subjective thought and consciousness is something we still don't really understand.

Cogito: So we might profitably look back to Descartes as a source for anti-reductionistic views about the mind, views which are clearly very much still with us?

Cottingham: I think there is something Cartesian in Thomas Nagel's approach to the mind, which invites us to address questions about *what it is like* to be an experiencing subject. Nagel focuses on problems about the relation between subjective experience and the objective description of the world, problems which can be traced back to Descartes. I'm not saying that Descartes provides any solutions to these problems, but what he has to say about them is very stimulating. In a certain sense, he defines the problem.

Cogito: Another area in which twentieth-century philosophers have looked back to Descartes is of course linguistics. The great American linguist Noam Chomsky even entitled one of his books *Cartesian Linguistics*. Why 'Cartesian'?

Cottingham: The central point Chomsky was making was that you can't explain language as the product of a stimulus-response system. Language is creative and innovative, that is, as Chomsky puts it, stimulus-free. Now that is more or less exactly in accordance with what Descartes says in Part Five of the *Discourse*, first published in 1637. Descartes points out that although animals do all sorts of complicated things, on analysis you find that each of their outputs is triggered by a particular input; whereas language is totally different in kind. Linguistic output is fresh, innovative, not tied to a specific stimulus. The problem with animals is not that they cannot talk, that they cannot physically produce the words (parrots, after all, can do just that), but that they are wholly non-linguistic beings. The special abilities of humans thus require a completely different explanatory account from the capacities of animals. In that respect, I think Chomsky and Descartes do link up.

Cogito: In what direction is your own research work taking you? Are you still working on Descartes; and if so, on what aspect of his work?

Cottingham: I'm working on ethics much more now than I used to, and some of these new interests do lead me back into Cartesian territory. Descartes spent a great deal of his later years working on the passions and their role in human life. His account of how we cope with the passions is, I think, of enormous interest. Although he is often described as a rationalist, he is in fact much less 'rationalistic' in this regard than some of the Stoics and Platonists. That is to say, he doesn't believe that the passions are wholly detrimental to the good life, worthy only of being curbed and suppressed. On the contrary, he says in a famous passage that it is in the passions that the greatest joy and felicity of human life is to be found. So he's alive to the idea that it's the emotions that make life worth living. He's also alive, I think (though this is more controversial) to what may seem a very modern thought, that a great deal of our emotional life is actually opaque to us as rational beings. This connects up with our earlier discussion of Descartes' dualism. In my view, Descartes' doctrine of the transparency of the mental – the doctrine that I have immediate access to all my mental states – applies *only* to the rational side of the mind. I can't form a propositional thought without being aware of doing so. But there's a great deal of our emotional lives that remains opaque to us, and it may require a lot of work to find out what's really going on when I become angry, or frightened, or whatever. This work, according to Descartes, will take us back to the causes of the passions, often to events in early childhood. So there are interesting ways in which Descartes' discussion of the passions has links *both* back to the earlier work of the Greeks and forward to the work of modern psychologists and psychoanalysts.

Cogito: Does Descartes have anything that we would recognize as a systematic account of ethics? Does he offer a worked-out view of the good life, or a set of rules of conduct?

Cottingham: He certainly doesn't have a public ethics, a standard of right action. Like most seventeenth-century philosophers he's miles away from consequentialism and calculations about benefits and costs. He's more concerned with the individual life, and how it can best be lived. There's no simple formula, but roughly his hope is to show how the irrational part of us, the feelings and emotions that we at present only partly understand, can become better understood and then retrained and channelled in such a way that, instead of being like mysterious forces that blow us off course, they themselves become part of the good life, sources of joy and felicity.

Cogito: This does of course suggest that disembodied existence might not be at all desirable. If it's in the passions that human felicity consists, and the passions appertain only to an embodied soul, or perhaps more strictly to the mind–body union, what is there to look forward to after the separation of mind from body?

Cottingham: Good question. There's not much speculation in Descartes about what the afterlife might be like, but if my interpretation of him is right, the part of a human being that survives death is something pretty abstract. You might spend some time contemplating the properties of isosceles triangles, but you are not going to have much enjoyment in the normal sense of the word.

Cogito: Perhaps that's a good place to finish, since we normally end by asking our interviewees what they enjoy doing when they are not doing philosophy.

Cottingham: Music is one of my interests. I'm a member of a choral society, though I wouldn't describe myself as a singer. I'm also a member of a local amateur dramatic society, and appear on stage from time to time. Skiing has become a hobby in recent years – it's a wonderful way of clearing the mind, but unfortunately rather expensive. And when my finances don't allow me to go skiing, I've also become fond of a more economical form of exercise, namely walking.

Cogito: All good activities, of course, for a substantial union of mind and body. Thank you.

19

JEAN HAMPTON

Jean Hampton was Professor of Philosophy at the University of Arizona. She wrote extensively on issues in political and legal philosophy, and was developing a distinct feminist perspective on some age-old questions about society and the individual. The interview was recorded during a recent visit to Bristol. During her time with us she was in good health and spirits. We were therefore shocked and saddened to hear of her sudden death, in France, as a result of a cerebral haemorrhage.

Cogito: Perhaps we could start by asking you, Jean, how you came to be a professor of philosophy at Arizona at what seems to be such a young age?

Hampton: I was born in 1954, in a town called Bayshore in Suffolk county, Long Island. When I was five I moved to a town called Albany, the capital of New York State. It was very cold there and boring, but a nice place to grow up. As I grew up I became desperate to leave. Then I went to University at Wellesley College, an all-women's college, where Hilary Clinton also went, and after that to Harvard. At Harvard I studied with John Rawls and finished up there in 1980. Then I went to UCLA and stayed there for seven years until 1987. My next appointment was in Pittsburgh where I had hoped to live for the rest of my life, because that was a wonderful department. I was just wined and dined and it was really terrific, but my husband Richard Healey, who is also a philosopher, did not have a proper job and we had to do something about that. UC Davis made us both offers so I went to Davis, where we stayed for a while. Then we got even more enticing offers from Arizona and I keep wondering if we'll stay there for the rest of our lives and die there, but it is a little too soon to say that.

Cogito: I believe there are other couples teaching at Arizona. Does this cause any trouble?

Hampton: There are three couples: Richard and me, David Owen and Julia Annas, and Alvin Goldman and Holly Smith. Actually I think it is wonderful – the nicest department that I can imagine. I guess because there are all these happily married people, it works out fine. We are all very different and the rule that Richard and I have worked out over many years is that he says what he wants and I say what I want and we do not try to persuade each other of anything because it never works anyway, so why bother? That is the way Julia and David cooperate too; Alvin and Holly are quite different. So you do not have this feeling that there are gangs of two, which I guess would worry most people. So it works out very well.

Cogito: Your work in philosophy obviously involves quite a broad knowledge of law. Have you any background in law?

Hampton: I have never been to law school, but when I was at Harvard I sat in on a course by Charles Fried, who was for a while solicitor attorney general under Reagan's administration. He taught a Contracts course, which attracted me as I was interested in Social Contracts. I also did a lot of reading on my own. Bob Nozick also taught in the law school on an *ad hoc* basis and knew a fair amount so I got involved. I attended his seminars and even though he wasn't a law professor he did the same thing that I have done, which is just make connections. Over the years I have developed quite close connections with a number of lawyers and the law school of Arizona. It is a very easy field for a philosopher to make connections in, because there is so much overlap.

Cogito: Tell us more about your work in philosophy. You have done a lot of work on what are apparently different themes and topics. Is there some theme you think ties these things together?

Hampton: I have been told by other people that the theme that pulls it all together is self-interest. So in Hobbes, for example, that is the driving engine of his argument. The work in law on punishment is very much interested in self-respect and the way punishment is meant to vindicate value from a self-interested point of view, so you pick it up there. With the rationality theory the interest is in projects which attempt to reconcile rationality and self-interest, like Gauthier's project. Even the feminism has a lot of that in it: I have written papers in which I lament the extent to which feminists in moral theory celebrate women's propensity to care. It seems to me that they care to the point where they are easily abused, and become servants, while I argue that women should value their own interests, so the subject of self-interest seems to come in there too. But I don't plan it in that way, that is not the idea.

Cogito: Alongside this Hobbesian streak I detect a Kantian streak in your work as well.

Hampton: That has also been said: people have said that I have put together Kant and Hobbes and since you can't put those two together they find this puzzling. In 'The Two Faces of Contractarian Thought' I talk about Hobbes and Kant and separate the two of them out. But there I leave out the Hegelian synthesis. The paper talks about the two kinds of contract thought in the moral tradition: there are moral contractarian theories and political contractarian theories. In the moral domain there are two kinds: the Hobbesian and the Kantian. My background, upbringing and temperament are all supportive of the Kantian style but I have a taste for Hobbes, the *bête noire*. I think there must be something right about Hobbes if he is that appealing. One of my projects, suggested in my 'Feminist Contractarianism' piece, is to try to redo a Kantian perspective with more self-interest in it. To think about morality which makes it less self-flagellating, less awful. Duty with a capital D just makes the whole project seem very unappealing, brutalizing in many respects. One of the projects that I am thinking about now, is to rethink what morality could be so that it is perceived as good for us, so I suppose it is sort of Greek, but I do not resonate with the Greek tradition as much as, for example, my colleague Julia Annas would like. It is the purely self-interested perspective that you get from people like Hobbes and Hume which I think is more interesting.

Cogito: Let me press you a little on this. There are a number of people now writing who are trying to make morality a little less demanding. And there is a reply to them which claims that in this world where we have so many starving people the demands of morality are inevitably very high. So high that people just want an intellectual reason for shirking their responsibility. Now describe yourself as not a shirker.

Hampton: There are two ways of getting people's perspectives back in the right place. One is to think about Virginia Woolf's 'Angel in the House' which I believe is in *A Room of One's Own*. She writes about this angel in the house which she tried to ward off, and it sounds as if she was thinking about her mother who was, as far as I can tell, just like this wonderful angel who does everything for others. I don't have the passage with me but she talks about how if there is a draught in the room the angel will sit in it; if there is chicken and every one else wants white and there is only dark meat left over she takes the dark meat. Whatever other people need she is there to supply it. Virginia Woolf describes how she felt she had to kill this angel because if she had not killed it the angel would have killed her. If you really lived in the way that this angel (which I take to be the voice of traditional morality) lived, it would be completely self-destructive. Surely the point in life is not to destroy ourselves by helping others? Indeed, such self-sacrifice often does not help others at all. I see this over and over again in the way a lot of women lead their lives: there is enormous pressure on young girls to be other-concerned. That is something that some feminists have rightly picked up in their research: not that this is a better way or worse way, but that it is what you would expect from a group that has been under pressure to be subjugated in a certain way. When you see these people growing up and dealing with children the way that I have (because having a child I have been exposed to many mothers with small children) in nursery schools for example, you become very aware of the extent to which they are unable to pursue their own projects. There was a woman that I knew who had three small boys under the age of five, which is hellish. She was very depressed and over-tired and was complaining to me at this nursery school about what she should do. So I said 'You really need about five hours a week where you just do what you want', and she said that she could never do that; 'How about three hours?' I suggested. No, she could not do that; even an hour a week she couldn't manage. I thought that this is somebody who has been so taken over by the demands of others that she is destroying herself. She was indeed miserable and eventually went into therapy and is now doing much better. Anyway, that is what I take to be the implications of this kind of view of morality: it will destroy you, and I do not see that any moral theory can place such an obligation upon us. It is in some sense defeating what morality is supposed to be about. So: 'How do you build self-interest back in?' is what I take to be the project. Unlike Susan Wolf, who says that morality must be put in its place, my prescription is different. We have been badly confused about what morality is. Indeed I have a theory about this, which is that morality, in some Marxist sense, has frequently been used as a whip to get certain sorts of people to be subordinated in the right kind of way, particularly women. One of the things that you find is that many women are incapable of taking into account their own points of view, whereas if you talk to a man, boy or a teenager they do not seem to have any trouble at all in factoring in their own self-interests. So there are obviously some very different things going on in the raising of kids, that I think play a role in how people think about their duties. Carol Gilligan, who talks about people's propensities to care in a way that I think is not very helpful, interviews two children in the beginning of her book *A Different Voice*. She says that the boy, when asked how would he weigh his interests against the interests of somebody else, replies that he would give three-quarters to himself and one-quarter to the other. He had it all worked out and boy, did he get a lot! Whereas the little girl, when asked, just went on and on; she had trouble answering the question but she finally said that maybe if you do not know the person then even if they want you to do something, then maybe it is OK if you put yourself first. So the extent to which she was able to advance her interests was minimal. There is clearly something going on about how people think they fit with others which is not uniform across society, and that needs to get fixed. Their underlying conception of what morality is, is badly skewed by contemporary unsuccessful social relations.

Cogito: Here you have taken a very abstract philosophical question and given it a feminist twist, which is something you do with other bits of your work too. Would you like to say more about that general issue?

Hampton: I do not mean to give anything a feminist twist. It just sort of comes out that way. When I was a graduate student there was a lot of interest among other graduate students in feminist theory, but I had no interest at all. Some women were quite cross with me in the department because I would not join their discussion groups, but I was interested in other things. Then in spite of myself I got interested. I have a feeling that this is just natural because all of us bring our distinctive backgrounds, our histories and our interests, to our work. If you have been raised in a certain way then that will turn up in your work. As a female I was raised in a certain way with certain perspectives and had certain experiences, and it is inevitable that they come through. I am a parent and went to this nursery school and talked to these people and it became part of my life, which is not a part of the life of an awful lot of philosophers, so of course for them that would never turn up. But it would be unnatural if I blocked these influences: it gets factored in with all of the other things that I think about. In a way you could wonder why all these kinds of twists, ideas, and perspectives have not been considered before. The obvious answer is that there have not been people with these kinds of experiences in philosophy, so you just have not seen them. But I think that it is extremely predictable that such perspectives turned up once women were in the field.

Cogito: You suggest that if you do not factor self-interest into an analysis of morality, in some way, then morality will become inherently exploitative, an idea that I find appealing.

Hampton: There is a Hobbesian remark that maybe is the only true thing that the man said. (I love Hobbes, but there is very little else that is true.)

He says in Chapter fifteen of *Leviathan* that we are not under any obligation to make ourselves prey to others. In the Hobbesian context that makes sense: it would violate rationality for you to do that. But if you extract that remark and think about it from a slightly different moral perspective it seems that it should be every person's credo, that you do not have to make yourself prey. Surely, that is politically very important. Another place where you can see the importance of self-interest in political terms is in a few books by an African-American woman writing in the early part of the twentieth century, Zohra O'Neil Hurston. She has written a wonderful book called *Their Eyes were Watching God* and another called *Jonah's Vine Gourd*. What she does in those novels is talk about the extraordinary pressures that are on young black females growing up in the early twentieth century who believe that they are worth nothing. Both of her heroines are able to buck these messages and are able to come out OK, through a lot of thinking, courage and bravery. You can see there the connection between being in an oppressed group – and if you are female it is in some ways doubly oppressing – and not having any self-confidence, any respect, any sense of yourself, any feeling that you are owed anything, and being imbued with the disposition to be a tool for the interest of others. That she despised and fought against. Another example, this time English, comes from Charlotte Bronte's *Shirley*. I quote from this in one of my papers. At one point the heroine in that book talks about how old maids are told that life is best when you are serving others. The heroine says that this is a very convenient doctrine for those who require the services of these women, and claims at the end of this passage that each person has his allotment of rights and we should cling to these. Imagine the political implications if we do not do that. This is not to say that you want to be greedy, abusive and completely self-serving, but if you do not have that perspective in life then you are just ripe for exploitation, no matter what group you are in, what job, what career. So I think this is something any decent political theory must accommodate.

Cogito: You have done some work trying to formulate an acceptable version of a retributive theory of punishment. This is a theory which amongst many liberal philosophers has been thought of as unsavable, but you have done your best to save it. Can you explain?

Hampton: Maybe the feminism also comes in here, as well as my religious views. I think punishment is in many ways an important issue, particularly in countries like the United States where crime is really out of control and where women are targets of some of the worst sorts, both inside and outside the home. Living in Los Angeles this all came to the fore because it was a very frightening place to live, and I just got sick of being scared all the time. A lot of my students got sick of being scared all the time:

the female students were legitimately much more scared than the male students. Lots of rapes, lots of attacks; you could be followed home by some man when driving and you would have to run from your drive-way into your house. It was a mess – it was just awful. So the topic of crime and its remedies came naturally to the fore. I also talked to a lot of students about some of the awful things that would happen to them. Rape was a common topic, the suffering that rape victims go through and the difficulties those victims have in getting those who raped them to justice. So you start thinking, what is it that these victims really want? Then I have had my share of wrongs: not legal, not a felony or misdemeanour, but life always allows us to get wronged by people, often our friends. We get betrayed or lied to or whatever, then certain kinds of feelings get generated. So you put all that into the mix and start wondering what is it that makes you so angry. Why does the anger take this form that you would like to inflict pain on the person that hurt you? Although I had been quite hostile to retribution – in fact I had written a paper called 'The Moral Education Theory of Punishment' which openly attacks the retribution theory – I slowly came to decide that retribution was the foundation of punishment and also the foundation of moral education. So I set about trying to give it a basis that made sense. A lot of people find my theory intriguing, but very few are persuaded, so I do not think that I have been successful yet. But I will keep trying and hoping that there is something to it. I know there is something to retribution; I am not sure that my theory gets to it.

Cogito: You are a philosopher working in the United States in the 1990s, which is a culture going through some crises. Do you think there is function for philosophers in the States at the moment?

Hampton: The philosophical community does not enjoy a high profile in American political discourse. That is partly our fault: there has been in the latter part of the twentieth century a real fear of getting involved in the public fray, partly because it can be so painful, difficult and distracting. So the profile is low. Some philosophers have got involved to some degree. People in applied ethics have entered the arena in certain areas. There is the occasional philosopher who will talk to Congressional committees. I believe that Thomas Nagel addressed a Congressional committee on affirmative action. Last spring I was an expert witness in a trial in Canada and there was some controversy about whether or not philosophers should be pronouncing upon the theoretical foundations of the law. Unlike, I think, in Europe, there is the feeling that academics are to be distrusted, that they are elitist, that they are living in the clouds and not engaged with the world in a way that would make them useful. There is a certain amount of resentment of them that I do not fully understand. So the philosophers are reluctant to enter the fray and in some ways the public keeps them at bay. There is not the kind of engagement that I would like to see, except for this applied ethics area where you are starting to see it more. Also I think you are seeing it more in feminist theory. The public is more interested in hearing feminist theory, so some of that is entering into articles in, for example, *The New Yorker*, magazines that are aimed at certain segments of the population. Outside that area I have been quite frustrated about how little attention is paid to moral theory done by philosophers. You get it in some areas like the law, this being where moral and political theory will have its greatest impact because the lawyers will listen to it. There is some role that philosophy is playing with artificial intelligence, although you see some of the same dispositions to keep the philosophers of mind at arms length here. There is another aspect of the situation which worries me. I am an analytic philosopher and I am very committed to that methodology as a way for philosophy to continue, which is not to say that I do not criticize analytic philosophy and worry that it can be too narrow, too critical, insufficiently expansive, unwelcoming of new ideas and new theorizing. All of that seems to me to be legitimate criticism. However, it still seems to me that the concern for analytic rigour and the use of logic is very important. That, I think, is under pressure in the US right now. I worry about how long that kind of philosophy – the kind called Anglo-American philosophy – is going to remain robust and healthy. The postmodernist movement seems to be advancing on our subject, not just in areas like English and social studies but in philosophy too in certain departments in certain ways. While I do not want to be hostile to new ideas and new theories, and while I am ready to be welcoming, when these new approaches are destructive of deeply-rooted ways of reasoning and thinking that are right and promising, then I get concerned.

20

MARTHA NUSSBAUM

Martha Nussbaum is Professor of Law and Ethics at the
University of Chicago. Her many publications include *The
Fragility of Goodness: Luck and Ethics in Greek Tragedy and
Philosophy* (1986), *Love's Knowledge: Essays on Philosophy
and Literature* (1990), *The Therapy of Desire: Theory and
Practice in Hellenistic Ethics* (1994), and *Poetic Justice* (1996).
She also edited, with Amartya Sen, the collection *The Quality
of Life* (1993). She is currently working on a theory of the
emotions.

Martha Nussbaum (interview 1996) is still Chicago-based, and has recently
published *Sex and Social Justice* (1998).

Cogito: Perhaps we should begin at the beginning, philosophically
speaking. How did you come to take an interest in philosophy in general,
and in ancient philosophy in particular?

Nussbaum: I think I was always interested, from a very early age, in some
of the problems I would later write about: the nature of the emotions,
moral dilemmas, practical reasoning, and so on. I remember starting to
think about these subjects when I was in high school. At that point, since
there was no philosophy curriculum in school, I wrote essays on
Dostoyevsky and other literature authors. I began to wonder, at that time,
why literature shouldn't be part of philosophy. So I was already thinking
about philosophical problems in connection with works of literature, especially Greek tragedies. When I went to college, there was a bit of a hiatus
because I didn't like my first two years at college much. I didn't find much
challenge in the instruction I found at Wellesley, and decided I wanted
to take some time off and become an actress. I got a job acting in a reper-
tory company, but it was a company that performed Greek tragedies.
So I was actually acting in the tragedies, and dancing. This made me

understand more, from a different point of view, about the problems of emotion and of human vulnerability. When I decided I wanted to go back to school, I was already hooked on these plays, and on some of the insights of classical culture, so I majored in classics as an undergraduate. At that point, I took a lot of classical philosophy, but my plan was to go to graduate school in classics, and to write about the tragedies. Then when I got to Harvard, I found that the people who were talking about literature were not raising the questions I was interested in. They were either doing technical philological work, or a rather impressionistic – and to my mind not very rigorous – kind of literary interpretation. On the other hand there were people over in philosophy – Gwil Owen, who became my thesis supervisor, in particular – who were doing very exciting work, though not on my problems. So I decided it was best to go where the intellectual rigour and excitement were, and thus went into Owen's programme, although my PhD remained, officially, in the classics department. I spent the rest of my time at Harvard working on Plato, Aristotle, and the Presocratics. So where were the tragedies? Well, it was always in the back of my mind that I wanted to write about the issues raised by Greek tragedy, and I never felt that Owen and I shared the same philosophical starting points or obsessions, which was probably a good thing as it made it easier to be an independent pupil. On my own, I began writing up some of my ideas. It was when Bernard Williams came to Harvard as a visitor in 1972 that I recognized that it was perfectly possible to address the questions that obsessed me within philosophy. To me Williams's seminar on moral luck was inspiring, both in itself and, perhaps even more importantly, as a sign of possibility. It made me feel that I could bring out the things I was writing on tragedy and still call them philosophy. At that point I was already working on *The Fragility of Goodness*. I had written a couple of chapters before Williams's visit, but I wrote it slowly, while still working with Owen on my PhD thesis on Aristotle's *De Motu Animalium*.

Cogito: You are best known in the philosophical world for your work on Greek ethics in general, and on Aristotle's ethics in particular. It seems to be rather a striking feature of moral philosophy in the second half of the twentieth century that Aristotle is making a comeback in a very big way. Do you have any explanation of why this should be the case?

Nussbaum: When I was in graduate school, there was the beginning of a tremendous revival in systematic moral and political philosophy. I studied with John Rawls, and still regard him as one of the very small number of really first-rate thinkers of this century. On the other hand, the idea that you had to choose to be either a utilitarian or a Kantian left some people dissatisfied. They felt that there was a need to investigate, in more detail than those theories were then doing, the role of the emotions in the moral life and the nature of practical choice. There was a hunger for a more ethically complex, even messy, approach to these problems of real life, and a feeling that the two dominant traditions were failing to provide it. At that point, people started turning to Aristotle. But they did so in a number of different ways, and for very different purposes. I'm increasingly worried about associating myself with Aristotle, because it can give such contradictory signals to people. At a recent conference in Germany, for example, Jürgen Habermas advised me to warn the audience that my Aristotle isn't the Aristotle of the Thomist natural law tradition. There are now so many different Aristotles before the public mind: there's MacIntyre's conservative authoritarian; there's the related Aristotle of the Thomists; then there's the more liberal Aristotle of Ross and Barker that I would like to defend. So I increasingly stress the liberal affiliations of my view, and often find myself talking about Kant, in order to stress that I am not one of those people who want to bash the Enlightenment and dismiss its aim of giving us a life enlightened by the critical use of reason.

Cogito: I find that reference to Kant interesting, because at least at first sight, there appears to be a fundamental tension between the Kantian and Aristotelian approaches to ethics. Aristotle's ethics is about the search for *eudaimonia*, the good life or human flourishing, rather than with 'morality' in its Kantian or Christian sense. But might it not turn out, as Bernard Williams has argued, that the pursuit of the good life may lead us to reject morality itself?

Nussbaum: I think Williams probably does think that, though I'm not sure how far he really wants to go. Is he prepared to give up the idea of a critical culture dedicated to equality and justice, which I think is the great legacy of the Enlightenment? I don't think he is willing to give that up. But to articulate that ideal we need Kant as well as Aristotle, because Aristotle's ethics, although it has many good features (in particular, a much richer account of the emotions than Kant provides) none the less has no idea of human liberty and human rights, at least not one that is fleshed-out enough to be useful politically. So I think that if we are to operate in the context of international politics, as I increasingly find myself doing, we need to be able to use the language of the Enlightenment. I see no reason why the pursuit of the good life should lead us to reject that language. Assuming, of course, that it's other people's lives, not just your own, that you are concerned for.

Cogito: In your work on Aristotle, you emphasize his commitment to a plurality of distinct and incommensurable values, goods that cannot be weighed against one another in terms of units of some common measure.

But this frank acceptance of incommensurability faces two types of objection. On the one hand, some people will say, 'If we can't weigh these things against one another in terms of units of a common measure, then choices between competing goods must simply be irrational.' Or they may turn the argument around and say, 'If we do trade one value for another in everyday decision-making, we must be implicitly committing ourselves to some common unit of measure.' How do you respond to these objections?

Nussbaum: The first thing to say is that the crucial point Aristotle is making when he says that these are all distinct parts of *eudaimonia* is that we need them all. A large amount of one good isn't going to compensate for the lack of another. So if your account of *eudaimonia* is to have implications for politics – and Aristotle thinks it does – what it tells the policy-planner is that you don't want to go for, say, the maximization of physical comfort at the expense of, say, friendship. These are two distinct goods, and you have to aim at both. Now suppose that in some very bad situation you have to make a choice between them. You should see this as a tragic choice, in which no amount of one good adequately compensates for the loss of the other. Then you have to make a choice, based on your overall picture of your situation. But I see no reason to believe that in making such a choice you are operating with a hidden metric. I think that's just a dogma that people have given no reason for.

Cogito: This issue about incommensurability is of course closely related to debates about the nature of practical reasoning. Until quite recently, the 'instrumental' theory of practical reason has been dominant in economics and philosophy. But on the instrumental theory, practical reasoning is simply a matter of working out means to pre-existent ends; the ends themselves cannot be objects of rational enquiry. So it looks as if your choice of ends is just a matter of brute irrational commitment. Many people in the late twentieth century have found this a very unattractive feature of the instrumental theory of practical reason. But are you in a position to offer us something better?

Nussbaum: I think Aristotle had already done so. What Aristotle thinks is that we start out, certainly, with an end in mind, but we may have only a very vague and general conception of that end. In our notion of *eudaimonia*, we start with the rough idea of human flourishing. We can perhaps agree that the most choiceworthy life is one that would be lacking in nothing that would make it better and more complete. But then we have to begin the job, not just of working out instrumental means to that end, but of specifying it, saying in more concrete detail what counts as realizing that kind of life.

That's true not only of *eudaimonia* as a whole but also of its constituents. If I decide that being a doctor is for me the best kind of life, then of course I have to think of instrumental means to that end (like getting into medical school), but I also have to ask myself, 'What counts as being a (good) doctor?' Thinking about that will have a great bearing on how I pursue it and how I relate it to my other commitments. Indeed, in order to get a good specification, I will already need to consult my other commitments. Let me give you a very trivial example to illustrate what I mean. I say to myself, 'It's my end right now to make a good dinner. Here's what I've got on hand. What specification of the idea "good dinner" shall I choose?' In seeking to answer that question, I'm going to have to look to other ends: How much work do I need to get done tonight? What friends are coming to dinner? What am I pursuing in my relations with those friends? My choices will be made by consulting a whole range of ends, not by just focusing on one and then working out instrumental means to it. I think Aristotle already gave some good examples of this sort of reasoning, but David Wiggins has developed this idea much further. And there's another book that I particularly like on this subject. It's called *Practical Deliberation of Final Ends*, by Henry Richardson, and is published in the Cambridge Studies in Philosophy series. I think that Richardson does the best job of working out this idea of the specification of ends in rich and rigorous detail, showing elaborate examples of how a person might specify, in Aristotelian ways, a final end. What I particularly like about Richardson's book is that he takes Sidgwick's instrumentalism seriously, gives the best argument for it, and then turns round and tries to show that the very things that motivated Sidgwick to be so fond of instrumentalism and commensurability can be accommodated within the Aristotelian picture. I think it's very important not simply to dismiss the various types of instrumentalism. It's much more valuable to see what their philosophical motivation is, to appreciate the strength of that motivation, and then to try to show how the Aristotelian picture can provide an answer to it.

Cogito: The great attraction of instrumental theories was, of course, that they offered – at least in principle – some sort of decision-procedure. But on the Aristotelian theory that you are articulating, there isn't going to be any such thing. According to Aristotle, 'the decision rests with perception', that is, the person of practical wisdom just sees what to do in a given situation.

Nussbaum: You can use instrumental reasoning too – often, you have to. You can use all the tools that these people give you, but you need others as well. What I think has happened with the dominance of instrumentalism in fields like law and public policy is that people think that it's only the instrumental part of decision-making that is rational. On such a view, your ends are simply a matter of brute preferences that are completely given by your nature, and cannot be changed or shaped by law and public policy. Milton Friedman famously asserted that 'about differences of value, men can ultimately only fight'. That's the attitude I come across every day in the law school of Chicago, where the influence of Friedman remains very strong. What that means is that these people are saying a lot of controversial ethical things about ends, but they think they don't have to give arguments to support their claims. They suppose, let's say, that the maximization of wealth is the end. But who is to say whether it is a good end? Let's see the argument. They don't feel they have to provide any argument, because the view that the choice of ends is irrational acquits them of having to say anything at all. So they just posit an end and get going on the instrumental reasoning. I think Aristotle is a very good antidote to this – I guess that's one reason why they wanted me to come to Chicago and fight with them about this matter. I always find myself saying to these people: 'Look! You think you are being so rational. You think you're the rationalists, but you are really selling reason short, because at the most crucial point in your project you just posit some goal, and you think there's nothing further to be said about it.'

Cogito: So someone who is really and wholeheartedly committed to reason will think of ends as things that can be argued for and can be shaped by public policy? Could you explain how this works?

Nussbaum: How do you argue for an end? Not, I think, by showing that it approximates to some norm fixed by Nature. You argue for an end in a holistic way, by showing that it fits best with other things that human beings want and that we think we have good reasons to pursue. So that's one role for reasoning – to look at how well one proposed end fits with other accepted ends. Another thing you can do is to entertain different specifications of the one end. In this process, you often come to recognize that people's preferences for ends are not simply given. Economists in the past (although this is changing) have thought that there's no point in asking which specification we should prefer, or which ends we should include in our scheme of other ends, because it's all fixed beforehand by our desires. On this view, desires are just brute facts of Nature, and there is nothing that ethical argument or public policy can do to modify them. But that seems just false. Even Gary Becker, who is the greatest of Friedman's disciples remaining at Chicago, now recognizes this fact. He grants that the way that society arranges race relations, for example, will shape the desires of African-Americans for a certain amount of education. The desire for a college education is not a brute fact of Nature, but is shaped by what you think about yourself, what amount of self-esteem you are led to have by your society, what your society tells you about the opportunities that are likely to be open to you, and so on. In his 1992 Nobel Prize address Becker had quite a lot to say about how people – he mentions both African-Americans and women – 'under-invest in their human capital', as he puts it, because they are led to expect that they won't have many opportunities. I think that this realization that preferences are not a neutral bedrock, but are malleable, and often shaped by public policies, is one of the greatest revolutions in modern economics. I'm happy to be a part of it. But it does seem funny to me that this revolution in economics had to wait until the 1990s, because Aristotle and the Hellenistic philosophers already had a sophisticated account of the social deformation of preferences. The economists could surely have done a little more reading in the history of philosophy.

Cogito: Perhaps we could shift now to your views about the emotions. In Aristotle's ethics, the emotions play a central role. To be virtuous, he says, it is not sufficient to act rightly; you must act rightly because you feel rightly. He also held that the emotions were not thought-less, but had some essential or intrinsic relation to belief. Many philosophers have now come to accept this view. It seems extremely difficult, though, to specify the precise nature of the relation between an emotion and a belief or cluster of beliefs. What is your current view about this?

Nussbaum: I've come to the conclusion that, basically speaking, the Greek Stoics were right. Emotions are not just internally related to a certain type of evaluative belief; they are identical with such beliefs. It isn't just that grief, for example, centrally involves the thought that someone extremely important to my life is lost; that's what grief is. Other people say that grief certainly requires this thought, that it's part of the definition of grief, but argue that it's not all there is to grief. But what are the other parts? Here we run up against two great problems which I haven't been able to solve, though I retain an open mind. The first problem is the great plasticity of human beings in the way that they experience emotions, both as regards the same person at different times and between different people. Some of the times I've experienced grief I've felt surges of energy, felt like going out and running ten miles; at other times I've felt crushed with fatigue. There seems to be no one bodily feeling or special, introspectible phenomenological condition that is always present when grief is present, even in me, much less across different people. That's one problem that people have not solved. The other great problem facing rival theorists is that I would like to say that emotions can have psychological reality, can influence our behaviour, even though they are not part of our conscious experience at a given time. A good example is the fear of death. I think this fear is, for most adults, psychologically real – it motivates their behaviour in ways that can be shown by looking at their patterns of action. And ultimately it can come to be acknowledged by them if you question them in the right way. None the less, we're certainly not aware of it all the time, so it seems highly implausible to suppose that there is any one phenomenological 'feel' that is an essential part of this fear. A third problem that interests me is that the philosophical tradition is full of accounts of the emotions of God or of gods. It looks as if people in those traditions are prepared to say that a bodiless substance can have emotions. I'm not prepared to say that they were all talking nonsense. The fact that many great thinkers have thought it perfectly coherent to imagine the emotions in this way seems to me a sign that we ought to take seriously the idea that maybe we can do it all with just the quality of the thoughts. There is obviously a lot more to be said about this, especially about the nature of the cognitions involved. I do think that the Stoics went badly wrong in two places, and my current project is an attempt to modify their view in such a way as to make it hold water. First of all, the Stoics thought of the cognitions involved in emotion as propositional attitudes. They thought that what we were grasping was a linguistically formulated, or at least formulable, proposition. If so, we can't give an adequate account of the emotions of non-human animals and very young children. The Stoics were forced to conclude that animals don't have emotions, which seems to me to be an extremely counter-intuitive consequence of their theory. I've done a lot of reading in recent cognitive psychology, and I think it's fair to say that the current consensus is that the best account of animal emotion is a cognitive account, but one that uses a looser notion of seeing X as Y, endowing an object with some content pertinent to the animal's own well-being. But this doesn't involve the potential use of language: the content is not something that is, even in principle, linguistically formulable. Much the same is true, I think, of human infants, and probably also of a great deal of our adult emotional life. The second major modification that I want to make to the Stoic theory concerns the history of an emotion. The Stoics didn't think about the past. They just thought that at a certain time you become capable of certain propositional attitudes: there they are, and they don't have a history. But if you think about any case of human emotion, the immediate object at hand is very often shadowed by traces of other earlier objects. Proust gives a wonderful description of this: when Marcel embraces Albertine with love, at the same time he is embracing his mother, mourning his own childish neediness and insufficiency, and doubtless more besides. So we need a story about how the emotions unfold from an initial situation of great helplessness and great longing, which is very likely therefore to be characterized by ambivalence towards the object of that longing, who both fulfils our needs and then doesn't, but goes off on his or her separate way. We need to unfold that story and see how the structure of that emotion, in particular the ambivalence of infant love, tracks the emotions of adult-hood and poses problems for adult emotional life. That's one of the things I'm doing in my current project, and it's the reason why, in these lectures I'm giving at Oxford, I've focused on philosophical accounts of the ascent of love. The crucial question seems to me to be this: given that our love is in its genesis mixed with hate – as thinkers like Spinoza and Proust say – how can we purify it? How can we make it more beneficent, more compatible with our general social aims? To me, this is a tremendous question. If we can't answer it, we really can't rely much on the emotions as good guides in public life.

Cogito: That leads on neatly to something else I wanted to ask you about. In *The Therapy of Desire* you attribute to the Stoics what I thought was an interesting and highly plausible doctrine of the unity of the passions. If you love something, you fear its possible loss, you grieve if you lose it through misfortune, you are angry if someone takes it away from you. So in virtue of the cognitive structure of the emotions, it looks as though you can't seek to cultivate those that we label 'positive' and rid yourself of those that we label 'negative'.

Nussbaum: I think that's true in general, but it's not the whole story. In addition to the belief that some important object has been damaged by another person, anger requires some beliefs about agency and causality. When I talk about mercy, both in *The Therapy of Desire* and in a more recent article, I say that one of the things people can do is to qualify their attribution of deliberate badness to the agent who has wronged them by coming to understand the narrative history of the wrong-doing. Not by saying that there is no moral responsibility, but by realizing that people grow as moral agents in a complex social and personal environment that very often gives us reasons not to withhold blame but to mitigate any punishment we might want to assign. In this way we may come to temper anger with mercy. This is one reason why I became so interested in compassion. The Stoics want to say that compassion is one of the same family of emotions, that you can't have pity or compassion without having anger. So, they conclude, you should do without it, and perform your public works through a sense of duty alone. But I think they are wrong in this. When we have compassion, what we are doing is to make people at a great distance part of our own system of goals and ends, like members of our own family. This ought very much to work against, or at least to mitigate, the anger that we might tend to feel against them should they do us a wrong. Thus the sense of common human affiliation can undercut the anger that we feel towards our political enemies. This is something the Stoics do actually say, and it's strange that they don't connect it very well with their theory of the passions. Marcus Aurelius, for example, portrays himself in his *Meditations* as very prone to anger and resentment. And he knows that in political life there are going to be plenty of occasions for such emotions. So he gives himself the following advice: 'Say to yourself in the morning', he writes, 'that when you go out you will see people who are bad-tempered, malicious, out to do you wrong, and so on' – it's a long list. But then he continues, 'But I, who know that the wrong-doer is of one blood with me, not indeed a family relation but sharing the same portion of the divine, I cannot be angry at any of them and no one can involve me in shame, because I know that we were born to work together.' We were born to co-operate, he says, like the hands and the eyes, or the upper and lower teeth – indicating perhaps a certain residual level of animosity! The idea, I think, is this: that when we think we're in the same boat together, that these other humans are members of my family, that I'm bound to them by the compassion I feel for all human weakness and vulnerability, then this thought militates against your hatred of an enemy, and provides a way of coming to a different view of your relationship. So I do feel that the Stoics' doctrine of the unity of the passions is not airtight. They themselves give some good reasons to think that we can work against anger while strengthening compassion.

Cogito: According to the Stoics, the emotions are not irrational in the sense of being thought-less, containing no belief component, but are irrational in the quite distinct sense that they involve mistaken judgements of value. Most importantly, they involve placing too high a value on external goods. Now I'm sure most of us are Aristotelians rather than Stoics in this regard, that is, we do place external goods among the conditions for *eudaimonia* or flourishing. This clearly lays us open to simple misfortune: what you love may be lost through sheer bad luck. But the Stoics are saying, are they not, that it's worse than this – that the passionate person is vulnerable not merely to misfortune but also to moral evil? And that's a much more disturbing thought.

Nussbaum: That is indeed what they are saying. They think that if you once form very strong attachments to someone outside yourself, you cannot guarantee that the course of life will not bring you into a situation where either that person will wrong you, or in some way the world will assail that valuable relationship, and then you will quite naturally – out of the relationship itself – feel anger. I think that's true, and that we could probably put it even more strongly. In the very attachment an infant has to its parents this ambivalence is already built in. Here is this helpless creature, unable to walk for longer than any other species in Nature, yet from a cognitive point of view immensely mature from a very early age. This perception of one's own dependency on these powerful external figures for all good, even life itself, combined with the growing awareness that those figures have independent lives and may simply walk away and cease ministering to one's needs, must generate a powerful ambivalence. Here I think Spinoza was right. So are we bound to feel anger towards those we love, simply because we are so dependent on them? Can we do anything about this, or must we just accept that love and anger are inseparable? I think there are several things we can do. First of all, in gradually developing compassion, I think children come to understand that all human beings are similarly vulnerable, very much in the same boat. Rather than seeing our parents as omnipotent figures who could minister to all our needs but choose not to, we come to see that they too are vulnerable like us, and have needs and demands on life similar to ours. This realization helps to undercut the anger that we feel against people who withhold from us things that we want from them. Another thing that we can do is to develop a sense of justice. Psychoanalysts like Fairbairn have interesting things to say about this. They claim that when the child comes to realize its own ambivalence towards its cherished objects, usually parents, this provokes a profound crisis, because it's rather horrifying to realize that you hate the one you love. But then arrives on the scene what Fairbairn calls, nicely, 'the moral defence'. This is the idea that bad can be wiped out through good, that there can be a righting of the balance through reparations and good deeds. To the child, says Fairbairn in a very moving passage, this is a tremendous discovery, because it means that you aren't stuck with limitless badness in yourself, but there's a way in which you can make things good by making amends. If you want to put it in religious terms, he says, just to imagine it more vividly, it's as if you had been living in a world that was OK but was ruled by the devil, and now you're living in a world where you're going to have to suffer, but at least it's ruled by God – that is, there's some principle of justice that governs things. That's a tremendous improvement over the blackness that you felt before. These are ideas that I'm working on now, because I've come to think that the arguments in *The Therapy of Desire*, which focused simply on trying to temper anger with mercy, didn't really go to the root of the problem and didn't have enough to say about how compassion is combined with justice. So that's a big part of my current work.

Cogito: So you don't extract from *The Therapy of Desire* the very pessimistic message that I thought was implicit there. I thought you had come perilously close there to an impossibility-proof, a demonstration that Aristotle's *eudaimonia* is unattainable for a human being. It looked to me as if it might turn out to be impossible to reconcile the moral virtues of Books 4 and 5 of the *Nicomachean Ethics* with the recognition of the importance of *philia* in Books 8 and 9. If both are necessary for the good life, but they can't be combined in a single life, then the good life is impossible.

Nussbaum: What I was saying there was that you can't count on it with the kind of confidence that Aristotle does. Aristotle does seem to think that, given the proper direction by reason, the emotions will fall into line pretty easily, and he thinks this partly because he doesn't have a sense of the boundless dependency of children on things outside themselves. The Stoics, as I have said, don't actually provide a genetic account of the passions, but oddly enough they have deep instincts about the human situation that Aristotle seems to lack. So it's very easy for people like Spinoza and Proust to take a basically Stoic conception of the passions and provide it with a genetic account. Aristotle, I think, writes about people as though they were always well-balanced adults. What I was saying is that we can't count on this. To the extent that we have great love we will always be at risk, not just of grief and loss, but also at risk morally. The lesson I drew from this is that we had better learn to have mercy on ourselves as well as on others, because otherwise we shall always hate ourselves.

Cogito: Perhaps we could turn now to what might be called your aesthetics, although it seems rather important, on your view, that this is not a separate and distinct branch of philosophy. One distinctive feature of your view is that you see art, either principally or at least in large part, as having a moral task.

Nussbaum: I certainly don't want to say that mine is the only way of looking at art, but I do think that a very important tradition in the arts, and especially in literature, is the ethical tradition. This makes claims for the ways in which art reveals the world, and insists that some of these ways of revealing the world are highly pertinent to good thought about how to live, and so 'ethical' in the broad Aristotelian sense. This way of thinking about art opens up some very fruitful questions about how a work of literature shapes attention and desire, what kind of desiring subject it makes me while I am reading it, and so on. These were questions that the Greeks were obsessed with in their discussion about how tragedies constitute us as pitying and fearing subjects, while Plato's dialogues, by contrast, call us away from the passions and activate our intellectual faculties. I think we need to reopen these ancient questions when we think about the role of literature in our own societies, and not just approach the works with the kind of aesthetic detachment that I think real-life readers rarely have anyway when they are reading a novel. It is better, I think, to view works of literature as partners in a search for how to live.

Cogito: Much of what you write concerns the effects of literature on the reader, the way in which reading can hold our attention and give shape and discipline to our desires. But what about the artist's point of view in making the work? How does that fit with the idea of art as a moral task?

Nussbaum: I'm not particularly interested in the biographies of the writers themselves. The figure I'm interested in is the figure Wayne Booth has nicely called 'the implied author' – that is, the figure that animates the text itself, who is very often close to the implied reader, that is the kind of posture of desire and attention that is demanded for a full appreciation of the text. So far as the implied author goes, I think very often there is a claim that the form of desire and attention that is embodied in the text is of superior human value in some way. The claim may be that the literary artist has a kind of intensity and particularity of focus, can see all around about an object, in a way that is characteristic of the highest kind of love – something that we don't often achieve towards one another in real life, when we are so distracted by petty egoism and daily cares. So I think there is a claim that the attention of the implied author is morally exemplary.

Cogito: Then what are the discontinuities between art and morality?

Nussbaum: That depends on how you are using the word 'morality'. If your conception of morality is that of, say, Bernard Williams, then the answer to your question will probably be that the complexity of art is more adequate to life than the simple demands of morality. But let's agree to use the word 'ethics' to refer to a broader view of the subject. The kind of contribution that I find in the novels of Henry James, for example, fits well with a certain ethical tradition, stemming from Aristotle, in which a central ethical task is the fine-tuning of perception and desire, making them more accurate, more subtle, and more flexible. How would other ethical traditions find a role for literature? I think it's most obvious that the imagination of a narrative artist is very hard to reconcile with utilitarianism. This is what my new book, *Poetic Justice*, is all about. It's all about Gradgrind's schoolroom in Dicken's *Hard Times*. In writing that novel, Dickens is of course representing the struggle between a literary style of imagining and the utilitarian style; but he's also enacting it, because in his very way of telling the story he's going to work on revealing the world in a way that Gradgrind can't see it. Showing you what is salient in this world, what stands out for the narrative artist, is also a way of showing you what Gradgrind is missing and leaving out. So we don't even need *Hard Times* to make the point, although I like using it because the explicit subject matter fits so neatly. You could use any fine novel which shows you the salience of qualitative distinctions, and of the difference between one person and another, which depicts the tremendous importance of agency and choice, and shows you that human beings are not just parts of a single system of satisfaction but distinct agents. Any work with this structure – and I think most realist novels have these features – will be doing battle with the utilitarian.

Cogito: Is there any room, then, for an aesthetic which is divorced from love, obligation, loyalty, precision of feeling, articulation of ethical perception, and so on?

Nussbaum: I think the idea of aesthetic detachment, in so far as it has any power at all, is at its strongest when we are thinking about the visual arts. I can at least understand what people like Clive Bell and Roger Fry were saying about how we should look at a painting. I don't necessarily agree with it, because I think that we rarely get a very rich understanding of an artist's work by abstracting from all questions about desire and intention. But for the visual arts I can at least understand what they are saying. Try to imagine, however, what they would say about reading a novel by Dickens. Why would we read the work at all if it wasn't because we were captivated by the peril of the characters, by their struggles in a world of poverty and uncertainty? So the bonds that hold us to the text, that sustain our readerly interest, are far from being detached. The bonds are the emotions of pity and fear, as Dickens in fact says in his description of the people of Coketown. When they go to the public library, he says, they read about the lives of men and women like themselves, and it is the emotions of fear and pity that make this reading fascinating to them.

Cogito: How do you see the role of 'aesthetics' within philosophy as a whole? In the article 'Flawed Crystals' in *Love's Knowledge*, you seem to be suggesting that this subject completes the task of other parts of philosophy – philosophy of mind as well as ethics.

Nussbaum: I think I was only talking there about moral philosophy. If you think about the task of moral philosophy as I do, as involving the working through of all the major alternative views in the tradition, holding each up in turn against our judgements and intuitions – a picture I borrow from Sidgwick and Rawls, as well as Aristotle – then we have good reason to think that the reading of novels is an ineliminable part of that task. This is because there is a distinctive conception of ethics, namely the Aristotelian approach, that can't be fully understood, nor the case for it fully made, without works of an extended narrative nature which show you what the discernment of perception is. Aristotle of course talks a lot about moral perception, but presumably when he lectured to his students he didn't just use these vague terms but exemplified them, and I think we need to understand for ourselves what that exemplification comes to.

Cogito: I actually had in mind what seems to be an even stronger claim. In the article on Beckett, 'Narrative Emotions', in *Love's Knowledge*, you say in your endnote that much of the interest readers have had in a certain style of philosophical writing has traditionally been connected with an interest in transcending everyday humanity, 'an aspiration problematic at its best'. Now that remark seems to contain an implicit critique of philosophical method, stemming from considerations about the role that literature plays in the philosophical task.

Nussbaum: Now it comes back to me what I meant about the relevance of literature for the philosophy of mind. Even to understand our own emotions, we really do need stories, because it's only through an extended story that we can get any purchase on a complex emotion like grief. To give a lecture on grief, I'm going to have to start with a fairly extensive story, and I think the point is a general one – that an emotion always has a trajectory. I was thinking of Spinoza when I wrote that footnote, and of the way in which he chose a particular style of philosophical writing – one modelled on geometry – to write about the emotions. He chose it deliberately, in order to free us from our bondage to the passions by representing objects in the way that they would look if they were not objects of passionate attachment, and we were not intimately involved in stories concerning them. If you are Spinoza, and this is your project, that is all very well and good; but people shouldn't just adopt this style and employ it without thinking carefully about what it does. I do in fact think that Spinoza's aspiration is morally problematic, and that we shouldn't be too quick to borrow his method without thinking of its deeper results.

Cogito: I'd like to ask one more question about the role of perception in ethics. How close is the connection, on your view, between the primacy of perception and the Aristotelian theory? Won't any moral theory have to find some role for perception? After all, morality is about practice, and we act and suffer in a world of particulars. So a utilitarian needs a sub-theory concerning our capacity to perceive the pleasures and pains of other people, and a Kantian needs to be able to see what actions count as cases of exploitation, and hence as violations of the categorical imperative.

Nussbaum: Perception plays very different roles in the different theories. Is it just that we hold the general rule completely fixed, and need perception merely to take the extra step that leads us to the action? Or is there a richer and more substantive role for perception? It might be that the general rules are so far provisional because we know that the contexts life throws at us are endlessly complex and still changing and evolving. In a new set of circumstances perception may lead us to go back and revise the general rule. This was a very important part of Aristotle's account, not only of private, but of public and legal morality. His account of equity says that, if you have laws the right way to think of them is as provisional guidelines that are to be filled up, and in some cases changed, by the good situational judgement of the juror or the judge. Historically, if you look at the orators, they did appeal to juries in just this way. They insisted that they weren't asking the jurors to depart from the intentions of the lawgiver but actually to fulfil those intentions. What those intentions were was precisely that you should take your current circumstances into account and not feel entirely constrained by the past, but do what is sensible and reasonable in the new circumstances. Now that I have part of my appointment in the law school, I see that this is a tremendously important part of the legal tradition in a number of areas, everything from torts to constitutional law to criminal law, which is what I'm particularly interested in. We are always being asked to think, 'what is reasonable here and now?' The whole procedure is very Aristotelian, because in all these areas there's a figure called 'the reasonable man', who is Aristotle's *phronimos*, and it's this reasonable man you are supposed to think about when you are considering your individual case-judgements. In many areas, legislators tried to encapsulate judgements into systems of explicit rules, but they found they couldn't do it because life is too complicated and too changeable. Let me give you one example. There used to be a rule about negligence which stated that, when crossing a railroad track, the reasonable thing to do was to stop your car, get out, look both ways, get back into your car, and then proceed. If you hadn't done this, you were guilty of negligence. Now trains got faster very quickly, and only twenty years later this came to seem very bad advice. I think it was Chief Justice Holmes who said, at this point, that it had been stupid to lay down so much in advance. What we really want to do is to get the jury to think, knowing the circumstances of their own lives, what a reasonable person would do now. And that is what typically happens in the tradition of common-law adjudication. Here's another example which is relevant to this point. I've just written an article on conceptions of emotion in the criminal law, dealing especially with the notion of provocation. If you have killed someone, when will you get a reduction of the charge from first degree murder to voluntary manslaughter on grounds of reasonable provocation? Once again, legislators tried to provide rules for this, but the rules were really quite funny. They would say, for example, that a blow on the ear was not sufficient, but a blow to the face was sufficient. But by now such rules have been abandoned, and juries are simply asked to consider the circumstances and make up their own minds about the degree of provocation involved. The judge will sometimes still rule that, as a matter of law, certain kinds of things are not reasonable and can't go before the jury. Racial hatred, for example, is ruled out: I cannot claim to have been provoked to violence simply by the presence of black skin, no matter how real my anger and hatred might have been. But anyway, the judge and jury between them struggle to work out a norm of reasonableness that fits the situation they are dealing with. This procedure has made the law a flexible and evolving instrument. I think that the ethics of Aristotle is extremely valuable in informing our thinking about these sorts of issues. I'm not sure whether or not Kant too can accommodate such flexibility about rules – there's a lot of dispute about this among Kant scholars, and I'd rather not pronounce judgement. I suspect that the amount of flexibility in Kant's ethics has perhaps been underestimated; but certainly Aristotle is the most obvious case of someone who gives perception more than just the minimal role of finding application for fixed and rigid rules.

Cogito: Perhaps we could end by asking about the implications of Aristotelian ethics in the political domain. Here Aristotle himself is often accused of elitism, of setting out an account of *eudaimonia* or the good life which only a tiny proportion of the population will ever be able to attain.

Nussbaum: I try to make a distinction between perfectionism and elitism. Aristotle is certainly a perfectionist in that he has a rather exigent conception of *eudaimonia*, one that makes big demands on the world. But I don't think that he's an elitist in the sense of thinking that only certain aristocrats can obtain *eudaimonia*. He does, admittedly, have objectionable views about slaves and women, but there is no need for his modern followers to take those views seriously because he provides no argument for them. But if we stick to the people Aristotle is concerned with, he does think that most people, 'anyone who is not maimed in respect of excellence', as he puts it, can, given sufficient support and care, come up to the mark. But that gives politics a very demanding task, as Aristotle sees when he comes to write his *Politics*. It's not enough, he says, just to spread some resources around: you have to direct them in accordance with a conception of the human good. Given such a conception of the good, you face the daunting task of getting to all the people the things they need if they are to attain the good life. So I think that this form of perfectionism gives a valuable set of guidelines to people who are thinking today about the quality of life. In our volume on the subject, Sen and I drew a lot on Aristotle, and especially on the idea that if you are to think well about the distribution of resources you shouldn't focus on those resources as though they were ends in themselves; rather, you have to ask how they go to work enabling human functioning. This forces you to ask which functions are the most important, and what kind of support they need. So Aristotle gets us to ask all the right questions, although of course we have to try to answer those questions for our own time and in our own way. We wouldn't, of course, draw the lines between the sexes in the way that Aristotle does. Indeed, one of the biggest preoccupations we had in our quality of life project was to bring the necessary conditions for *eudaimonia* to women, holding them to the same mark as their menfolk. This is a very radical thing to do, because very often quality of life assessments are made simply by asking how much a household has, and not asking, within each household, how much in the way of resources each of its members commands. We are insisting on asking this question about people one by one, thereby addressing and bringing to light some of the gross inequities in the distribution of resources within the household.

Cogito: This of course connects neatly with your earlier remarks about preferences, and about not taking them simply as brute 'givens'. You mention, for example, a study of Indian widows who make no great demands on health care, although to an external observer they seem far from healthy. Such women might not articulate any distress, might answer, if asked about their health, that they are OK. But on the Aristotelian, 'perfectionist', approach you are employing, that needn't be the last word on the subject.

Nussbaum: No, absolutely not, and I think there's plenty of empirical evidence that such preferences are not just 'given'. The study I was referring to was one of Indian widows and widowers. The widows, asked about their health, replied that they were doing fine, while the widowers made lots of complaints, even though, by a neutral medical examination, the women had many more diseases, particularly nutritional diseases, than the men. It may be that some of these women simply felt intimidated, unable to say what they really felt. But another deeper possibility is that if you have never been well nourished, and if you have always been brought up to think that women are weak and can't do certain things, you won't know what you are missing. What happened in that study was that, after a period of information-giving and consciousness-raising, they repeated the study and found that the women's complaint-level had gone up. Their health had not improved, but now they made a lot more complaints. And I think that's great progress.

Cogito: Thank you.